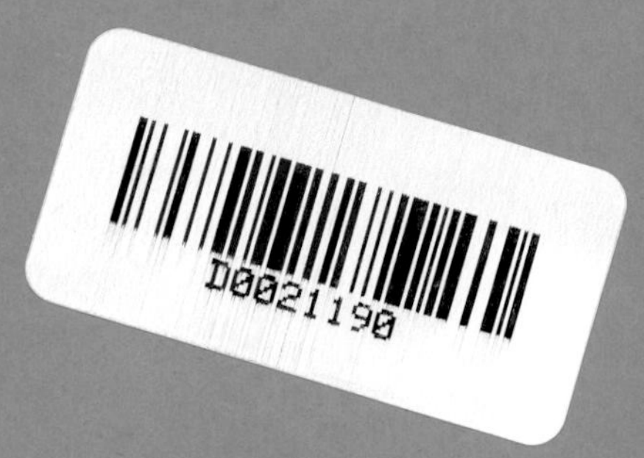
D0021190

ZINFANDEL

CALIFORNIA STUDIES IN FOOD AND CULTURE

DARRA GOLDSTEIN, EDITOR

1. *Dangerous Tastes: The Story of Spices*
   ANDREW DALBY
2. *Eating Right in the Renaissance*
   KEN ALBALA
3. *Food Politics: How the Food Industry Influences Nutrition and Health*
   MARION NESTLE
4. *Camembert: A National Myth*
   PIERRE BOISARD
5. *Safe Food: Bacteria, Biotechnology, and Bioterrorism*
   MARION NESTLE
6. *Eating Apes*
   DALE PETERSON
7. *Revolution at the Table: The Transformation of the American Diet*
   HARVEY LEVENSTEIN
8. *Paradox of Plenty: A Social History of Eating in Modern America*
   HARVEY LEVENSTEIN
9. *Encarnación's Kitchen: Mexican Recipes from Nineteenth-Century California, Selections from Encarnación Pinedo's* El cocinero español
   ENCARNACIÓN PINEDO
   EDITED AND TRANSLATED BY DAN STREHL, WITH AN ESSAY BY VICTOR VALLE
10. *Zinfandel: A History of a Grape and Its Wine*
    CHARLES L. SULLIVAN, WITH A FOREWORD BY PAUL DRAPER

Sullivan, Charles L. (Ch
Zinfandel : a history
of a grape and its wine
c2003.
33305213637717
sa 04/22/08

ZINFANDEL

A HISTORY OF A GRAPE AND ITS WINE

CHARLES L. SULLIVAN

FOREWORD BY PAUL DRAPER

UNIVERSITY OF CALIFORNIA PRESS
BERKELEY · LOS ANGELES · LONDON

Unless otherwise noted, all photographs and drawings are from the author's collection.

University of California Press
Berkeley and Los Angeles, California

University of California Press, Ltd.
London, England

© 2003 by the Regents of the University of California

Library of Congress Cataloging-in-Publication Data
Sullivan, Charles L. (Charles Lewis), 1932–.
Zinfandel : a history of a grape and its wine / Charles L. Sullivan ; foreword by Paul Draper.
p. cm.—(California studies in food and culture ; 10)
Includes bibliographical references (p.) and index.
ISBN 0-520-23969-5 (cloth : alk. paper)
1. Grapes—California—History. 2. Viticulture—California—History. 3. Wine and wine making—California—History. I. Title. II. Series.
SB389.S94 2003
634.8′09794—dc21 2002156534

Manufactured in the United States of America
12 11 10 09 08 07 06 05 04 03
10 9 8 7 6 5 4 3 2 1
The paper used in this publication meets the minimum requirements of ANSI/NISO Z39.48–1992 (R 1997) (*Permanence of Paper*). ♾

For Gail Unzelman

NO WAYWARD TENDRIL

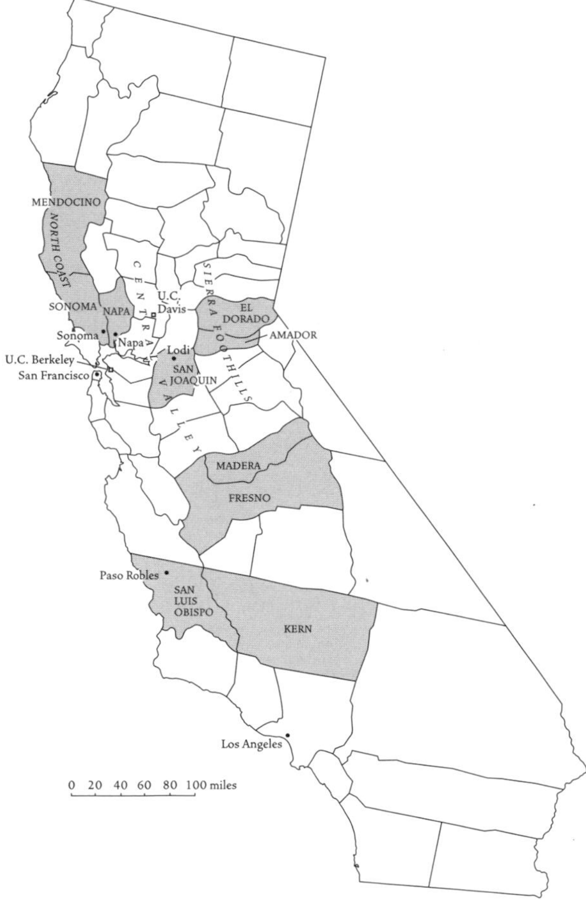

Zinfandel country. Shaded counties are the leading Zinfandel producers in their regions.

CONTENTS

ILLUSTRATIONS

Figures

Tables

FOREWORD

PAUL DRAPER
WINEMAKER, CEO, RIDGE VINEYARDS

CHARLES SULLIVAN'S TIMELY BOOK PRESENTS A FULL HISTORY OF THE grape that is at the heart of California's contribution to the world of fine wine. Just as Bordeaux established the reputation of Cabernet Sauvignon, Burgundy of Chardonnay and Pinot Noir, and the northern Rhône of Syrah, so California has established Zinfandel and set its standard of excellence. California today challenges, as do other wine regions of the world, the supremacy of the great wines of France. But with those varietals we are the challengers; we did not establish their reputation.

Zinfandel cuttings from California thrive in Australia, South Africa, and the south of France, as well as in a number of other countries. The same grape variety has been grown in southern Italy since the late eighteenth or early nineteenth century under the name Primitivo, yet the wines produced have failed to establish a reputation for quality. As all these wines improve, they, too, will become challengers. I hope they will push California Zinfandels to still higher quality.

We now know that Zinfandel is not originally from Italy, but some California producers are worried because of that country's extensive Primitivo plantings. There are clonal variations within any old varietal; on this basis, these Californians have asserted that the two are not the same. In France and elsewhere, however, an even larger number of Pinot Noir clones differ as much or more than do Zinfandel and Primitivo—yet no one would think of claiming that they are not the same varietal. On the scientific evidence, the European Union has declared Zinfandel and Primitivo synonymous; since the United States accepts any wine label certified by the country of origin, Primitivo wine can be sold in this country under the name Zinfandel. The concerned producers feel that the Italians could take unfair advantage of the name and reputation we have built. But I fear memories are short. We in California continue to take advantage of our European colleagues by using designations such as Champagne, Burgundy, Chablis, and Port—and think nothing of it. I am sure Bordeaux producers have been less than delighted with the competition provided by California Cabernets, but they have been challenged to improve their own wines. In any case, the market will distinguish between California Zinfandel and Italian Zinfandel, just as it distinguishes Chilean and Australian Cabernets from California Cabernet.

The author also covers the organization Zinfandel Advocates and Producers—affectionately known as ZAP. In addition to its work with the Heritage Vineyard collection, ZAP sponsors trade and consumer tastings around the United States and Europe. The largest and most unusual of these takes place in San Francisco each year on a Saturday late in January. In 2002, ten thousand people tasted their choice of more than six hundred wines from roughly three hundred California producers. This alone is impressive, and unmatched by any tasting of a single varietal anywhere in the world. More important, however, and most encouraging for the future of wine as a part of our culture, has been the attitude of the majority of tasters. They are judging what is in the glass rather than the name on the label—a sure sign of a maturing attitude toward wine in America.

In 1998, geneticist Dr. Carole Meredith of the University of California at Davis traveled to Croatia to investigate claims that the major Croatian red wine grape, Plavac mali, was the same variety as Zinfandel. Working with two researchers from the University of Zagreb, she determined that this was not the case. But genetic testing did prove that the two grapevines share half of their DNA—they are closely related. In the fall of 2001, the Croatian researchers found a vine, called Crljenak (Tzerl-yen'-ak), that is the same variety as Zinfandel, and several other varieties that are closely related to Zinfandel but not the same. As Sullivan explains, "One of the principles of crop plant genetics posits the high probability that a center of genetic diversity in the form of close relatives is also the place of origin of the specific plant to which all appear related. Because the Zinfandel has numerous close relatives in Croatia, it is probable that Croatia is the place of origin." By fall 2002, nine vines had been confirmed in one vineyard, and several other strong candidates were under investigation; scientific evidence had demonstrated an overwhelming probability that Zinfandel had originated in Croatia.

Sullivan meticulously lays out the history and recent genetic research that together confirm the origins of the Zinfandel grape and explain how it reached California. He sets the historical record straight, definitively laying to rest the myth that Agoston Haraszthy was involved in its introduction. I will admit to becoming lost at times in the detail surrounding Zinfandel's arrival on the West Coast—the records of acreage, yields, and prices are formidable. But Sullivan has provided an invaluable reference work, and a truly entertaining detective saga.

MONTE BELLO RIDGE
NOVEMBER 2002

PREFACE

BEFORE THE UNIVERSITY OF CALIFORNIA PRESS PUBLISHED MY ENcyclopedia of California wine history in 1998, my senior editor asked me to explain why the Zinfandel entry was longer than the entry for Cabernet Sauvignon. I'm sure she already had a good idea of why this was so and simply wanted to get all the arguments straight.

I pointed out that the Zinfandel entry was actually the longest in the book. Then I went through all the reasons I could think of, which you, the reader, have probably already heard. It is one of the most versatile grapes in the world. There are several wine types: table, dessert, sparkling. There are the table wines: red, white, and pink. It can be used in brandy production. And the Zinfandel grape is good to eat, as raisins or fresh.

But what I concentrated on was the history of Zinfandel. Numerous mysteries have surrounded the variety's origins. A myth had even developed about it. And no history had ever been written on the Zinfandel from the time that it became the darling of the California wine industry in the 1880s until it became popular as a premium varietal in the late 1960s.

Many wine grape varieties are of mysterious origin, but none is as important as Zinfandel. Few would be interested in reading a book on the history of the Green Hungarian or the Cabernet Pfeffer varieties. But Zinfandel is different. Until 1998, when it was superseded by Cabernet Sauvignon, it was California's most widely planted red wine grape—and had been since 1975, when Carignane was king for a few years. One might also say that it has been for years California's signature wine. Who else produces Zinfandel?

Cabernet Sauvignon may be more important in California than Zinfandel in many ways, but it has nowhere nearly so intriguing a history. In fact, intrigue has been a major component in what purported to be Zinfandel's early history in the Golden State. That intrigue and the mysteries of its origin are what piqued my interest in Zinfandel three decades ago. And I presume that they have a lot to do with your reading this book.

We need to look carefully at the mysteries. The first is the mystery of origins, for the vine is clearly a vinifera variety and therefore European. But there is no variety of that name in Europe, nor do we have evidence that there ever has been. An almost complete unraveling of this mystery has taken place during the past twenty-five years. The history of this mostly scientific undertaking is an important part of this book.

The second mystery is easily understood. These questions need answering: How did what we call Zinfandel come to the New World? Where did it come from? Where on our shores did it land, and how did it get from there to California? Although the solution to the first mystery comes from the work of scientists, the historian must solve the second.

The most fascinating aspect of this mystery is that from the 1880s until the 1970s it was apparently no mystery at all. Everyone knew the story of how a flamboyant European nobleman had brought the vine from his homeland and spread the word of its virtues to the four corners of the Golden State. But it wasn't true. It was a tale manufactured by the son of a famous father, told in the 1880s, a package of lies and partial truths about the introduction of the vine thirty years earlier.

This tale became a solidified block of historical concrete, copied by virtually every interested historian and wine writer for almost a hundred years. I cracked the concrete monolith of this myth in the 1970s by going back to the period between 1852 and 1880 and examining the contemporary record, the primary sources from which a true history could be pieced together. And I went to the East Coast to examine the primary sources there, which gave a fairly clear picture of the Zinfandel's arrival on that coast in the late 1820s.

In 1989 historian Thomas Pinney wrote, in his *History of Wine in America*, "The notion that Haraszthy first brought the Zinfandel to California has persisted and now seems to be so firmly fixed that no amount of historical bulldozing can dislodge it. Still, it is not true." In chapter 6, I fire up the bulldozer anew.

A third mystery is built into the destruction of the Haraszthy myth. After it arrived in California from the East Coast, how was this grape, grown in Boston for the table, discovered as an excellent wine grape? And how did its fame spread in the 1860s so that it became the leading variety planted in the state during the first wine boom, in the 1880s? Who were the heroes in this story in the 1850s and 1860s?

The fourth mystery is really an unanswered question. What is the history of the Zinfandel between the 1880s and 1960s? This history has never been written. In attempting to answer that question, I'll explain why I call it the "stealth grape" in the years before Prohibition, and I'll show how Prohibition made the name "Zinfandel" a part of the American wine vocabulary in a way that it had never been before. I'll also explain how Zinfandel meant two very different things to consumers in the years after the repeal of Prohibition.

An important part of the modern story comes from the fact that, unlike all the other world-class varieties that have become a part of California's premium wine production, Zinfandel has no model of European perfection for comparison. When we sit down at a blind tasting to evaluate and compare a few red Bordeaux and California Cabernets, we can have a good time thinking and talking about what we perceive. Which do we like better? Which will be better in years to come? Have the California producers used the *grand cru* wine of the Médoc as a model? But such an event involving California Zinfandels and a world-famous European counterpart never takes place. This fact has added to the complexity of Zinfandel's history as a table wine in California. In some ways it has been bothersome to producers. In others it has been a tantalizing challenge, which, in recent years, seems to have been gloriously met.

When I was learning how to be a historian, my professors impressed on me the idea that we all bring our personal history, our values, our beliefs to the task. There is no such thing as perfectly objective history since it must be filtered through the mind of a fallible human being. Historians must be aware of their values and beliefs, knowing that they certainly affect the final product, which is as much interpretation as fact. And the historian's reader should be made aware of these values and beliefs. So I need to come clean.

My wife, Rosslyn, and I love wine. We are particularly fond of red wine and drink a bottle with dinner regularly. We are claret drinkers. We have a cellar full of claret, that is, California Cabernet Sauvignon, red Bordeaux, and Zinfandel.

Over the years I have been made to believe by friends, mentors, and critics that the history of Zinfandel is not to be understood unless Roz and I are characters in it. That is, the reader has to understand how we have put all this together, from Los Gatos to Berkeley to Davis, Boston, Beltsville, Austria, Hungary, Italy, and Croatia. With this in mind, I will begin my story at home.

ACKNOWLEDGMENTS

THIS HISTORY OF ZINFANDEL HAS BEEN ABOUT THIRTY YEARS IN THE making. Along the way I have profited continually from the advice, the hints, the practical assistance, and the good will of numerous individuals. Often the assistance has been the understandable consequence of institutional relationships. And there have been scores of people who just wanted to help.

Chief among the latter has been Professor Thomas Pinney of Pomona College. He has labored through every word of this work in draft and has left me and other wine lovers in his debt. As I have written of his previous help, "How could I hope to have had a better advisor than an English professor who is also an expert on wine history?"

John McGrew, formerly of the U.S. Department of Agriculture, set me straight on the history of eastern American viticulture. He is the final authority on that subject. And he introduced me to the wonderful viticultural collections at the National Agricultural Library in Beltsville, Maryland. There the staff provided my wife and me with a week's happy labor.

In Boston the staff of the Massachusetts Horticultural Society and the Boston Public Library helped make my research on early New England viticulture possible.

At home I value the help provided by the staff of the Bancroft Library, at the University of California at Berkeley, as well as the staff at the university's Shields Library at Davis, where Axel Borg and John Skarstad have been solid viticultural connections. The teaching staff at the Davis campus of the university also deserves my thanks, particularly James Wolpert, James Lapsley, and Carole Meredith. Readers will appreciate Professor Meredith's contributions when they read about the unraveling of the mysteries of Zinfandel's origins.

The ample resources at the Sonoma County Wine Library in Healdsburg have also been of great value. I owe special thanks to the continued assistance of Bo Simons, the keeper of the library's treasures.

When I wrote on the dedication page that Gail Unzelman, founder of the *Wayward Tendrils Quarterly*, was no wayward tendril, I meant that she was not wayward. But no tendril I know is more tenacious. She, more than any other person, is responsible for my research resulting in this book.

The story of the Italian Primitivo presented here depends on the advice and the documentary resources supplied to me by Darrell Corti. Professor William Marchione of the Art Institute of Boston helped me to understand that city's early nurseries. And Walter Hamböck introduced me to the horticultural collection at Vienna's Schoenbrunn Palace.

I must also express my special appreciation to a tireless group of wine lovers whose keen eyes and ready scissors have provided me with a steady flow of wine-related periodical and newspaper clippings. Margaret Dealey and Ed Shaw cover Southern California. My mother, Charlene Sullivan, and Mike Donohoe handle the San Francisco Bay Area, and Elizabeth Polansky is in charge of the East Coast.

Anyone who is familiar with the work that has gone into this book knows how much my wife, Rosslyn, has contributed to it. She has been my research assistant, my reader and critic, my fellow wine taster, and my best friend throughout. With her at my side, this has been a labor of love.

CHAPTER ONE

HOW I SOLVED THE HISTORICAL MYSTERIES SURROUNDING ZINFANDEL—SORT OF

I HAVE NOT ALWAYS BEEN A WINE LOVER. IN FACT, UNTIL I WAS WELL into my twenties, I drank beer at family dinners while others drank wine. But that changed in the mid-1950s when my wife, Rosslyn, and I were caught up by the early enthusiasm of what is often called the modern "wine revolution." This was the time in the 1960s and 1970s when table wines became the dominant product of the California wine industry and when drinking wine with meals became a regular part of the lives of many Americans.

Our first love was for slightly sweet German whites, but this passion was softened in the late 1950s as we began discovering California Cabernet Sauvignon and red Bordeaux. Our first case of great claret was sold to us personally by André Tchelistcheff, the famed winemaker at Napa's Beaulieu Vineyards. He happened to be in the tasting room at BV when we stopped there in 1961 on our first trip to the Napa Valley. The wine was the BV 1956 Private Reserve Cabernet Sauvignon.

On that trip we also visited Lee Stewart's Souverain Cellars on Napa's Howell Mountain. I had heard of Zinfandel, though in my mind I associated it with inexpensive jug wine. But when I tasted Stewart's 1959 Zinfandel, I knew that there was much more to that strange-sounding variety than I had thought. I was pleased to note that the Souverain Zinfandel was only two dollars, a real quality bargain after having paid five dollars for the BV Cabernet. I loved them both and thought the Zin a very close second.

On a beginning schoolteacher's salary, such expensive wines as these had to be saved for special occasions. But it did not take us long to discover the country wineries in the Santa Clara Valley, where we live, and in the nearby Santa Cruz Mountains and Livermore Valley. We found that many of these family operations sold very inexpensive and very good red wine in gallon jugs. These became our wines for daily consumption.

Every few months the family headed out in the station wagon from our headquarters in Los Gatos and returned with the four kids crammed into the second seat. The back was always loaded with cases of gallons, mostly Zinfandel.

I read a few books on wine and discovered that some hearty red wines improved when aged in individual bottles. A few early experiments convinced me that the bright young Zinfandels in our gallon jugs, with their explosive raspberry flavors, could be transferred to "fifths" and corked up. Just a year or so under the house produced amazing results. This bottle aging softened the wines' rough edges and added to their complexity. By the mid-1960s I had become what some today call a "Zinfanatic."

When we visited wineries in those early days, I always talked to the owners, asking about their wines, the grape varieties, their operations, and their winery histories. I took notes from the outset and read what I could on California wine history. A good touring guide was available that had a little history of the individual wineries.[1] But the only serious, scholarly work to be found contained little that gave me any sense about the past of the California wine industry I was looking at in the early 1960s.[2]

I had been well schooled in the job of the historian and had been writing articles and a portion of a book on my specialty, Baltic-German history. But the more I learned about California wine from the people who were producing it, the more I became convinced that the state's wine history was where I wanted to concentrate my research efforts.

I started in 1963 by reading *Wines & Vines,* the leading wine industry trade publication. It was loaded with just the sort of information on the current wine scene that I hoped to find concerning the earlier years. So I began getting bound volumes of *Wines & Vines* from the State Library and reading them in reverse, back to 1919, when Horatio Stoll founded the publication as the *California Grape Grower.* Then I read its predecessor back to 1883. All the time I was taking copious notes and learning about a wine industry whose history really had never been written.

My next step was to read newspapers. I started with the local *San Jose Mercury,* which has always been an outstanding wine country periodical. With this source I was able to reach back into the 1860s. It was a treasure trove of wine and viticultural information, almost none of which could be found in standard printed sources. Then came the San Francisco *Alta California* and the *California Farmer,* and then into the North Coast wine country with the *St. Helena Star* and the *Sonoma Democrat.* By the end of the 1960s I had read and indexed most of the wine country newspapers, the beverage trade journals, and the government publications on wine and viticulture from the years before Prohibition.

One of the largest sections of indexed material was the last one in my file, headed "Zinfandel." But I was intent on gathering information and did nothing to bring it together as written history. In 1976 this situation began to change when events at a friendly dinner directed my first steps toward solving some of the mysteries concerning the Zinfandel's origins in California.

Our guests were Dave and Fran Bennion, founders of Ridge Vineyards, today and then a leader in the production of outstanding Zinfandel. The other couple was Joe and June Swan, whose little winery in Sonoma's Forestville had become a Mecca for Zinfandel lovers.

Late in the evening, after I had probably been pontificating on some historical matter, Dave fixed me with a serious look and said something like, "Charles, all you do is talk about California wine history. Why don't you do something?"

"What should I do?"

"What do historians do? They tell stories about the past, don't they?"

"Yes, but they also try to answer questions about the past. The answer isn't always a story."

"So, answer a question; solve a problem."

"Like what?" I asked. (I honestly hadn't given it a thought.)

"Aren't there any historical mysteries about California wine that need solving?"

"Well, there is always Zinfandel. The Haraszthy story—I just don't buy it anymore."

At this point, I think, Joe Swan cast his stern gaze on me. "Charles, why don't you just do it?"

I thought I could. The previous summer I had read a fascinating and lengthy 1885 article from the *San Francisco Evening Post* by a Sonoma journalist/historian.[3] In it he quoted a letter from an 1857 neighbor of Agoston Haraszthy, telling in detail how the Zinfandel came to Sonoma from a Napa vineyardist who had acquired the vine from a friend, who in turn had brought it from the East Coast in the 1850s. The *Post* challenged the idea (at that point becoming current) that Haraszthy had brought the vine to California in the early 1860s. It was clear to me from my research into the 1860s that no one at the time credited him with this introduction.

It was the memory of that article that moved me to take up the dinner challenge of those two masters of Zinfandel. I put together all my notes, read some books on East Coast viticulture, and concluded that the story accepted by practically everyone in the California wine industry for years was almost pure hokum. Agoston Haraszthy had not introduced the Zinfandel to California. It had come here in 1852 from the East Coast, where it had been grown for many years as a hothouse table grape, its name usually spelled "Zinfindal."

I wrote to Professor A. D. Webb at the University of California at Davis and told him of my findings. I wondered whether they would be of interest at the annual conference of the American Society for Viticulture and Enology. He invited me to present my paper. This I did, and my findings were then published in several periodicals.[4]

Simply showing that Agoston Haraszthy had not introduced the Zinfandel to California did not explain its arrival in America, however, nor did it give any hints as to its history in Europe. An exchange of correspondence soon put me on this track. John McGrew was the research plant pathologist at the U.S. Department of Agriculture's Agricultural Research Center in Beltsville, Maryland. He read one of my Zinfandel articles and sent me a powerful clue he had seen in a manuscript collection at the National Agricultural Library (NAL) there. In letters in this collection, he had read of some early vine shipments to an East Coast nurseryman from the imperial botanical collection at the Schoenbrunn Palace in Vienna. There was a good chance that our Zinfandel was involved.

I suppose the smart thing would have been to head for Beltsville. But it was 1980, and our plans to go to the Moscow Olympics had been thwarted by the American boycott. Roz's brother was the American chargé d'affaires in Vienna, and we decided to see the Olympics on television from the Austrian capital. Naturally the Schoenbrunn was in my mind before we left. When we arrived and it transpired that my brother-in-law was a good friend of the director of the Schoenbrunn botanical collection, a light went on in my head.

Although John McGrew had given me the approximate dates of the vine shipments he had discovered, I soon found that the older Schoenbrunn records were stored in various locations, unindexed as to date or topic. When we flew home, I still had some hope, having collected a list of the agencies I would need to contact in order to find an official record of a vine shipment. But I knew that I would next have to spend some time on the East Coast examining agricultural journals, newspapers, and manuscript collections. I hoped that these might reveal how the Zinfandel arrived there and how it was used for the twenty-five to thirty years before its journey to the Golden State.

In the summer of 1983 Roz and I took off by train for Boston, where excellent collections of nineteenth-century agricultural journals and newspapers are stored in several area libraries. We were soon leafing through such all-but-forgotten periodicals as the *New England Farmer, Massachusetts Ploughman, Yankee Farmer,* and dozens more. Not one was on microfilm, but many had detailed annual indexes. We paged through them, year after year, piling up sheaves of notes on anything vaguely touching on viticulture on the East

Coast. The dust from the old newspapers played hob with our sinuses, and the skin on our hands became desiccated and rough. But we were dauntless.

When we boarded the train to head south, we were content in the knowledge that the New England story of Zinfandel was tellable and that the picture of its arrival in California in the 1850s that I had put together in 1976 was basically accurate. A table grape had come almost unnoticed to California from Boston, and almost by chance it had become a very useful California wine grape.

At the NAL in Beltsville, just outside Washington, D.C., we dug into everything that John McGrew could find for us that might throw light on the Zinfandel story. Specifically, I wanted to search the Prince Family manuscript collection. The family's Linnaean Botanic Gardens in Flushing, Long Island, had been the first commercial nursery in the United States. Anyone conversant with American viticultural history knows about William Robert Prince's 1830 *A Treatise on the Vine.* In it the author made an oblique reference to Zinfandel.[5] And, the year before our trip east, I had learned from UC Davis Professor Maynard Amerine that the yearly catalogues of the Prince nursery also had interesting references to the grape. John McGrew had warned me to bring lots of notepaper for work on the rest of the gigantic Prince collection, which the library had acquired at the end of the nineteenth century.[6]

Our hopes about the trip to Beltsville were richly rewarded. The Prince manuscripts yielded loads of "Zinformation," including some persuasive hints as to how the vine got here from Europe. Clear evidence demonstrated that what became known as the Zinfandel in America came to this country from Europe in the late 1820s, first to a certain nurseryman on Long Island. But it did not come as Zinfandel or Zinfindal. There is no evidence that an Old World vine called Zinfandel ever grew under that name in Europe. Nevertheless, what we call Zinfandel in California today is clearly a vinifera vine from the Old World.

One of the mysteries concerning Zinfandel has been our longstanding inability to find the genetic forebear of the vine growing in Europe. With my mind on this question, I had another goal at the NAL.

I wanted to look at material on nineteenth-century Italian viticulture, because UC Davis scientists had discovered in the early 1970s that a vine grown today in southern Italy called the Primitivo is probably the same as the California Zinfandel. I went through several Italian sources and found good information on the Primitivo growing in the Puglia area in the nineteenth century. This region is high on the heel of the Italian boot, much of it facing the Adriatic.

My sources in the Prince manuscripts clearly indicated that the Austrian Empire was the source of the unnamed vines that arrived on our East Coast in the 1820s and came to be called Zinfandel. I had no trouble imagining a historical connection between vines grown in Puglia and others grown farther north along the Adriatic, much of which was part of the Austrian Empire in the nineteenth century.

Since then, the DNA research at UC Davis led by Professor Carole Meredith has confirmed that the Italian Primitivo and our Zinfandel are genetically identical. Later in this study I will focus more closely on this remarkable research, to show how another grape variety, this one from the northern Adriatic, has helped to fill out much more of the historical picture of Zinfandel's European origins.

My hopes of finding nineteenth-century documentary evidence in the Schoenbrunn archives for shipments of the vine to the East Coast were doomed by what I learned from my correspondence with Austrian officials over the next three years. I had the years for the shipments nailed down—the late 1820s, probably 1829. But the director of the Austrian State Archives informed me that no record existed in the appropriate account books for such transactions. But, he counseled, I shouldn't take this fact as a decisive negative. A warehouse full of transaction documents was the most likely repository of the primary sources. Though his department, of course, could not afford the perhaps hundreds of hours such a task might entail, Herr Direktor Rill invited me to apply for a permit to do it myself.

Such documents would be handwritten in the old German Sötterlin script used in the nineteenth century. I had learned how to read it in my youth but recalled that once, when I had to read a few pages in an old diary, each small page had taken me more than an hour. So much for the Austrian connection on the European side, as far as historical documentation was concerned. But the documents in the NAL were convincing enough. Why should they not be? And in the course of my narrative I hope to show how the recent genetic evidence from European sources has enhanced my conviction.

So now to that narrative. Let us go first to the East Coast of the United States in the 1820s and 1830s, when James Monroe and Andrew Jackson were in the White House, when Thomas Jefferson was still alive and writing delightful letters to the editors of eastern farm journals, and when Americans were developing a passionate interest in a scientific approach to all aspects of agriculture and horticulture. Not the least of these interests was viticulture.

CHAPTER TWO

SOJOURN IN THE EAST

AMERICANS IN THE ENGLISH COLONIES OF NORTH AMERICA GREW grapes from Florida to New England. In the early days of the republic, they took vines west to the Ohio and Mississippi Valleys. The growers were most successful when they raised grapes to eat. There were no great successes in the field of winemaking, although there were some admirable failures.

The grapes the Americans used fall into three categories: the native varieties found growing in North America, the European vinifera varieties transported to the New World, and the chance hybrids between the two. (In the nineteenth century American nurserymen began deliberately producing such hybrids.)[1]

In the more southerly climes, winegrowing demonstrated the most potential, thanks to the warmer climate and the heterogeneity of the population. But as one looks north along the eastern seaboard, one finds fewer and fewer persons who thought of viticulture in connection with wine production; such views were rare north of the middle colonies (later states). You could draw a line north of Long Island and west to the Hudson River Valley as a sort of geographer's limit of serious winegrowing.

Viticulture as a source of table grapes was another matter. Between 1810 and 1835, Massachusetts saw the development of an interesting horticultural fad that gradually grew to be something of a small but serious commercial enterprise: the growing of grapes in hothouses. This hobby, which soon began to earn serious money for some of its adherents, was not simply intended to protect the plants from the icy winter climate. The special fad, developed from ideas already flourishing in England, called for vines to be forced by artificial means of heating so that they produced marketable bunches of delicious dessert grapes as early as March and April, when the ground outside the hothouse might still be deep in snow. New Englanders could draw on extensive English experience with this complex culture, first described in detail in a nurseryman's handbook in 1724.[2]

It sounds easy, but in fact it was tricky. The first requirement was plenty of free time and a bit of capital. (I have yet to hear of a humble dirt farmer involved in such a venture.) A grower would begin by building a glass greenhouse facing south with adjustable lights (windows) to let in a little air on clear, cool late-winter days when the vines might fry in temperatures over 95°F. To take care of the freezing days, and particularly the nights, a heating system had to be installed nearby with pipes that conveyed heated air to the greenhouse. Usually there was a hot-water furnace with many cords of wood stacked to fuel it. A trusted servant was often employed to keep the heat up during the night.

In the first year the vine received a normal greenhouse regimen. Then, the following March, forcing began. In the second year the heat was turned up on February 15; in the third year it was turned up on February 1. Each year the date was moved back fifteen days until eventually the furnace was fired up on December 1. By then the vines were dormant in the New England climate. The idea was gradually to trick the vines into thinking that spring had arrived only two months after they had lost their leaves in the fall. It worked. (And it still does. I put a potted Zinfandel plant through such a routine for five years, substituting a refrigerator and a short period in a freezer for the New England climate. The vine finally leafed on December 23 and made a remarkable New Year's table decoration the year before it died.)

J. Fisk Allen, then the leading American authority on the process, tells us that buds on forced vines started pushing around January 20. By February 10 many vines had shoots two and three feet long. By late February most varieties had blossomed, and Allen figured he would usually start thinning bunches for higher flavor in early March. Dark grapes were well colored by April. Allen noted that his Zinfindal (note the spelling) colored later in the month. He usually was able to harvest this variety in May or early June.[3] Of course, Allen was describing what he thought were the best practices for top quality. Growers who pushed earlier and harder, with earlier ripening varieties, didn't have to wait until May. April bunches on the Boston market brought up to $2.00 per pound (a price comparable to more than $25.00 in the year 2000, when corrected for price inflation in constant dollars). Grapes ripe in May commanded only about $1.25.

One incentive that helped propel this forcing culture beyond the simple greenhouse stage in the 1830s in Boston was the news of London prices for top-quality April grapes, as reported in English gardeners' publications, which were widely copied by American newspapers. Bostonians rightly surmised that such prices might be had at home. Allen tells us that a price equivalent to more than $50.00 per pound in year 2000 dollars was not unheard of when this market was first developing.[4]

Several New England greenhouses had been built in the eighteenth century, the first in the Boston area by Andrew Faneuil in the 1750s. Between 1800 and 1810, when the forcing fad was still a few years away, several families of means built them with the specific intent of raising vinifera grapes for the table. One such gentleman central to the solution of part of the Zinfandel mystery was Samuel Perkins, who built his greenhouse near Brookline and had marked success at an early date, particularly with the Black Hamburg and Muscat of Alexandria varieties.[5]

Perkins and others like him, from Long Island to southern Maine, read English gardeners' publications and ordered vines from English nurserymen. They were often just as interested in apples, plums, and pears, but those are part of a different story. We can get a very clear picture of the grape varieties available by reading English books and periodicals from the 1720s onward and from American horticultural periodicals. (None dealing strictly with viticulture had yet appeared.)[6]

Of these imported varieties, virtually every one that proved successful in New England could have been found in English nurseries before it arrived in America. We would classify most of these varieties today as table grapes, but a few have been used successfully to make good wine.

The following list of such varieties is partial, perhaps amounting to less than a quarter of the varieties we know were grown in New England greenhouses. But together these probably account for 95 percent of the grapes grown in this manner. One variety well known in Boston in the 1830s is not on the list, however, because it never appeared on any English nursery list or in any English horticultural publication from the 1720s to the 1860s. It is the vine that Bostonians were calling the "Zinfindal" in the 1830s. But the list does include a grapevine grown in England (marked +) that, when it arrived in California under this name, was the same as the Zinfindal. The list also includes four varieties usually classified as wine grapes (marked *) that Allen and others thought were good for eating and that were usually raised for this purpose in New England.

—Black Hamburg (or Hamburgh)
—Black Lombardy
—Black Prince
—Black St. Peters+
—Cannon Hall Muscat
—Golden Chasselas
—Grizzly (grey) Muscat
—Muscat of Alexandria
—Muscat of Frontignan*
—Red Traminer*
—Royal Muscadine
—Sweetwater

—Syrian
—Verdelho*
—White Riesling*

The Black St. Peters is something of a mystery variety before it became settled in California. Many vines with "St. Peters" in their names were known in England and were imported into New England and Long Island. What this vine was on the East Coast is not clear, although Allen's description is almost identical to that of his Zinfindal. But we know for sure that whatever arrived in California in the 1850s under that name and survived in the state's vineyards in later years was the same vine that was by the 1870s universally accepted as the Zinfandel in the Golden State.

The Zinfandel/Zinfindal came to Boston in the nursery pots of George Gibbs of Long Island, an amateur horticulturist much interested in viticulture. His name is all but forgotten, though his wife's name survives, attached to a grape variety she brought from Smithsville, North Carolina, to Long Island in 1816. She presented it to William Robert Prince, the noted nurseryman, and he named it for her—the Isabella. It became one of the East Coast's most popular native varieties.[7]

Beginning in 1820 Gibbs imported several shipments of vines from Europe. We have a partial record of his acquisitions from the Austrian imperial nursery collection in Vienna. In 1820 he imported twenty-eight varieties, five of which originated in the Kingdom of Hungary, then and until 1918 an important part of the Austrian Empire. The names Gibbs listed for the vines in this shipment included some that may be slightly familiar to us today: for example, "Chasselas," "White Muscat," "Frontenac." Others, perhaps not so familiar, included "Early Leipsick," "Faketi," and "Schumlauer." There was also the Frankenthal, which J. Fisk Allen later likened to the Zinfindal.[8]

Gibbs had a very close relationship with his neighbor William Robert Prince, whose work *A Treatise on the Vine* (1830), written with the help of his

1. The Zinfindal was one of the many vinifera table grape varieties sold by William Robert Prince in the 1830s at his great Long Island nursery, the Linnaean Botanic Gardens. (Source: L. H. Bailey, *Standard Cyclopedia of Horticulture,* vol. 3 [New York: Macmillan, 1944], p. 1591.)

father, was described by historian Thomas Pinney as being "of an entirely different and higher order" when compared to any previous text on American viticulture.[9] (In 1793, Prince's father, William Prince Jr., had established the Linnaean Botanic Gardens in Flushing, Long Island, discussed in chapter 1; William Prince Sr. had earlier established the country's first commercial nursery.)

The Princes also imported vinifera vines from Europe in the 1820s, many from England, and many too from the Austrian Empire. William Robert Prince's catalogue entries for these vines in later years can be confusing without a clear understanding of the political geography of central Europe in the nineteenth century. Vines from the German-speaking portions of the empire he listed as being from "Germany," meaning from a land where German language and culture dominated. (There was, of course, no country called Germany until the unification process of 1870–1871.) The capital of the empire, and the site of its imperial collections, was the very German city of Vienna. Vines from the Kingdom of Hungary, which comprised lands covering more than half of the empire, Prince listed as being from Hungary. (It goes without saying that the king of Hungary was the Austrian emperor.) These terms, "Germany" and "Hungary," in the Prince nursery catalogues have been a continual cause for misunderstanding from the 1880s until recently.[10]

In 1829 Gibbs received a shipment of vines from Vienna and sent Prince a note listing them. "You may depend on [them] as genuine as I recd. them from the Imperial Garden at Schoenbrunn."[11] No vine labeled anything like Zinfandel was listed, but there were some unnamed vines that must attract our attention. One was a "rough black" grape taken from Hungary to Vienna, "prolific, a very good grape." Was this the Zinfandel? We can't be sure, but later, when Prince began listing Zinfandel in his catalogue, he noted that it had been "introduced by the late George Gibbs . . . from Germany," meaning from Vienna. We can't be certain which one of Gibbs's shipments he meant, but we can be very sure that Prince knew that the vine had come to Long Island in these shipments from the Schoenbrunn nursery collection.

At this point we should take a closer look at the geography of the Austrian Empire, both to understand previous references to Hungary and to see how its political components were related. Later this knowledge will also make recent scientific discoveries concerning the origins of Zinfandel more understandable.

The Kingdom of Hungary had been reconquered from the Turks by the Hapsburg rulers of the Austrian Empire in the seventeenth and eighteenth centuries. These Hungarian territories, the so-called Lands of St. Stephen, were dominated demographically by Magyars (Hungarians). But many other peoples were included. The kingdom was huge when compared to today's Republic of Hungary and included much of what is today Croatia and Serbia. It also included much of Slovakia, Slovenia, and Romania. It may help to illustrate this complexity by noting that the Hungarian (Magyar) Agoston Haraszthy, of California wine fame, was born in the kingdom, although his home village is today in Serbia, not far from Belgrade.

Vines from all parts of the empire, including those from Croatian areas along the Dalmatian coast, were referred to in the Prince catalogues as being from Hungary. And such vines were collected and made part of the general imperial collection in Vienna. It is not difficult to understand how a person might be confused trying to find historical viticultural remains from the old kingdom in today's Republic of Hungary, which is about one-fifth of its size.

One can't help wondering about the origins of the name "Zinfandel." There is no record of any vine with such a name in European vineyards in the nineteenth century or before, nor is there any record of a vine with that name being shipped to the American East Coast. And yet Prince's 1830 *Treatise* contains a list of foreign varieties of recent introduction with two entries for the "Black Zinfardel of Hungary," one of them being "parsley leaved."[12] Could this be a reference to the vine in the Gibbs 1829 import shipment? It is certainly possible, and Prince also used this exact notation in his 1831 catalogue.

I am inclined to believe that it was not, for, as we will see, the Zinfindal later in the Prince nursery came to Long Island from Boston, by way of Samuel Perkins. But somehow Prince had this word, "Zinfardel," in his mind in 1830, before Gibbs's vines traveled to Boston. Later J. Fisk Allen, the country's most learned viticultural scholar, the first ever to give a detailed description of the Zinfindal/Zinfandel, carefully and explicitly avoided such an assumption. We may never know where Prince picked up that word, but he, Allen, and Gibbs all knew where the popular Zinfindal of Boston in the 1840s had come from and who had brought it here. And has anyone ever seen a parsley-leaved Zinfandel?

We are not through with 1830. That year George Gibbs went to Boston for the annual meeting of the Massachusetts Horticultural Society (MHS), of which both he and Prince were corresponding members. There he made a fine display of his "foreign"—that is, vinifera—vines, his European imports.[13] The aforementioned Samuel Perkins acquired some of Gibbs's vines and was soon advertising cuttings of the "Zenfendal" for sale in Boston.[14] Two years later William B. Roberts, who ran Perkins's nursery, advertised "Zinfindal" vines for sale in Boston. By the next year Perkins was selling rooted "Zenfendel" vines and displaying their grapes at the MHS annual meeting.[15] By 1835

2. The leading nurseryman in the Boston area between 1830 and 1860 was Charles M. Hovey. He sent loads of nursery stock to California by sea and was an early advocate of the Zinfandel, grown under hothouse conditions as a table grape. (Source: Massachusetts Horticultural Society.)

Charles M. Hovey, Boston's leading nurseryman, was praising the flavor of the "Zinfindal" and recommending it as a table grape. (Hovey's spelling soon became standard on the East Coast.)[16]

For the next ten years horticulture publications in the northeast were full of notices for Zinfindal.[17] It had become a fairly popular table grape for the forcing house, or "early grapery," as some writers termed it.[18] Its grapes were usually on the Boston market by June.

We might ask why no one thought to test the Zinfandel for its winemaking potential. In this situation, the answer is obvious. New Englanders had given up considering vinifera, no matter how the vines were grown, for wine in their frigid environment. In 1825 John Lowell had summed it up in the *New England Farmer:* "Cider tastes good here. . . . Wine tastes terrible." To the south, people such as Prince did keep up hope for years. But New Englanders who drank wine bought it from other climes. For the year 1840, the census figures for wine from grapes in Massachusetts listed only 1,095 gallons.[19]

The grape-growing fad in New England remained strong through the 1840s. Professionals and serious amateurs exchanged vines and technical information, they held their shows, and they contributed learned papers to the local press and to agricultural journals. By the last half of the decade, the whole set of scholarly and commercial interrelations had become well organized enough for one man to bring it all together in one volume for the interested reader.

John Fisk Allen of Salem was a scholar and a practical botanist, the first person in America to produce a really good hybrid grape variety, when he crossed the Isabella, which he got from Prince, with the vinifera Chasselas de Fountainbleau. U. P. Hedrick, later one of America's leading viticultural experts, considered Allen's feat in 1844 one of the greatest events in the history of American viticulture, "surpassed only by the introduction of the Concord" in 1852.[20]

In 1846 nurseryman Charles Hovey, the publisher of the *Magazine of Horticulture,* encouraged Allen to bring his knowledge together in an extended article for that publication.[21] The article was published the next year and was soon followed by a slightly extended version in book form (55 pages). In 1848 Allen's 247-page detailed guide to viticulture, titled *Practical Treatise in the Culture and Treatment of the Grape Vine,* appeared. It went through numerous printings and five editions into the 1860s. In the 1847 article, Allen described the varieties with which he had personal experience. He gave more lines to the Zinfindal than to any other variety. His description was of the vine we know as Zinfandel. He noted that he could not find the vine described in any book, a point he continued to make in later editions of his own work. He further said that it probably was a "German" grape and had first been grown around Boston by Samuel Perkins, "who received it from a gentleman in New York State. . . ." You will recall that "Germany" in 1847 meant the vast region of central Europe where German was the dominant language. And we know full well that the gentleman in New York was George Gibbs.

In 1855 Allen addressed the fact that Prince had written about a "Black Zinfardel of Hungary" in his 1830 *Treatise,* but Allen had no idea what that vine was or whether it was the same as his Zinfindal. In 1847 Allen had had little to write about the Black St. Peters, but his later descriptions of that grape were very close to that of his Zinfindal. Samuel Perkins in 1830, and perhaps others in New England, had acquired this variety from England and had supplied Prince with the variety in 1830. As we will see, vines with this name arrived in California at about the same time as the Zinfindal, in the 1850s, and vineyards planted to the Black St. Peters in the 1860s were generally understood to be the Zinfandel in later years.

So what do we know from all this? I think that the traceable Zinfandel line is clearly Gibbs-Perkins-Prince. Unfortunately we have no "smoking gun" reference to the vine's arrival in Gibbs's nursery. Could it have been that "rough black" grape? Or was it Prince's Zinfardel, which he had received from Gibbs?

Did it come from the imperial collection in Vienna? Probably. From Hungary? Quite likely, so long as we keep in mind how huge that area of the Austrian Empire was in the nineteenth century.

In the 1850s William Robert Prince came to California, taking his chances with some placer mining and collecting seeds from native plants to send home to Long Island. Later, in a notebook now in the National Agricultural Library, he commented on the Zinfindal in California, noting, "Zinfindal fine for raisins in Cal. Drying perfectly to Raisin." Of course, this was before the chance discovery that this eastern "table grape" made a very good red wine. Prince also wrote that he thought the Zinfindal in California was the same as the "Black Sonora" there.[22] I have no idea what he meant by this reference.

Some writers recently have wondered how we can be sure that what was called Zinfindal on the East Coast was the same as what came to be called the Zinfandel in California. Prince had seen the vine growing in California and knew it from home. Those troopers from the Massachusetts Horticultural Society who came to California and remained there, helping to establish Northern California viticulture after that state joined the Union, certainly knew what the vine looked like. Those who have questioned the identity of the vine on the two coasts might consider whether a man such as Frederick Macondray, who grew the Zinfindal in Massachusetts and brought it on his sailing ship from the Bay State to California, might not have known what he and his fellow New Englanders were doing. James L. L. Warren, founder of the California State Agricultural Society, was another former Massachusetts grower, whose nursery near Boston listed the "Zinfendel" for sale in its 1844 catalogue.[23]

Before we end our sojourn in the east, it is worth noting what happened in later years to all the vinifera growing in New England. To make a short story of it, the fad of hothouse forced growing petered out. In the 1850s the discovery of the Concord variety, perfect for outdoor culture, turned almost everyone's head. I have traced the change in popularity by reading the proceedings of the MHS to the 1920s, searching in vain for some reference to Zinfandel after the 1850s. By the late 1850s native varieties, crosses, and hybrids had become all the rage. The Concord made a satisfactory wine in the Massachusetts environment, and it was to New England taste. By 1857 a Boston grower was producing twenty thousand commercial gallons of wine per year from the variety.

The Concord, Delaware, Iona, and Allen's Hybrid varieties were the darlings of the 1860s. In 1865 Hovey wrote, "The grape fever here rages higher and higher each succeeding year."[24] But he was not referring to vinifera grapes. By the 1870s vinifera table grapes were arriving from California via the new transcontinental railroad.

Vinifera varieties still appeared at the MHS exhibits, but they were of such little moment that they were rarely named in the proceedings. When Allen died in 1876, Hovey lamented that the "circle of old cultivators is narrowing."[25] No vinifera vines were shown at the annual meeting in 1878. In an editorial on the matter, the secretary of the MHS did not lament the decline. There were now better native grapes to grow at home, and good vinifera grapes were available directly from California.

GRAPES.—*Vignes.*

The abbreviations are as follows:

1. *Form of the bunch:* comp. compact, when the berries are very closely set; loose, when they are loosely set.
2. *Color:* bl. blackish; g. green; w. white; pur. purple; r. reddish; y. yellowish; p. pale; d. dark.
3. *Quality:* 1. first rate; 2. middling; 3. indifferent.
4. * Native; † Foreign.

NAME.	Form of the bunch.	Color.	Form of the berry.	Qual.	REMARKS.
†White Chasselas, - - *Royal Muscadine.*	loose	y. w.	round	1	A superior variety.
†White Frontignac, - - *White Constantia,* *Muscat blanc.*	comp.	w.	round	1	Excellent and highly esteemed.
†White Muscat of Alexandria, - - - - *Frontignac Alexandrian.*	long	w.	oval	1	Superb—much esteemed.
†White Sweetwater, - *Chasselas Royal.*	loose	w.	round	1	A hardy foreign sort, and much cultivated in the
Black Hamburg, - - *Red Hamburg,* *Frankenthal,* *Valentine's,* *Admiral,* *Languedoc,* *Troller,* *Purple Hamburg.*	large	b.	round	1	Well known to be one of the most valuable varieties. The berry is uncommonly large and very productive, and is, as it deserves to be, more extensively cultivated than any other variety.
†Black Prince, - - *Black Spanish,* *Lombardy of some.*	large comp.	bl.	oval	1	A good bearer and colors well.
Black St. Peter's, - - *Black Palestine.*	loose	b.	round	1	Ripens late.
*Catawba, - - - -	loose	r. p.	round	2	A very productive, hardy grape, of musk flavor.
†Chasselas of Frontignac,	loose	r.	oval	1	Very good.
†Constantia, - - -					
†Grisly Frontignac, - - *Muscat gris,* *Grizeline,* *Red Constantia.*	long	y. r.	round	1	Muscat flavor and excellent.
*Isabella, - - -	loose	pur.	oval	1	Well known and productive. Hardy variety.
*Jewett's White, - -					
†Miller's Burgundy, - - *Le Meunier,* *Black Cluster.*	comp.	bl.	round	1	An old variety—a first rate wine grape.
†Oval Malaga, - - - *White Muscadel,* *White Jar Grape.*	large	w.	oval	1	Excellent for table use—keeps well.
*Pond's Seedling, - -	long	p.	round	1	Sweet, thin skin and very good.
*Schuylkill, - - -					
*Scuppernong White, - " Black, -	loose	bl.	round	1	Muscat flavor—excellent for dessert.
†Zinfendel, - - -	long, loose	bl.	round	1	An excellent variety, the flavor superior—grows in very large, long clusters of a conical form.

3. James L. L. Warren was the founder of the California State Agricultural Society. Before he came to the Golden State in 1849 from Massachusetts, he had owned a commercial nursery near Boston. Grapes were one of his specialties. Here is a portion of his 1844 catalogue, which lists the table grape varieties he had for sale. Note the last item in the Grapes section, as well as the "Black St. Peter's" earlier in the list. (Source: Professor William P. Marchione, Boston Art Institute.)

Then, in the 1880s, vinifera began to reappear at the annual shows. But the varieties were very limited in number, mostly Black Hamburg, Muscat of Alexandria, Syrian, and Muscat of Frontignan. There were a few others, but never a mention of Zinfindal/Zinfandel. In 1926 Archibald Wagstaff presented a paper to the MHS entitled "Growing Grapes Under Glass." The tone of his comments suggested that he believed he had come up with something new.

Now let us turn to California, where the lure of gold would draw argonauts by the tens of thousands from all over the world. Among these were thousands of New Englanders. Many brought with them a sound knowledge of horticulture; a few would soon bring in their precious nursery stocks.

CHAPTER THREE

HO! FOR CALIFORNIA!

JOHN SUTTER'S LADS ON THE AMERICAN RIVER, WHO DISCOVERED gold there on January 24, 1848, were building a sawmill in the Sierra Foothills to provide lumber for their boss to sell to the growing trickle of Americans who had been traveling cross-country and entering the Mexican province since 1841. California had been conquered almost bloodlessly by American forces in 1846. Nine days after the gold discovery, Alta California became part of the United States under the Treaty of Guadalupe Hidalgo. This sparsely populated land was ill equipped to receive the thousands of adventurers who would begin pouring into Northern California after word of the discovery was fully broadcast in the summer of 1848.

The pastoral Mexican province had about 15,000 non-Indian inhabitants when James Marshall and his men made their historic discovery. Four years later the state census counted almost 225,000. Most of those who came to the Golden State in those years were young men looking for gold; a few did make their fortunes in the mines, but an overwhelming majority did not. To some of the newcomers, it was clear from the beginning that surer wealth would come to those who supplied the gold seekers with tools for digging and food to live on. Except for beef cattle, the food supply in early Gold Rush California was mostly imported. Some remarkable fortunes were made by those who could produce a field of potatoes or onions in these early years.

Fruit was another matter. You can't produce a pear, an apple, or a bunch of grapes as quickly as a sack of potatoes. And the orchards and vineyards of the ranchos and pueblos of Alta California could not begin to meet the needs of the new population. Most of the domestic fruit sources were located in Southern California, previously the far more populated area. But now the gold and the new markets were in the north.

New Englanders constituted one of the most numerous, talented, and influential groups of newcomers to California during these years. Many brought with them a solid knowledge of fruit culture. It is instructive to read the names of the pioneers of horticulture in the new state and compare these with earlier membership rolls of the Massachusetts Horticultural Society. Chief among these pioneers was James Lloyd Lafayette Warren, the man historian Walton Bean has dubbed the "godfather" of California agriculture, which, in the 1850s, was passing through a difficult infancy as the stepchild of mining and ranching. Warren's *California Farmer,* first published in 1854, was the new state's first agricultural publication and is an important source of our knowledge of California viticulture in the 1850s.[1] His wide circle of Yankee friends included several who would help to supply Northern California with vineyard nursery stock. Of these, Captain Frederick W. Macondray is the most important for this investigation.

Warren arrived in the riotous village of San Francisco in 1849. He was quick to notice the remarkable climate and soils of California's coastal valleys. This was a Mediterranean climate, perfect for raising wine grapes. And, like others, he bemoaned the fact that the only grape variety then available was the Mission, which made a fair sweet wine but never a very good dry table wine. This variety had been planted wherever a rancho or pueblo was to be found in the old Mexican province. It had also been widely cultivated at the Franciscan missions—the first of which had been established in San Diego in 1769, the last in Sonoma in 1823—although these vineyards had mostly declined or disappeared since the secularization of the missions in the 1830s. And most of the commercial vineyards in the late 1840s were located in Southern California, in and near Los Angeles.

Between 1852 and 1862, California nurserymen, hopeful vineyardists, and potential winemakers brought in loads of vinifera grape cuttings and rooted vines to correct this situation. The economic outlook was obvious. The young adventurers who were pouring into California brought with them a prodigious thirst for alcoholic beverages. The figures for imported wine, beer, and spirits entering the state through the Port of San Francisco are staggering. In 1855 alone the annual total for still wine came to almost 14,000 barrels and 120,000 cases, not to mention about 20,000 "baskets" of sparkling wine.[2] The high prices paid for these vinous products tempted many Californians to try for a piece of this action. But anyone with a sense of taste and smell knew that the wines made from the local Mission grapes could not compete with the foreign imports, mostly from France, no matter how mediocre the latter might be. And if we can trust the judgment of those on the scene, who seem to have known good wine, the quality of most of the imported wine was very mediocre indeed.

Early grapevine imports came from two sources. The first was the East Coast, which had, as we have seen, a small and flourishing viticultural industry aimed at the production of table grapes. The other source was continental Europe, specifically France and Germany, which, in the minds of the few who knew anything of such matters, produced the best wines in the world. (A third, but less important, source was South America. Some Spanish varieties were brought north from Peru in early days.)

Word of the Gold Rush had hardly reached San Francisco when ships from the outside world began dropping anchor in the great bay, many of them left abandoned as the crew and officers headed off to the mines. Others sold what they had on board at marvelous prices and headed home for more.

New England sea captains had been sailing the California coast for years and knew all the tricks of rounding the Cape and tacking north. One of these was Frederick W. Macondray, who had first sailed into the Pacific in 1822 aboard the *Panther*. Later he visited California several times and took part in

4. Frederick W. Macondray was a Massachusetts sea captain and a member of the Massachusetts Horticultural Society. He settled in California in 1849 and imported nursery stock from Boston. His 1852 importation included a large collection of vinifera grapevines. The Zinfandel was one of them.

the profitable China trade between the Far East and New England.[3] Historian John Walton Caughey was referring to men such as Macondray when he wrote, "For New Englanders the sea route to California was the natural one, both from habit and for convenience."[4]

Macondray arrived in San Francisco and set about establishing his trading company, Macondray & Co., which still does business out of the Macondray Building in that city. He was an old friend of James Warren, both having been longtime members of the Massachusetts Horticultural Society. When Warren finally was able to establish the California State Agricultural Society in 1854 and start promoting its state fairs, Macondray became the society's first president.

In 1852 one of Macondray's import shipments to the Golden State from Boston included grapevines. By no means were these the chief element in this large horticultural shipment. Macondray in fact was more interested in pears, apples, and plums. Back in the Bay State he had been something of a pear specialist. The vines he brought into California were thought at the time to be useful primarily for producing table grapes. But he and James Warren were intent on giving them a fair and full trial to see what they could do in this new environment. There was the Black Hamburg; the Muscats of Alexandria, Frontignan, and Cannon Hall; the Chasselas, both black and white; and several others, one of which was the Zinfindal, which Boston viticulturists and nurserymen knew well and liked—as a table grape.[5]

Many other shipments of vinifera varieties arrived from New England. Anthony P. Smith, who sailed from Boston in 1849, imported nursery stock in 1853 for his historic Pomological Gardens near Sacramento. He is one of the sources for the Zinfandel vines planted here and there in the Sierra Foothills between 1854 and 1860. His "Zeinfandall," exhibited at the 1858 State Fair, brought the vine's first official mention in California records. In 1860 he made his first wine from the variety. New Englander Wilson G. Flint also supplied Zinfandel vines to others in the Sacramento area. Other sources included James R. Nickerson of Folsom, Charles Covilleaud of Marysville, and Charles M. Weber of Stockton.[6]

In 1860 at the Santa Clara County Fair, Weber was the first to show the "Zinfindal," under that name, in the San Jose area.[7] (We will see, however, that the vine was already in San Jose under another name.)

Bernard S. Fox, the superintendent of Boston's Hovey & Co., accompanied a huge shipment of nursery stock to California in 1852. He then established the San Jose Valley Nursery, for years Northern California's largest. Before long he was in print, remarking on the wonderful way the Massachusetts vinifera vines took to the California environment.[8]

But his neighbor Antoine Delmas, a French nurseryman, proved far more important in the history of California viticulture than Fox. (Fox's gravestone is decorated with a huge pear; Delmas's, properly, boasts several bunches of grapes.) Delmas's 1852 importation of French wine grapes was the first to Northern California and included "Cabrunet," "Merleau," "Black Meunier," "La Folle Blanche," and "Charbonneau."[9] In that same year he acquired a shipment from New England, perhaps through Bernard Fox, although Del-

5. Antoine Delmas, a leading nurseryman in San Jose in the 1850s, is shown here with his sons Joseph (*left*) and Delphin. In 1852 he imported vines both from France and from the East Coast. Included was the Black St. Peters, later discovered to be the same as the Zinfandel.

mas never clearly identified his source. Thirty years later he thought that a certain mystery vine important to our investigation had come from France, but I have my doubts. I believe that it was among his other New England imports.

Whatever it was, he called it the Black St. Peters, that variety so similar to the Zinfindal in New England in the 1840s. Two Northern California vineyards planted to the Black St. Peters survived into the 1880s, and they were both clearly Zinfandel in the later years. One was the R. T. Pierce vineyard in the town of Santa Clara; the other was William McPherson Hill's planting near Glen Ellen, in Sonoma County.[10]

In 1856 Delmas also sent Black St. Peters cuttings to Victor Fauré, General Mariano Vallejo's winemaker in Sonoma. A few years later Thomas Hart Hyatt, publisher of the *Pacific Rural Press,* found that both the Zinfandel and Black St. Peters varieties were going into the Buena Vista winery's Sonoma Red Wine. The date of Hart's visit was either 1865 or 1866; by then, several Sonoma vineyardists were growing Zinfandel.[11] Thus, some of Sonoma's Zinfandel came to that county from the San Jose area as Black St. Peters. Certainly, Hill's Glen Ellen plantings originated there, as did Vallejo's. But by the mid-1860s it became impossible to trace all the possible sources. It is worth noting that by the late 1860s, after the Zinfandel had started to get its rave notices, one could find no Black St. Peters in the Santa Clara Valley. It appears that the Black St. Peters vineyards all quietly became Zinfandel vineyards. But this was not a process, obviously, that received any kind of publicity; and it is impossible to document.

From this rather sketchy and selective synopsis of various introductions of Zinfandel to California, we can logically infer that there must have been others as well. This narrative simply outlines the course of events as it appears in the public record. I have chosen to focus on Macondray's introduction because it can be traced in the contemporary historical record and because in the 1880s those who could recall the confused horticultural events of the 1850s in California chose to award the palm to this adventurous and entrepreneurial sea captain.

Before we begin to follow the trail of Macondray's Zinfindal as it became Zinfandel, we should note that in the 1850s there was little talk about making wine from these New England vinifera varieties. Many did argue for trying them, to see whether any might work. But it was understood that great wine would probably come from great European wine varieties. I have already mentioned the Delmas vines in San Jose. The Pellier brothers, also French nurserymen in that town, arranged an important importation, as did Almaden's Charles Lefranc, who brought in a huge load of first-rate French vines in 1857. Several Germans, notably Emil Dresel in the Sonoma area and Francis Stock in San Jose, brought in White Riesling, Sylvaner, and Traminer vines before

1860. On the Napa side Samuel Brannan made a sizeable importation of European vines in 1860 for his vineyards near Calistoga.

Years later most of these documented early imports would be largely forgotten. It is a sad and ironic fact that Agoston Haraszthy's later imports in 1862 ended up in a tangled mass of commercially useless vineyard at Sonoma's Buena Vista in the late 1860s. It will be obvious as we examine the construction of the so-called Haraszthy myth from the 1880s that this importation by the Hungarian vintner had almost no impact on California winegrowing. And yet over the years this 1862 importation got practically all the press for its significance, right down to recent times. It is even more ironic that Haraszthy should have been credited almost universally for bringing the first Zinfandel to California, while the names of Macondray and Delmas were all but forgotten. These two and several others were initially responsible for the success story that follows.

CHAPTER FOUR

PLANT YOUR VINEYARDS! BEGIN NOW!

IN THE MID-1850S FREDERICK MACONDRAY BUILT A SMALL GLASS-enclosed grapery behind his new San Francisco home at Stockton and Washington Streets. There he began propagating his vines as he had done in New England, but without the added heat for forcing. The city's very cool summers and intrusive summer fog convinced him that he would never ripen grapes in open culture there. (People are still trying, with poor results.)

Later he expanded his horticultural operations, which were by no means confined to viticulture. He bought land in San Mateo County, south of the city, and there built up his beautiful 260-acre Baywood estate, where he created what the *Alta California* termed "the finest grapery in the state." [1]

In 1855 Macondray's friend James Warren began a campaign in his *California Farmer* newspaper to promote viticulture and winegrowing in Northern California. "Cultivators of California! Plant your vineyards! Begin now! No better investment can be made." [2] To promote the kind of systematic and intelligent agriculture that Warren had known in New England, he helped local growers and breeders organize regional and county fairs, where prizes were awarded in a broad range of categories. Eventually they organized a series of districts whose competitions led up to the State Fair, which in the early years was held in various parts of Northern California. These regional fairs invariably handed out medals, diplomas, and cash awards and always held competitions for the best grapes, wines, and brandies.

During the first years of the state and regional fairs, the wine awards could go only to products of the Mission grape, because it was the only kind of bearing vine in the area at the time. But very soon the imports began bearing, and careful distinctions began to be made in the categories of competition. "Native" grapes, meaning Mission grapes, did not compete in the same category as "foreign" grapes. This latter category was for vinifera varieties brought in after 1850. At first the only varieties entered were from the New England importations of Macondray and others. Not until 1855 were any real European wine varieties to be seen, these from Antoine Delmas's 1852 importation.[3]

By 1857 a clear pattern among the "foreign" grape varieties had developed at these competitions, held around the San Francisco Bay Area, from San Jose to Napa and Sonoma. The winners were almost entirely predictable: F. W. Macondray, A. Delmas, A. P. Smith (Sacramento), and J. W. Osborne (Napa). There were others, of course, but these four won about 70 percent of the awards between 1854 and 1860.

We have already encountered three of these men, but not the gentleman from Napa County. Joseph W. Osborne, also a New Englander, had acquired a huge tract of land north of Napa City in 1851. He was a close friend of Macondray; when the sea captain was president of the California State Agricultural Society, Osborne was its vice president.

Osborne was a brilliant man, interested in all aspects of agriculture and reputed to have had the finest library on the subject in the state. Had he not been murdered in 1863, he might have gone on to be the "father" of Napa's premium wine industry. He called his wonderful estate Oak Knoll and was awarded the medal for the best cultivated farm in California at the 1856 State Fair in San Jose. (Today the Trefethen Winery and vineyards rest on a portion of the old estate.)

Both Macondray and Osborne exhibited their Zinfindal grapes at the district and state fairs. After the competition at San Francisco's Mechanics' Institute in 1857, James Warren rhapsodized over the captain's collection of "foreign" grapes: "They were truly superb, and reminded us of the exhibitions we had been engaged in in former years in the good old Bay State."[4] That year the State Horticultural Society recommended the Zinfindal for further trial, but it is clear that this list of recommendations was not aimed at future winegrowers.

Osborne had acquired most of his "foreign" varieties from Macondray, and he grafted them onto mature Mission vines. Thus did the Zinfandel arrive in Napa. But far more important at that moment was its arrival in Sonoma, for it was there that the variety's winemaking potential was nailed down, at least under this name.

Sonoma winegrowing from the Mission variety was fairly well established in the 1850s, but little resembling a wine industry had developed. Mariano Vallejo, the former Mexican commandant in Sonoma, had a large vineyard and a real winery under the supervision of Victor Fauré. Beyond that, several other farmers were making a few hundred gallons here and there and selling what they couldn't consume wherever they could.

In 1857, however, a new entrepreneurial spirit emerged in the Sonoma Valley. Led by men such as Agoston Haraszthy, Emil Dresel, and Jacob Gundlach, a large number of locals and outside investors rightly came to see the Sonoma Valley as an ideal environment for the center of the new wine industry that they hoped would soon be flourishing in Northern California. Their products would be dry table wine and brandy. Their object was to compete with the huge flow of European imports, in quality and price.

But first they needed better grapes. Partly for this purpose the Sonoma Horticultural Society was organized in 1859. At its first meeting, on March 14 in Santa Rosa, Haraszthy and Napa's Osborne spoke on the need for better varieties for wine production. Haraszthy was elected president, and William Boggs was elected a director and secretary of the society. For those days, Boggs was an old-timer, having arrived in 1846 with his family. He had bought a tract of land next to the one Haraszthy later purchased in 1857 and became quite close to the Hungarian. Boggs eventually became an avid vineyardist and a keen observer of the viticultural scene. As early as 1855 his Sonoma red wine, from Mission grapes, had won recognition from James Warren; in 1861 Boggs was awarded the silver cup at the county fair for developing Sonoma's best small vineyard.[5] I stress the importance of this pioneer from Missouri, for in the 1880s it was his testimony that set matters straight on the coming of the Zinfandel to California's North Coast region.

The Sonoma men knew the progress Osborne had been making at Oak Knoll with the New England varieties he had acquired from Macondray. Accordingly, late in the 1859 season, they contracted to buy cuttings from Osborne to act as the base for later propagation at the Sonoma Horticultural Society's gardens. Osborne's gardener carefully labeled the cuttings and, with Boggs, drove them over to Sonoma, in two wagon loads. The chief varieties were two kinds of Chasselas, Muscat of Alexandria, Reine de Nice, Red Lombardy, Black Hamburg, and Zinfindal. Boggs stored them in the society's gardens, adjacent to his property. But the spring frosts were cruel, and most of the cuttings were killed. In fact, only the Zinfindal was unhurt. Boggs recalled that it "grew better in the nursery than any other variety."[6] Later, when these surviving vines had been planted in the society's vineyard and yielded enough grapes to make a little wine, Boggs took them to Fauré, General Vallejo's winemaker, probably in 1862. Boggs and his friends thought that the acid in the Zinfindal was too high to make good wine, but Fauré told them that this was precisely what they needed to make a good claret. He also told Boggs that the grapes might have been from a red Bordeaux variety. Later Boggs did not recall that the Frenchman had named any particular variety. He also wrote that his original intention had been to trade the grapes with Fauré for some vinegar.

Later, after they tasted the young wine Fauré made from the grapes, Sonoma vineyardists quickly developed a solid respect for this strangely spelled variety. Fauré, of course, planted Zinfindal cuttings in 1863 for Vallejo, as did Haraszthy at Buena Vista. These were the vines that Thomas Hart Hyatt saw growing at Vallejo's place in 1866, along with the Black St. Peters vines that Delmas had previously sent to the general.[7]

Meanwhile, back in San Jose, Delmas's Black St. Peters had won the gold medal for the best red grapes at the Santa Clara County Fair. Then in 1858 he made some experimental wine from this variety, and the next year he decided

6. General Mariano Vallejo was Sonoma's leading wine producer in the 1850s. This is his Lachryma Montis estate, which is a state park today. His winemaker, Victor Fauré, may have been the first to identify the Zinfandel under that name as a good wine grape for California.

to enter it in the State Fair competition. The committee awarded him the first prize, but in their report the committee members expressed surprise that the French nurseryman's grapes "had been selected more as table fruit than for winemaking" when they were first planted. The *Alta California* was soon crowing that the Delmas red wine was the best claret in the state and that it could easily be taken for the French article.[8]

Thus it was that the Zinfandel, under various spellings and under at least one other name, came to be recognized in Northern California as a valuable red wine grape. It was not long before growers in the Sierra Foothills and the Sacramento Valley also discovered that it was something more than just another good table variety.

But we should not infer from the story of these events that anyone at the time understood the importance of this discovery. Its importance was recognized only in retrospect, in the 1880s, when the variety became the darling of the wine industry (and at that time the story was purposely obscured). In the 1860s the wine "industry" in the Sonoma, Napa, and Santa Clara Valleys was small potatoes, and few paid any attention to it.

To tell the tale of the Zinfandel during the 1860s is to pick and choose among scores of random references in the press. In the 1870s no one tried to reconstruct the history of this variety in California. Not until the late 1870s did the Zinfandel really become important, and not until the 1880s was its preeminence manifest. I cannot even fix the exact time when it became, once and for all, Zinfandel, but it was sometime in the 1870s.

The *Transactions of the California State Agricultural Society* for 1860 contained several references to the new grape. Folsom's James Nickerson now thought the "Black Zinfindal" the best variety they had for red table wine. Wilson Flint, a Sacramento New Englander, also praised it. Even James Marshall, the man who had discovered gold in 1848, had the variety in his Coloma nursery. References to the Black St. Peters here and there in the Sierra Foothills can also be found, though none appear after the 1860s.[9] The *California Farmer* had referred to the Zinfindal on several occasions, but the variety had not attracted Warren's close personal attention until he visited Charles Covilleaud's Marysville vineyard in 1861. His description of this "rare variety" was perfect, and he also noted that it was from Germany. (Since Warren knew Prince and received his catalogues from Long Island, the reference makes perfect sense, because Prince had consistently written that Gibbs had acquired it from "Germany.")[10]

Agoston Haraszthy's 1861 trip to Europe, just about the time the guns at Fort Sumter were sounding the beginning of the Civil War, was something of a nonevent in the history of California Zinfandel. His purpose was to collect European vines of all sorts to test in the California environment. He had sought and received a commission from the state legislature, "as a dignity without emolument." But it did not authorize him to purchase vines, and certainly not at state expense.

Before he left, he advertised for subscribers to support his venture at fifty cents per vine. He apparently got very few takers, if any. When he returned, he had a list of hundreds of varietals, both well known and obscure, but it contained no mention of anything that might be taken for Zinfandel.[11] (The list included 157 varieties from Hungary.) In fact, we have no contemporary evidence that this most prolific of California wine writers ever mentioned the variety either in writing or in conversation between 1856 and 1866.

Between 1863 and 1867, we can find clues that the Zinfandel was gaining a bit of stature beyond its discovery. By 1865, at the huge Natoma Vineyard near Folsom, Benjamin Bugby had decided that Zinfandel was one of the top vines in California for red wine. The next year the report of the California State Agricultural Commission lamented that no more than 1 percent of the 1866 Sonoma wine crop would come from "foreign" varieties, although the report directed special praise for the wine being made there from the "Black Zinfandel." But in the minds of the *Alta California*'s editors, "much of California wine is bad."[12] At this point, there were still more commercial vines in the hot lands of Los Angeles County than in Napa and Sonoma combined.

The first big year for Zinfandel was 1867. The *Alta California* asked Napa's Jacob Schram for the name of the best red grape available, and he told them it was the "Zenfenthal." Later he spelled it "Zinfendel."[13] On the Sonoma side, William McPherson Hill made what I believe was California's first really famous Zinfandel from vines he had planted in the early 1860s. Thomas Hart Hyatt discovered it in 1870 and recalled that he had seen the Zinfandel growing in Sonoma in 1866. This is a portion of his review:

> We sampled . . . a bottle of wine from the cellar of Wm. Hill . . . made from the Zinfandel grape, a new variety that is growing rapidly in favor with winemakers of this county. This wine . . . was pronounced by the gentlemen who tasted it to be superior to any they had seen in the state.[14]

Later the *Alta California* claimed that Hill's Zinfandel "would take the first premium at a National Exposition."[15] Such language in years to come might be rejected as fulsome puffery, for California newspapers became experts at booming the state's products. But at this moment in California wine history, these writers were looking for a good wine any place they could find it. They were not touting the quality of California wine in general. That would come soon enough.

There had been a flurry of Zinfandel planting in Sonoma in 1867. What might have helped to promote this rush was a U.S. Department of Agriculture report appearing that year that praised the Zinfindal for making "a very fine red wine, resembling the finest brands of claret imported." [16] During the dormant season of 1867–1868, the *Alta California* described a stampede of growers looking for Zinfandel cuttings, "whose demand far exceeds supply." There was also talk in the press about using Zinfandel to upgrade the quality of ordinary Mission wine in order to produce an acceptable claret.[17] That year Sonoma's John Snyder was awarded a silver medal at the Mechanics' Institute for his "Zinfenthal." In the next year J. H. Lockwood gave us our first descriptive picture of Zinfandel claret in his long report to the California State Agricultural Society: "The two prominent excellencies of its wine are tartness and a peculiar and delightful flavor resembling the raspberry." This was the variety, he predicted, that would allow California to compete with the French imports. He discussed dozens of good wine grapes, but closed by remarking that if a winegrower could plant only one, it should be Zinfandel.[18]

From a grower's point of view, the most significant information about the variety concerned wholesale prices. At the end of the 1869 vintage, new Sonoma Mission "claret" brought forty cents per gallon; new Zinfandel in bulk brought ninety cents.[19]

Press surveys of winegrowers in the early 1870s focus on the varieties favored in Northern California's coastal valleys. The market most demanded white wines in the German style; the vines to plant were the White Riesling for style and elegance and the highly productive Burger (Elbling) for stretching and blending. For red table wine, virtually everyone was touting the Zinfandel, straight or used to upgrade lesser varieties, particularly the still ubiquitous Mission, which continued to be the number one variety in the Sonoma, Napa, and Santa Clara Valleys.

The other red wine variety most often mentioned in these booming post–Civil War times was the Cinsaut, also spelled Cinsault. At the time it was usually referred to as the Malvoisie or Black Malvoisie. Today this variety is widely planted in southern France. It makes a good blending wine, as it did 125 years ago. Viticultural expert Jancis Robinson has given the variety faint praise for playing "third or fourth fiddle in blends of good Châteauneuf-du-Pape today."[20] But in the 1870s it played an important second chair to the Zinfandel, even becoming concert master for a brief period, at least in some winegrowers' minds. By the 1880s it had lost much of its quality luster and had become a matter of concern to persons worried about the quality of California Zinfandel, since blends of the two were common and always, if we are to believe critics of that age, greatly inferior to straight Zinfandel.

In the early 1870s Sonoma was still the home of the best dry table wine in California, so far as the press and the leaders of the young and rather insignificant California wine industry were concerned. But Napa was catching up, particularly for red wine. Sonoma whites, especially those with a good lacing of White Riesling or Sylvaner in their blends, were still champs. But in the mid-1870s the area around St. Helena in Napa Valley had edged into the lead for red wines. And there Zinfandel planting was frantic in these years.

Unfortunately for the nascent dry wine industry, much of the rest of the 1870s was an economic disaster. The Panic of 1873 triggered America's first great industrial depression, and the wine industry suffered from a collapse of consumer buying power and plummeting wine prices. To make it worse, the vineyards that had been planted before the crash came into full production when business conditions were at their worst. But through these unhappy years, Zinfandel's reputation grew to a remarkable extent. Toward the end of this dismal decade, it became the basis for economic renewal for the tiny California wine industry.

CHAPTER FIVE

BOOM! 1872–1890

This was the first grape from which
good red wine was made in California.
PROFESSOR GEORGE HUSMANN, 1896

THE INDUSTRIAL AND AGRICULTURAL DEPRESSION THAT GRIPPED the United States from 1873 to 1878 hurt California wine producers and acted as a brake on vineyard expansion. The prices of all agricultural products were battered, and yet the amount of wine shipped out of state to the East Coast grew—partly a result of a decline in wine imports from France, whose vineyards were being wasted by the phylloxera root louse. The producers of California's best table wines, such as Lefranc and Pellier in the Santa Clara Valley, Krug and Groezinger in Napa, and Dresel and De Turk in Sonoma, made money and survived. Even though prices were rock-bottom, they and several others clearly demonstrated that good table wine could be made profitably in the northern coastal valleys of California. Their efforts provided strong evidence for the growing belief that this region, not Southern California, would be the future home of California's premium table wine industry.

What reputation Northern California was gaining for its table wines derived primarily from its whites in the Germanic style. Red table wines, usually labeled claret or burgundy, were made mostly from Mission grapes, which still dominated, even in Napa and Sonoma in the early 1870s. Whatever California vintners thought of the Zinfandel and Cinsaut, the reality was in their wine vats at the end of the vintage, full of grapes from vines planted in the 1860s. These were mostly Missions.

In his 1880 report as head of the state viticultural commission, Charles A. Wetmore looked back at the 1870s: "In clarets we are notably deficient, not withstanding the glories of our Zinfandel."[1] If he had been privy to the kind of acreage reporting we have come to expect today, Wetmore would have known that a wave of Zinfandel planting had been sweeping the Golden State for several months.

Looking back, we can see a small crack in the wine depression in 1877, when several Napa and Sonoma vintners received unexpected orders for bulk wine from new East Coast customers.[2] The situation wasn't rosy, but it encouraged a small amount of new planting in the 1877–1878 dormant season. The dike broke in the next season as national prosperity began to return, wine consumption began to increase, and French sources of table wine continued to decline. (The phylloxera helped to cut French production about 35 percent between 1870 and 1885.) Although most of these new orders were for white table wine, by 1884 California claret producers would be the chief beneficiaries of increased eastern demand.

The great California wine boom of the 1880s saw the state's vintage rise from an average of less than five million gallons in the mid-1870s to just over fifteen million in 1884, when the first wave of large plantings came to bear. The great surge in vineyard expansion came in the coastal valleys around the San Francisco Bay Area, in Sonoma, Napa, Alameda, and Santa Clara Counties, which soon were accounting for more than half of the state's production of table wine. Zinfandel was by far the leading variety in this surge. This is not to say that a majority of the planting was to Zinfandel. I calculate that about 30 percent of the new vines in this area were Zinfandel, but this was roughly double the number for the runner-up. (Believe it or not, California had no reliable state or county statistics by varietal until the 1960s.)

SONOMA AND NAPA

The image of the Zinfandel as a fine claret grape, which developed in the 1860s, had been reinforced well before the boom. Napa's Charles Krug was ever bemoaning the still huge number of Mission vines in the state's best viticultural districts and the relative scarcity of Zinfandel.[3] The *Alta California,* always the advocate of better California wine, was calling for Missions to be grafted over to Zinfandel as early as 1872. Sonoma's Isaac De Turk in 1877 contended that however overexpanded the wine industry appeared during the depression, there was no oversupply of good Zinfandel.[4]

Sonoma and Napa were the centers of the Zinfandel craze after 1878. This was not by chance. The perception of these two areas as the home of high-quality red table wine had become fixed in the industry by the end of the depression. One Sonoma newspaper gloated that "in no other county has the Zinfandel so congenial a home" and predicted that the county would ride to prosperity on that variety.[5] Napa newspapers might have risen to the Sonoma challenge, but elsewhere in the state? Not a chance. By 1880 almost 80 percent of the new planting in the Alexander Valley/Healdsburg/Dry Creek area was to Zinfandel. To the north the new Italian Swiss Colony below Cloverdale reported that half of its first 300 acres were in Zinfandel. White Riesling was a distant second, with 35 acres.

In 1881 Isaac De Turk reported that Sonoma's vineyards amounted to 11,594 acres. In 1879 the vineyards had covered 7,248 acres, with 5,977 of those containing old vines planted to the Mission. Now there were about 2,500 acres of Zinfandel, making it by far the most numerous new variety in the county.

In Napa the emphasis on Zinfandel was even more pronounced, particularly around St. Helena. Charles Krug reported a total of 11,700 Napa County acres in 1881, compared with fewer than 4,000 in 1878. Zinfandel contributed more to this growth than any other variety. The distant second and third were the Palomino and White Riesling.[6] By 1887 Napa's Zinfandel accounted for more acreage (5,744 acres) than had all varieties six years earlier.

So great was the Napa passion for this grape that one of the tiny railroad stations below St. Helena was renamed "Zinfandel." By the 1880s Zinfandel Lane crossed the valley, and the steamer *Zinfandel* plied the bay waters between San Francisco and the wharves of Napa City.

PASSENGER
AND
FREIGHT LINE
BETWEEN
San Francisco and Napa
STEAMER
ZINFANDEL
H. G. BELL, MASTER,
Will leave Washington st. wharf, San Francisco, every Tuesday, Thursday and Saturday at 5 p. m., touching at all intermediate landings;
RETURNING, leaves Napa Tuesday, Wednesday and Friday, with the tide,
FARE, INCLUDING BERTH, $1,00.
Freight at Lowest Rates.
N. H. WULFF, Agent, Napa, Cal.
Telephone No., Napa, Red 72.
San Francisco, Main 1104

7. In the 1880s one could catch the *Zinfandel* at the dock in San Francisco and in two hours, after numerous stops, step off at the wharf in Napa City. (Source: *St. Helena Star.*)

SANTA CLARA VALLEY

Zinfandel was not a craze in the Santa Clara Valley. Some attributed this to the early and powerful French influence in the vineyards around San Jose. Why the French do not love our Zinfandel I don't know, but my impression is that this stereotype from the 1870s persists 130 years later. There have been exceptions, of course, such as Domaine Tempier's Lucien Peyraud, who has likened his French Bandol wines to California Zinfandel.

David Harwood's Lone Hill Vineyard was the largest in Santa Clara County in the 1870s. He planted varieties I have never heard of; he even had the eastern native Catawba. But he had nary a Zinfandel vine. His neighbor was Almaden's Charles Lefranc, who would have nothing to do with the variety. Nevertheless, by the mid-1870s, the *San Jose Mercury* was trying to draw the attention of local growers to the Zinfandel's Sonoma success.

By the early 1880s fairly sizeable plantations of Zinfandel were going into the Santa Clara Valley. Even the pioneer French winegrower Pierre Pellier had some at his vineyard above Evergreen. And all those Black St. Peters vines planted here in the 1860s were understood to be Zinfandel by the mid-1880s.

There was, however, sound logic in some vintners' doubts about the advisability of planting Zinfandel in the deep rich soils that would, by the turn of the century, be the home of some of the finest prune and apricot orchards in the world. In 1885 the *San Jose Herald* warned growers of the hazards of planting Zinfandel in the wrong places. This was soon a common concern, and it eventually became a *leitmotif* in the warnings of University of California Professor Eugene Hilgard to the state's vineyardists. He even specifically warned Santa Clara Valley growers about the hazards of overplanting Zinfandel on rich valley floors. The result would be a "heavy earthiness" that was difficult to blend out. Bacchus is said to have loved the hillsides, and so did Zinfandel.[7]

SANTA CRUZ MOUNTAINS

Zinfandel planted in the hills and foothills above Los Gatos and Saratoga gave a clear indication that complaints about local Zinfandels could not be considered a valid knock at the variety in general. These areas, today part of the Santa Cruz Mountains appellation, were producing some of the best Zinfandel claret in the state by the mid-1880s. Place names such as Glenwood, Lexington, and Alma attached to "Zinfandel" in the years before Prohibition would brighten the countenance of any knowledgeable lover of California red table wine.[8] On the hillsides above today's Cupertino, the famed Monte Bello Ridge, Zinfandel found a particularly congenial environment, eventually gaining a high reputation that has continued into recent years.

ALAMEDA COUNTY

One of the Bay Area's most important winegrowing districts grew up as a child of the first California wine boom. Before the 1880s agriculture in the Livermore Valley meant grain and grazing. There were fewer than 100 acres of vines there in the 1870s, and these were all scattered Mission of no commercial value. But by 1885 there were almost 3,000 acres of vines, planted in about one hundred separate vineyards. Forty-four different wine grape varieties were listed in a local survey in 1885; of these the leader was Zinfandel, outdistancing the second-place Mourvèdre (Mataro) by more than three to one. But Zinfandel amounted to barely 30 percent of the new planting, so eclectic was the selection of varieties in this coastal valley.[9]

By the 1880s Alameda County had two important winegrowing districts, the Livermore Valley and the area around the old Mission San Jose. There along the foothills of the East Bay, about twenty miles south of Oakland, viticulture had a long history, dating back to the mission days before the American Conquest. Many, including UC's Professor Hilgard, believed that this area had as great a potential for fine wine production as Napa and Sonoma. The vine planting craze struck here, too, with heavy emphasis on Zinfandel and red Bordeaux varieties. One vintner, Juan Gallegos, a Spaniard who had made millions growing coffee in Costa Rica, loved claret and planted more than 500 acres of vineyard for his Palmdale Wine Company between 1880 and 1882. Zinfandel dominated the numerous red wine varieties he planted here.[10]

When the new vines in these Alameda County districts came to bearing and their wines were shown at the state viticultural convention in 1887, delegates were astonished at the high quality of the wines, especially the reds, and most especially the Livermore Zinfandels. That valley's great reputation for premium white table wines was still to come.

CENTRAL COAST

South of the Bay Area in the Central Coast region, the effects of the wine boom were mild and Zinfandel planting a here-and-there occurrence. One exception was in the Cienega Valley near Hollister, where William Palmtag

8. In the Livermore Valley, Zinfandel was the Ruby Hill Winery's leading red wine variety before Prohibition. Here I often bought my Zinfandel in the 1960s and 1970s. The winery burned down in 1989.

planted eleven thousand Zinfandel vines after he acquired the historic Theophile Vaché estate in 1883. These were expanded in later years and became the basis for Palmtag's well-regarded San Benito Claret. Today the area around Paso Robles has an excellent reputation for first-class Zinfandel, but that distinction has developed only since Prohibition.[11]

SOUTHERN CALIFORNIA

In Southern California, where virtually all vines were of the Mission variety, the planting craze in the early 1880s was surprisingly strong, particularly when one considers that the large plantings of Mission vines here had been an important part of the overproduction problems suffered by the industry in the 1870s. The eventual key to success was better varieties planted in foothill localities. The elevated slopes above the San Gabriel Valley around Azusa,

Pomona, Duarte, and Monrovia were dotted with scores of new vineyards in the early 1880s. Glendale and Pasadena soon had several wineries. A good part of all this new planting was to Zinfandel for red table wine and Burger for white. In later years the Zinfandel grown on the foothill lands above Pasadena and Sierra Madre would acquire a good international reputation.

CENTRAL VALLEY

The chief enemy of high-quality table wine in Southern California was the hot weather. And so it was in the torrid Central Valley south of the Delta region. This area was not much more than a desert before the coming of the Southern Pacific Railroad and large-scale irrigation in the 1870s. Fresno was the center of agricultural development and an important grape-growing region in the 1880s. Since Prohibition, viticulture there has been concentrated on the production of sweet wines, brandy, and raisins. But in the nineteenth century land promoters likened the climate to that of southern France, and thousands of acres of wine grapes best suited for table wine were planted. Actually, the temperature summations of the region are more like those of Algeria.

In 1880 pioneer vintner Francis Eisen reported 172 acres in vines. The most common variety was Zinfandel, on 47 acres, followed by Malvoisie (Cinsaut), on 37 acres, and ten others. Virtually every new vineyard in this desert region, many of them very large scale, was loaded with vines that reflected the hopes of the owners for table wine production. But in those early years, investors in vineyard land had little understanding of the relationship between climate and individual grape varieties. In years to come, these acres of Central Valley Zinfandel would help to deflate that variety's early high reputation.

In the Central Valley to the north, in an area east of the delta and much influenced by the maritime conditions in the Bay Area, a somewhat different situation obtained. Here, north of Stockton in the Lodi area of San Joaquin County, the production of acceptable table wines was a possibility. George West had been doing it since the 1860s at his El Pinal Winery. And Zinfandel was one of his favorite varieties. In fact, it was the only red table wine he showed at the 1883 viticultural convention in San Francisco. West had also started making "white" Zinfandel, a pink wine, from his free-run juice in

1869. This was so successful that in his 1884 report viticultural commissioner Charles Wetmore specifically recommended that Zinfandel be classified a white wine grape in San Joaquin County and praised its wine there for its "delicate" flavor.[12]

I cannot fail to note that San Joaquin County today has more than 20,000 acres of Zinfandel, more than four times as many as second-place Sonoma County. This Lodi area is now important for its production of White Zinfandel, a wine that is still highly popular since its swift rise to fame in the early 1980s. Score one for George West and Commissioner Wetmore!

Farther north in the Sacramento Valley, the almost desert conditions return, although not with the intensity found near Fresno. But here too the planting of vines for table wine production became a real industry in the 1880s. In 1884 at the Natoma Vineyard Co., northwest of Sacramento, 2,400 acres of vines were in the ground, representing eighty-seven of the finest varieties, including a huge spread of Zinfandel. Within a few years 1,000 of these acres had been pulled, and brandy had become Natoma's claim to fame. Later, to the north in Tehama County, Leland Stanford would make the same mistake, planting huge tracts of vines best suited for table wine production. By the end of the 1880s brandy was the chief product at his Vina estate.

As the California wine boom began to slow in the late 1880s, most of these huge vineyard plantations in the Central Valley simply added to the sea of mediocre California wines made from varietals planted where they shouldn't have been. All too often, Zinfandel was a major component.

SIERRA FOOTHILLS

What of the Sierra Foothills, where viticulture had had such promising beginnings in the 1860s? (In 1866 El Dorado County had more vines than Napa and was producing twice as much wine.) By the late 1860s the *Alta California* could praise the foothill vineyards, noting that many of the old mining camps were "now embowered with vines."[13] But little was left that one could call an industry. The planting boom of the 1880s touched the foothills hardly at all. Amador and El Dorado Counties had only forty-nine small vineyards in 1884, although some of these would produce into the twentieth century, and a few of their vines were Zinfandel. One such vineyard is still in production. But the total amount was small then. In the 1880s less than 5 percent of El Dorado's 1,200 acres of vineyard were planted to Zinfandel. And yet we often think of the Sierra Foothills today when we rejoice over some of the best old-vine Zinfandel vineyards that have survived. Truth to tell, with but a few exceptions, these vines were planted between 1900 and 1910 and between 1920 and 1925. Eighty-year-old vines are old, but they're not over a hundred years old, as labels from this and other regions have all too often claimed.

By the mid-1880s the enthusiasm for California Zinfandel, grown in the proper places, was general among the state's wine leaders. The best Zinfandel did not usually travel under that name. In fact, among consumers, except for many on the West Coast, the name was virtually unknown. But in the minds of people closely associated with the industry, the Zinfandel stood tall. The vine gave a good-sized crop, and the quality could be excellent.

Frederico Pohndorff, a noted European wine expert, settled in the United States and spent a good part of his time evaluating California wines. He reported to the California press on the state's wines at the 1885 Louisville Exposition and was particularly impressed by the Zinfandels shown there. His report included some praise and a warning:

> California's most propagated vine, of prolific and excellent fruit, the Zinfandel has been the basis of the superior claret wines of the State for the last twenty years. You will find in the exhibits at the Louisville Exposition several really creditable Zinfandel wines, the oldest 1880, one from Sonoma and one from Napa. Zinfandel wine is for years known by consumers, be it straight under its name, or in the disguise of a French label. The true virtues, merits, and beauty the juice of Zinfandel is capable of are, in the minority of cases, apparent when grown in valley or level land. Only a small proportion of the wines are made rightly and show the real beauty of its fragrance and fruity taste. It has thus happened that the appreciation of the well-made and matured Zinfandel has remained limited.[14]

The great California wine boom started slowing in 1886, and by the end of the 1880s it was out of steam. By then, one could hardly find an acre of wine grapes being planted in the northern coastal valleys. And the new vineyards being planted in the Central Valley were mostly made up of varieties best suited for sweet wine and sherry production. Like most periods of agricultural expansion in American history, the expansion between 1877 and 1885 had gone too far. The result was surpluses and rock-bottom prices, a situation that worsened in 1893, when the depression became a national disaster, leaving the country in economic ruin until the recovery began in 1897–1898.

But the boom had firmly established the Zinfandel as California's own, the grape that would be the basis for the state's best standard red table wines, the backbone of the industry until Prohibition struck in the 1920s. Unfortunately, too much Zinfandel was being grown in places not suited to produce anything but very low-grade table wine; and these grapes were best suited for the production of sweet wine, brandy, and raisins. By the early 1890s this situation caused Zinfandel to become the whipping boy of analysts trying to explain the economic malaise torturing the California wine industry. When the national economy collapsed in 1893, people stopped bad-mouthing Zinfandel specifically, but the negative connotation stuck.

We'll look later at Zinfandel as part of a fairly mature and dynamic industry. And we'll talk more about the good and great Zins being produced. But first we need to examine the creation of a myth, in the 1880s, that totally confounded the history of Zinfandel for the next ninety years. I have already mentioned the historical cement of the Haraszthy legend. The details are complicated and often a bit tedious, but the story is worth telling. It is a good tale, full of skullduggery, heroics, perhaps even a little "recovered memory" or, better, recovered false memory.

CHAPTER SIX

THE HARASZTHY MYTH

WHEN THE MATTER CAME UP IN THE PRESS IN MAY 1885, THE FIRST thing anyone should have asked was, "Well, can't someone show me where Colonel Haraszthy mentioned the Zinfandel in his voluminous public writing on California wine?" It had been almost seventeen years since the extraordinary Hungarian had quit California for Nicaragua, where he apparently was devoured by alligators a year later. But he was well remembered as the man who, more than any other, had filled the Northern California press between 1857 and 1866 with letters, articles, speeches, and interviews on viticulture and winemaking. But if Agoston Haraszthy ever uttered or wrote the word "Zinfandel," not a trace of it remains, or remained even in the 1880s, except in the imagination of his son, Arpad Haraszthy.

The basic biographical data for the father has never been in question. It can be found in any good library in the *Dictionary of American Biography*, volumes that contain few, if any, nobodies. Haraszthy is truly an important figure in the history of the American West.[1] But what I and other writers have termed the "Haraszthy myth," or legend, has attached a powerful set of "facts" to the basic data. Added to the misinformation concerning the Zinfandel, we find the belief that Agoston Haraszthy was the father of the California wine industry, that he was the first to bring foreign wine varieties to the young state, and that these and his later imports were the basis for the success of the California wine industry. None of these ideas can be supported by the historical evidence available to us.

Agoston Haraszthy's birthplace was Futak, in the Vojvodina, then, in 1812, a part of the Kingdom of Hungary, which was part of the Austrian Empire (today located in Serbia, formerly part of Yugoslavia). His family was of the landed gentry and thoroughly Magyar (Hungarian) in ethnicity. He came to America in 1840, ending up in the Wisconsin Territory, where he helped to found the town of Sauk City. In that area he was involved in at least a dozen entrepreneurial endeavors. He also got into politics and was on hand when Wisconsin became a state in 1848. He had advanced to a position of power in the Wisconsin Democratic Party and campaigned mightily for Lewis Cass, the conservative Michigan senator and his party's presidential candidate in 1848. Cass lost by a whisker to Zachary Taylor; had he won, Haraszthy would probably have stayed in Wisconsin as a political beneficiary of his friendship with Cass.

A few months after the election, the news of gold in California reached Wisconsin. In April 1849 Haraszthy, his wife, father, and six children headed off on the Santa Fe Trail for San Diego. There he called himself "Colonel" Haraszthy, an honorific he had picked up in Wisconsin. No one knows when or how he became "Count" Haraszthy.

The rough frontier life in San Diego was too much for his wife and two young daughters, so Agoston sent them back to the East Coast, along with his nine-year-old son, Arpad. The boy and his father were not reunited until 1857 in Sonoma, and then only briefly.

Meanwhile Agoston began investing in San Diego County real estate, planting fruit trees and grapevines in nearby Mission Valley. In April 1850 he was elected sheriff, and his father, Charles, was elected to the town council. San Diego historians remember the two for their role in building the first jail there. There was a hint of graft involved, but no charges were ever brought against the Haraszthys.

9. This photo of Agoston Haraszthy was taken in New York City just before he set sail for Europe in 1861 to collect wine grapevines. For years it was thought, incorrectly, that the Zinfandel was among those imports.

Agoston became a power in local politics from the outset and joined the pro-Southern wing of the Democratic Party. In 1851 he was elected to the state assembly on a platform calling for a north-south division of the new state. The mission of the Southern California Democrats, many recently arrived from slave states, was to set up a separate territory that would eventually be a political ally of the "Cotton Kingdom." Haraszthy accepted the idea, but when he arrived in Northern California for the 1852 session of the legislature, he saw that this was where the action was. He did not return to San Diego.

Haraszthy saw that the type of agriculture that had served the sparsely populated Mexican province of California in earlier days was no longer adequate for the developing new frontier. Nurseries, orchards, vineyards, and truck farms were needed to feed the burgeoning population. A few had made huge fortunes in 1850 and 1851 by raising vegetable crops and by cornering certain parts of the state's slender fruit production. He decided to help meet this challenge, buying a piece of land near the old mission outside San Francisco to start a nursery. He called it Las Flores. He also made good money brokering fruit, particularly fresh table grapes. In 1853 he was able to acquire a 640-acre tract in the uplands on the San Francisco Peninsula near Crystal Springs. There he expanded his nursery operation and even took to raising cattle.

While there, he planted some Mission vines and may have imported grape cuttings from the East Coast. It is not clear whether such an importation was direct or through local connections in California. I know from reading the Macondray letter books that the sea captain's family knew Haraszthy. But he also had Hungarian connections on the East Coast, where the rest of his family was staying, who could have been the source of these vines. And anything brought from the east might have included Zinfindal, which was in regular use there. Later stories claim that he imported vines directly from Europe and that these included the Zinfandel. There is not a scintilla of contemporary evidence for such an importation, not a word in the press nor a word from Haraszthy himself.

During the next three years Haraszthy began engaging in endeavors substantially removed from horticulture. He became involved in smelting and refining the gold coming down to San Francisco from the Mother Lode. He, with several partners, opened a private smelting firm. In 1854 his Democratic political connections led President Franklin Pierce to appoint him assayer of the San Francisco Mint.

Over the next eighteen months his activities got him into trouble with the U.S. Treasury's special agent on the West Coast, J. Ross Browne. In January 1857 Haraszthy resigned his post, and in June Browne revealed his case against the Hungarian, whose accounts were apparently one hundred fifty thousand dollars short. Although it was a long and complicated affair, in 1860 the criminal charges against Haraszthy were dropped. The best research into the matter indicates nothing definitively. It does suggest that Haraszthy's guilt could not be proved, rather than that he was actually innocent. But comments later made by Browne indicate that he was then not convinced of any wrongdoing in Haraszthy's activities at the mint.

Meanwhile Agoston Haraszthy had set out on the venture that made him an important force in the history of California winegrowing. In 1855 he had visited the Sonoma Valley and tasted the wine made from the Mission grapes grown there. The depressed price of land, the quality of the wine, and the healthy appearance of the old unirrigated vineyards convinced him to make a serious move into winegrowing. He bought 560 acres of land east of town, including the old Kelsey place, called Buena Vista Ranch, whose wine he liked. He then had many of his young vines at Crystal Springs transferred to Sonoma. There were already several working vineyards in the Sonoma Valley, but it was Haraszthy who was able to focus the attention of the old-timers, and many newcomers, on commercial winegrowing. In 1857 he made six thousand gallons of wine at Buena Vista and began the estate's physical transformation.

During the next year he expanded the Buena Vista vineyard with vines he propagated himself, which he bought from others in the area and which he perhaps imported. But no contemporary evidence exists for such an importation. He also had tunnels dug into the mountainside to store his coming vintages, and he built a solid stone winery. He also raised grain and vegetables and planted an orchard. In 1858 he sold a large part of his grape crop fresh in San Francisco. By then he had 140 acres in vines; a year later he had 250 acres. And his neighbors were also doing well with their vines. Everyone agreed that Sonoma was having a boom and that Haraszthy, more than anyone else, was its author.

In 1858 Haraszthy wrote a report on grapes for the California State Agricultural Society.[2] From this and other of his writings that appeared in the Bay Area press, it is clear that he was concerned about the wine grape varieties available in California. He was convinced that the Mission would not suffice. But in his own report he stated that he had more than 150 varieties growing at Buena Vista. He never listed them. He couldn't. Such a claim was pure puffery. The Hungarian was employing the great American entrepreneurial tradition of substituting his hopes for facts in public statements about his enterprise.

In 1860 he gave an address at the State Fair calling for better varieties in California vineyards. At the end of the year he developed a plan to import a large number of first-class European wine varieties, and perhaps make a few dollars on the side. Working through the state agricultural society and political friends in Sacramento, Haraszthy got a bill through the legislature calling for the state to appoint a commission "to collect together all the useful and valuable grape vines . . . for distribution amongst the people." Meanwhile he advertised in the local press that he would supply farmers with several kinds of vines for a few dollars. He received virtually no response.

Haraszthy was on his own when he sailed from San Francisco on June 11, 1861, seemingly oblivious to the war that was tearing the country to pieces. Back in Sacramento, Haraszthy's pro-Southern cronies were calling for the nation to let the seceding Southern states go in peace. (Haraszthy himself never publicly supported the Confederacy, and Union men such as Warren and Osborne never questioned his loyalty.)

He stopped in New York to arrange for the publication of a book to chronicle his tour. He was on the high seas bound for Southampton when the Union armies were routed by the Confederates at Bull Run. He was accompanied by his wife and daughter Ida, and they soon met Arpad in France. Arpad was a young man now and had been studying sparkling wine production at Epernay in Champagne. They toured France, Italy, Germany, and Spain collecting vines, while Agoston took notes for his upcoming book. By October the party had amassed about one hundred thousand vines, which were later consolidated and shipped home. The collection contained about three hundred varieties.

The party arrived back in San Francisco in December. Agoston quickly set about trying to get some kind of compensation for his expenses. But the political scene had changed since his departure. Now Union forces controlled the state government, and Haraszthy's "Copperhead" friends were in total disrepute. The legislature was in no mood to hear about underwriting this

Hungarian grandee's vacation in Europe, particularly since his commission had specifically precluded any remuneration. If his collection was so valuable, his critics argued, why didn't he just sell it? The fact was that there was nothing special about the importation of good European vines. It had been going on since 1852. What made the Haraszthy importation unique and potentially valuable was that it might have been distributed to vineyardists, had an agency for such an operation existed. But there was none. The Delmas, Lefranc, and Dresel importations had been strictly private matters, although some of their vines and their offspring were sold to others.

Haraszthy took his vines to Buena Vista and planted them, and there most of them stayed, for want of a state agency with a mechanism for distributing them. Nevertheless, the claim that the Haraszthy vines were distributed throughout the state became part of the legend constructed by Arpad years later. There is nothing to support such a claim. And, of course, nothing in Agoston's list of imports even vaguely sounded like Zinfandel. So what? By 1862 the Zinfindal was already in place in much of the winegrowing country of Northern California.

The last chapter of Agoston's adventure in California wine came in March 1863, when he was able to promote the incorporation of the Buena Vista Vinicultural Society, a move that infused his venture with much-needed capital. But it proved to be a serious error on the part of the eight San Francisco businessmen who pumped their money into the Sonoma venture. Haraszthy served as superintendent, and the result was economic disaster. In 1864 the society's fiscal report tried to put a brave face on matters, but by July 1866 the directors were lamenting the "hopeless condition of the Society." Three months later Agoston was forced out of his position at Buena Vista. After its correspondent later visited the place, the *Alta California* wondered at the sorry state of the once-great vineyard. It now resembled a jungle, where it was next to impossible "to get enough grapes of any one kind to make a barrel of wine."[3] During 1867 Haraszthy produced brandy and planted a couple of vineyards for others in the upper Sonoma Valley. Then in 1868 he was off to Nicaragua to set up a distillery.

The lively Hungarian's demise received little notice in Northern California; the entangled vineyard and the lack of profits at Buena Vista were now symbols of his failure. Years later the slavish acceptance of the Haraszthy myth by journalists and wine writers meant that Agoston's real contributions to the California wine industry would be overlooked and forgotten. It was laughable to assert that he was the "father" of the industry, but I don't believe that anyone contributed more to its growth and development. He was a great publicist. He was the young industry's public conscience, promoting better wine through the use of better grapes and rational cellar practices. He advocated vineyard and cellar techniques in the 1860s that were considered prescient in the 1880s. Unfortunately, the picture of the man's contributions developed in later years emphasized a few material accomplishments that cannot be supported by the historical evidence. His introduction of Zinfandel into California is the most obvious and most frequently quoted of these errors. So say virtually all those who have examined the full record from the period between 1850 and 1868.

More than a month after Haraszthy's death in 1869, an unsigned obituary article appeared in the August 26 issue of the *Alta California.* The rhetorical style, the phrasing, even the vocabulary indicate that the piece was written by an indignant son, shocked at the callous forgetfulness of a once-admiring Northern California community to which Agoston Haraszthy had been a hero. The cadence of the words would echo through the son's writings on the California wine industry for the next thirty years, amplifying and refining these contentions:

—Agoston Haraszthy was the father of the California wine industry.
—His imports in 1861 were the basis for the eventual development of California's fine wines.
—He was the first to import foreign wine varieties to California.

The young lad who had been sent back to the East Coast from San Diego with his mother and sisters in 1851 had become the bright star of the Haraszthy children. Intelligent, energetic, full of curiosity, Arpad had been placed in academies in New York and New Jersey to advance his formal education. When he finally joined his family in Sonoma in 1857, he stayed only two months before heading off to Paris to study civil engineering. Then, in 1860, encouraged by his father, he changed course and moved to Epernay to study the production of Champagne in the firm of De Venoge. He stayed there two years and accompanied Agoston on his 1861 European tour.

Arpad was home in Sonoma in 1862 in time to supervise the crush at Buena Vista for his father. He also began experiments in making California sparkling wine. In the following year he and his brother Attila married two of General Vallejo's daughters. According to historians Ruth Teiser and Catherine Harroun, Arpad's wife, Jovita, "was considered the beauty of the Vallejo family." [4]

Arpad continued his experiments with sparkling wine after Agoston organized the Buena Vista Vinicultural Society, but the expensive failures involved forced him to resign and leave his father's employ. In 1866 he joined forces with wine merchant Isador Landsberger and within a year had produced what eventually would be California's first commercially successful bottle-fermented sparkling wine, known as Eclipse. By the 1870s Eclipse was a commercial success, and Arpad became known as something of a man-about-town, a "convivial boulevardier," in the words of historians Teiser and Harroun, and a charter member of the San Francisco Bohemian Club.

But Arpad was a troubled man. Although he and Jovita now had two children, their domestic life was unhappy. In 1877 she began divorce proceedings. General Vallejo was finally able to placate her and "avoid a scandal." Whatever the problem, Arpad had written his wife several letters "asking her pardon." In the general's words, Jovita finally gave in, "for the sake of the children." In the next year the couple's new baby died, and Jovita died soon thereafter. Symbolic of the couple's shaky circumstances, they had changed residence seven times in their twelve years in San Francisco before Jovita's death.

In 1879 Landsberger pulled out of the partnership, and Arpad was able to bring in Harry Epstein, a rancher and businessman who supplied twenty-eight thousand dollars for the firm to buy the Orleans Hill Vineyard in Yolo County. The land was totally unsuited for the production of fine wines. Historian Ernest Peninou has written that the place was nothing but "dry, hot

SPARKLING ZIN?

One of the main import items that flowed through the port of San Francisco in the thirsty Gold Rush days was sparkling wine. Californians who could pay the price couldn't get enough good Champagne. Early in the 1850s several producers in Southern and Northern California tried to make a good commercial sparkling wine, but even the best were commendable failures.

The main problem was the Mission and muscat varieties they had to employ. Too much sugar created too much carbon dioxide and too many exploding bottles. Too little acid meant that the resulting wines would taste flabby in comparison to the real thing from France. And the crude flavors that were imparted by the Mission variety could not be successfully covered with a shot of muscat juice.

The first to solve these problems were two winemakers associated in its early days with the Buena Vista Winery venture in Sonoma. Arpad Haraszthy had studied Champagne production in France, and Isador Landsberger was a successful wine merchant well acquainted with vinous matters. After he left Buena Vista, Haraszthy teamed up with Landsberger and began a series of experiments in San Francisco. These led to the first successful California sparkling wine. They called it Eclipse, after a famous racehorse. By the early 1870s it was the toast of San Francisco.

Haraszthy's success came from his experimental blends that eventually gave him a sparkler with plenty of small bubbles, but not too many, and good acid to make a crisp and pleasing beverage. He chose grape varietals that grew well in California and contributed flavors to the wine that satisfied many who were familiar with real Champagne. By the 1880s Haraszthy's formulas, which were always complex, rested on one major ingredient. Here is the formula for his 1885 Eclipse *cuvée:*

1 percent Folle blanche
3 percent Sylvaner
4 percent Pinot Meunier
4 percent Grey Riesling
4 percent White Verdal
12 percent Malvasia bianca
13 percent French Colombard
18 percent Burger
41 percent White Zinfandel!

sun-swept foothills." I join him in terming the purchase by a supposedly knowledgeable leader of the wine industry "unexplainable."[5]

Arpad and Epstein spent more money expanding the vineyard to 340 acres by 1885. Meanwhile they were producing still wine and "Champagne" at other premises. The following year, seemingly to secure the failure of the venture, they built a 250,000-gallon stone winery on the Yolo property. The folly of this endeavor can be guessed, given that the vintage there often began in

10. The Orleans Hill Winery, built by Arpad Haraszthy in 1886 in the desertlike western Sacramento Valley. Its failure added to his desperate personal problems. (Source: Unzelman Collection, Santa Rosa.)

July. They were dry-farming vines in the middle of a desert to produce what they thought would be premium table and sparkling wine.

It was during this period of Arpad's familial disintegration and financial folly that the Zinfandel question was raised in the press. But so far as his public image was concerned, Arpad Haraszthy was on top of the world. In 1878 he had been elected president of the California State Vinicultural Society. In 1880 he became the first president of the Board of State Viticultural Commissioners (BSVC).

No one who grew Zinfandel or was making Zinfandel wine in the early 1880s gave a hoot about the battle that soon began to rage in the press over the origins of that vine in California. The fight developed when a desperate man advanced a historical theory that simply did not fit the experience of the individuals who had lived through Zinfandel's arrival in the Golden State and its subsequent rise to prominence. Nevertheless, Arpad's fictitious characterization of his father's contributions became a historical block of concrete for almost a century.

The idea that the Zinfandel might have come from Hungary had been kicking around in California since the 1860s, for numerous copies of William Robert Prince's book *A Treatise on the Vine* were at hand, containing a clear reference to the "Zinfardel" of Hungary. It is doubtful that anyone noticed J. Fisk Allen's later unwillingness to equate this reference with the well-known New England vine that came to California. And few would have been aware of Prince's own recognition that Gibbs had brought what he now thought was Zinfindal to Long Island from Vienna. I find such Hungarian references in numerous sources with no mention of any role by Haraszthy.[6] It makes sense that some people would wonder a little about the vine's origins at the time that it was really starting to catch on.

The first squeak from Arpad Haraszthy on the subject seems to have been in 1877, when he was cited in the *San Francisco Bulletin* claiming that Agoston had transferred the Zinfandel from Crystal Springs to Sonoma when he moved north.[7] (One must keep in mind that when these events took place, Arpad was a teenager, studying either on the East Coast or in France.) From then on, Arpad began pushing the story to unbelievable limits. He passed it on to Charles A. Wetmore, who included it in his first report (1880) as executive officer of the Board of State Viticultural Commissioners. It is clear that Wetmore had been duped, for he gave Agoston thanks for his 1860 "princely gift to this State, including our now famous Zinfandel." (He didn't even have the date correct.) Wetmore went on to state that the vine "is now known more in America than in Europe. . . ."[8] That was true, since there is no evidence that the vine was ever known by that name in Europe. Wetmore surely blushed when someone pointed out to him that Agoston's complete 1862 list of vine imports, published as an appendix to his own 1880 report, included 157 Hungarian varieties brought back from the excursion—with no mention of Zinfandel.

There is no record of the events, but it is clear that Wetmore was subsequently challenged by those who had been on the scene twenty-five years earlier and knew what had and had not happened. His mistake concerning the 1862 listing was obvious. But what was the truth as to the original introduction of the vine?

Wetmore must have talked to dozens of old-timers and then developed a generalized theory concerning the Zinfandel's introduction to California. He had to be careful because he couldn't call Arpad Haraszthy a liar. And I'm not at all sure that he thought Arpad was lying. I'm not even sure that Arpad himself knew that he was lying. Family memory can be a very capricious and fragile thing. At that moment, his family life was in shambles, partly because of what appears to have been a dishonest indiscretion. And he had just invested virtually everything he owned in a very tenuous new venture that would eventually come down around his ears.

In his 1884 BSVC report, Wetmore did his best to clear up the mess he had made in his earlier report, which obviously had stirred up a hornets' nest. In tracing the history of California winegrowing, he praised Agoston Haraszthy for his contributions, although he correctly acknowledged Charles Kohler as "the pioneer and founder" of the California wine industry.[9]

Then he noted that Agoston Haraszthy had imported vines to California *before* the 1861–1862 trip and mentioned that among them was the Zinfandel, "which he knew in Hungary." He might as well have said, "Arpad told me that his father had known the vine in Hungary." He surely must have wondered why Arpad had told him that the Zinfandel had been in the 1862 importation and then changed his story.

Wetmore also backed away from his previous implication that Agoston had been cheated by the state, another piece of misinformation that had come from Arpad. Now the commissioner admitted that the collections had been made at Agoston's own private cost. He also backed away from his contention that these importations had been a great service to the state. Now he could list only a few table grapes in the collection that had been further propagated. Then he went on to praise the many earlier Californians, mostly German and French, who had made truly valuable importations in earlier years, which "laid the foundations of vineyards that are now successful." It is clear that Wetmore, who was but fourteen in 1861, had been given some powerful history lessons during the previous four years by some of the people who had made that history.

Later in his report Wetmore addressed the question of the Zinfandel. First he stated that Agoston's importation of that vine from Hungary "is known to his family." He was not unkind enough to add, "and to no one else." But he did give a very adequate generalized history of how the vine came to California, a history that does not differ from the one I have traced, except that he gave no names or dates. Zinfandel had come to California, in his words, in various small lots, "at an early day, from eastern nurserymen who called it Zinfindal." He also acknowledged Prince's historic reference in 1830. He continued that "it was not extensively propagated [in California] from the early nursery stocks, but became sufficiently scattered throughout the State to cause much present confusion in the popular claims for recognition as to the credit due for introducing it." As to the vine's European origins, Wetmore was as correct as he could have been at that time, given the material available to him. Zinfandel was "taken from collections in Europe that are as little known there as here, rare curiosities of viticulture which we have utilized...."

Commissioner Wetmore hoped this report would put an end to the matter. Haraszthy could make his claim through "family memory," and the people who had experienced the 1850s and taken part in the discovery of the Zinfandel had been saluted in a general fashion. Now the whole thing should go away. The industry's fortunes were soaring, and it didn't need this internecine bickering.

But the winemakers out in the country wouldn't let it go away. In Sonoma Robert Thompson, a well-known journalist and local historian, had been putting the whole Zinfandel story together, talking to everyone he could find who remembered. In May he wrote a long article for the *San Francisco Evening Bulletin* and made hash of Arpad's claims. He traced the Zinfandel from New England to California, citing the contributions of Macondray, Osborne, and Boggs.[10] A few weeks later Boggs himself wrote to the *St. Helena Star* and told the story of his personal involvement in the coming of the Zinfandel.[11] The Boggs letter was a reply to one written by Arpad Haraszthy to the *Bulletin* on May 11, in which he reasserted the claims he had made concerning his father.

Boggs first made it clear that "no disrespect was meant to the memory of his [Arpad's] lamented father," nor was there "any desire to detract from the credit due him for his enterprising interest promoting the wine industry of this State." But Boggs had been on the scene, and he knew what had happened. He had owned the land next door to Agoston's 1857 Sonoma purchase and had come to know the Hungarian on a daily basis. He told in his letter how he and Haraszthy had organized the Sonoma Horticultural and Viticultural Gardens in 1859 and how he had brought the Zinfandel over from Osborne's place in Napa. Boggs noted that until that time the only "foreign" grapes in Sonoma were a few table varieties and the Black St. Peters that Vallejo had acquired from Delmas.

Then Boggs told of the transportation of Haraszthy's vines from Crystal Springs to Sonoma. "There were no foreign vines shipped to Sonoma. . . . I know whereof I write. . . ." He had been there and helped to plant these Mission variety vines. "Col. Haraszthy may have had some foreign vines . . . in San Mateo [County], but there was no such grape planted by him at Buena Vista vineyard" until the Osborne cuttings arrived. Arpad was "mainly indebted to his own vivid imagination" in his claim that his father first brought the Zinfandel to Sonoma and had been the first to import foreign varieties to California.

At about the same time Antoine Delmas added his voice. He had imported the Zinfandel under the name Black St. Peters in 1852. (He thought it was from France, but I believe that it was in his shipment from New England.) He had planted the R. T. Pierce vineyard in Santa Clara to the Black St. Peters, and everyone knew that those vines were now Zinfandel. (William McPherson Hill told the same story from Glen Ellen.) A week later Arpad was in San Jose for a viticulture conference and was persuaded to look at the Pierce vines. He admitted that they looked like Zinfandel, but he stuck to his guns. He knew the vine had grown in his mother's vineyard in the old country but thought it might be a seedling of the Pinot noir.[12] He also noted Prince's reference to the Hungarian Zinfardel, to help prove his point, obviously unaware that Prince had later made it clear how the vine had come to the East Coast.

Arpad refused to back down; some of his statements became absolutely outlandish. According to a trade journal, he claimed that Macondray's gardener had told him personally that the sea captain had no Zinfandel in his

11. Arpad Haraszthy, pictured here, was a leading San Francisco wine merchant in the 1880s, who almost singlehandedly concocted the story that his father had brought the Zinfandel to California from his native Hungary. No contemporary historical evidence supports this story, whereas a great deal of evidence supports the history outlined in this book.

grapery. (Macondray had been dead for seven years before Arpad first mentioned the Zinfandel in print, in 1869.) Arpad told a Napa newspaper that his father had known the Zinfandel in Hungary and that it made excellent claret there. He also began questioning whether the Zinfandel's growing habits were similar to those of the Black St. Peters.[13]

By the fall of 1885 the public controversy had subsided. Now Arpad began mixing his historical concrete. In the spring of the next year he penned a four-page memo for historian H. H. Bancroft that detailed his father's contributions to the California wine industry. In July Bancroft produced a forty-five-page typescript titled "The Haraszthy Family." Most of this document is a fulsome encomium to Arpad Haraszthy, historically accurate, for the most part, but a tedious chronicle of the great works of a great man's more than great son. Only the first twelve pages are devoted to the father. They follow

Arpad's manuscript closely and contain some good history about Agoston's years in California. But squeezed in was the same historical nonsense Arpad had been recently peddling.[14]

There were some strange inconsistencies between the manuscript and the typescript. In the manuscript Arpad had written that his father had imported vines from Europe and the East Coast in 1853 and planted them at Crystal Springs in March 1854. Of course, the Zinfandel was included. Arpad has Agoston selling vines from this importation "to all parts of the state," years before moving to Sonoma. Concerning the Zinfandel at that early date, "ever after it was his pride to recommend its plantation as the best grape for red wine claret." In the final version put together by Bancroft, the importation takes place in 1851, while Haraszthy was in San Diego. Such a claim is nonsense, but what happened between the writing of the manuscript and the production of the final draft? Had Arpad learned of the pre-1853 importations by others? It would almost appear that Arpad participated in the composition of the final draft. This section of the typescript ends with the following sentence: "It is now universally admitted that to Col. Haraszthy is due the sole credit of the first introduction of foreign vines into the State of California."

Many a viticultural pioneer in California would have gagged on that line. But no one would see it except historians of a later time working at the University of California's Bancroft Library to investigate the history of the wine industry.

Another inconsistency is truly remarkable, though it does not relate to the Zinfandel. Concerning the 1862 importation, Arpad's manuscript contends that the vines "were sold throughout the state, for the first time causing a general and large plantation of foreign vines in every direction." But in the final typescript the vines were "scattered through the country," which "now conduce to the general confusion in nomenclature." These are the words of Charles Wetmore, not Arpad Haraszthy. But if Wetmore was consulted, how did the "first importation" silliness get through? We will probably never know. But this was the document later used by so many to outline the growth of the California wine industry in the early days. Historian Thomas Pinney is gentle, I think, when he rejects the Haraszthy document, judging that "its demonstrable errors make it unreliable in general." [15]

Next Arpad wrote a brief article that appeared in an obscure Northern California publication, the *Sonoma County and Russian River Valley, Illustrated.* Here he refabricated and embellished the Zinfandel story. Earlier he had written that the vines had simply been imported; now they came directly from Hungary, along with five other Hungarian varieties. Now the date of the importation was precise, February 1852, and all were then planted at Crystal Springs. This was impossible, of course, since at that time Agoston had just been elected to the state assembly and then headed north for the first time from San Diego. And he did not acquire the Crystal Springs land first, but rather the property near the Mission, Las Flores. It is understandable that Arpad might not have gotten the story straight, since at that time he was a young boy living in New Jersey.

Then Arpad moves the story in his article to Sonoma, with accurate detail. He supplies many useful names and numbers. And then he slips in the casual intelligence that Sonoma "suddenly became the supplying grape vine nursery for foreign vines for the whole State of California. It was from here that the Zinfandel was distributed to the four parts of the state prior to 1859. . . ." Nothing like this happened, but the list of vines he adds to the Zinfandel is the same list Boggs had brought over from Napa's Oak Knoll.[16]

Arpad then had his article reprinted in large quantities, and he distributed it to the press in California and on the East Coast, to trade journals, and throughout the industry. By the end of the decade the materials he had produced concerning his father's introduction of fine wine varieties to California were everywhere and were usually all a person could find. When journalists wanted a picture of the origins of the wine industry, this is what they got:

—Agoston Haraszthy was the first to import fine wine varieties from Europe, including the Zinfandel from his native Hungary.

—His later importations in 1862 were the basis for the great success of the California wine industry since the late 1870s.

—In Arpad's words, Agoston was "The Father of the Vine in California."

None of these contentions is true. Not a shred of evidence from 1851 to 1869 supports this outlandish view of California wine history.

We can get another view of the Haraszthys and Zinfandel in the early years by taking a look at what Arpad Haraszthy actually said and wrote about that variety when, as a young man, he was an important commentator on the viticultural scene in Northern California. (As noted earlier, I have never been able to find a word about the Zinfandel from the lips or pen of his father.)

Even before Arpad returned from France after his apprenticeship in Champagne, he had become a correspondent for the influential *California Farmer.* He sent publisher James Warren a series of articles on French wines and vines directed to the California reader. The articles began in June 1861 as letters to Warren. When Arpad returned, he continued writing for the *Farmer* until the spring of 1863, when he began writing articles on wines and vines for Warren's son, J. Q. A. Warren, who was now publishing his short-lived *California Wine, Wool, and Stock Journal.* To this point, Arpad had not written a word about Zinfandel, which, twenty-five years later, he would claim his father had been promoting and distributing "to the four parts of the state" since before 1859.

Arpad's articles for the younger Warren were knowledgeable, intelligent, and loaded with practical information for the California winegrower. He never mentioned Zinfandel, even in his article specifically aimed at describing the best red varieties for local production.[17] The University of California file of Warren's publication is actually made up of the copies from the library of Arpad's father-in-law, Mariano Vallejo. Arpad's file went to the university's Bancroft Library. In both these collections, someone had removed the issue that included Arpad's recommendation for red wine varieties. I do not know who removed it, but I have a clear suspect. It would have been embarrassing indeed, in the midst of the public fight over the Zinfandel's introduction, to have a famous son making claims that flew in the face of what he had written a quarter-century earlier.

To the best of my knowledge, Arpad's first mention of the Zinfandel in print was in the *Alta California* in 1869, where he described it as a good variety for sparkling wine.[18] Between 1871 and 1872 he wrote a series of articles

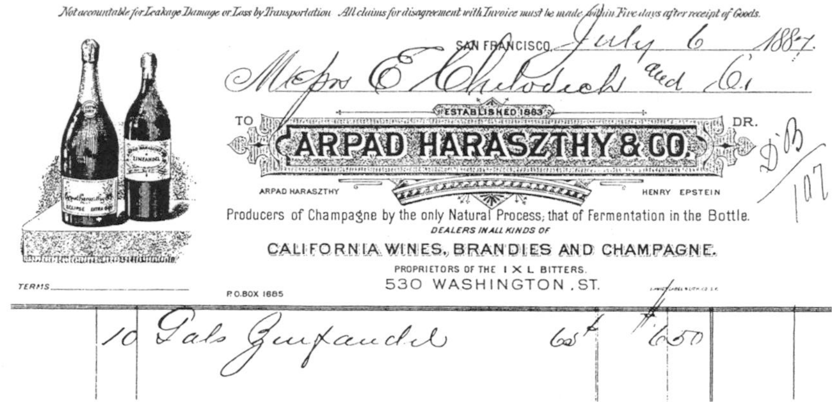

Not accountable for Leakage Damage or Loss by Transportation. All claims for disagreement with Invoice must be made within Five days after receipt of Goods.

SAN FRANCISCO, July 6 1887.

TO ESTABLISHED 1863 DR.

ARPAD HARASZTHY & CO.

ARPAD HARASZTHY HENRY EPSTEIN

Producers of Champagne by the only Natural Process; that of Fermentation in the Bottle.

DEALERS IN ALL KINDS OF

CALIFORNIA WINES, BRANDIES AND CHAMPAGNE.

PROPRIETORS OF THE I X L BITTERS.

530 WASHINGTON ST.

TERMS

P.O. BOX 1885

10 Gals Zinfandel 65¢ 6.50

12. A bill for ten gallons of Zinfandel wine sold by Arpad Haraszthy's San Francisco firm in 1887. (Source: Unzelman Collection, Santa Rosa.)

titled "Wine-Making in California" for the *Overland Monthly.*[19] He mentioned his father's 1862 vine importations and later listed a few varieties that were doing well in California, among them Zinfandel. But he made no familial claims.

In 1877 Edward Bosqui published the beautiful *Grapes and Grape Vines of California.* The unnamed writer of the section on Zinfandel had been primed by Arpad and declared that the variety "was first brought to this State by the late Col. Agoston Haraszthy, between the years 1853 and 1854" from Hungary to Crystal Springs, then to Sonoma, and finally throughout the state. Arpad had made this claim, almost verbatim, in the January 20, 1877, issue of the *San Francisco Bulletin,* just before this handsome ampelography went to press.[20]

It was likely this claim and Wetmore's mistaken conclusions in his first report for the BSVC that triggered Robert Thompson's ill-fated attempt to set the record straight. But he and William Boggs did not have the endurance, the resources, or the moxie to keep the fight going. By 1888 Arpad had won the battle. In that year the *New York Tribune* ran an article on the Haraszthys and Zinfandel without mention of counter-claims or controversy. Later the

Scientific American even thought that it was Arpad who had made the 1862 importation.[21]

As Arpad's fortunes declined after the 1880s, no one dared or wanted to bring more tragedy into his life. After 1894 everything fell apart for him. His Champagne company went under, and the Orleans Hill Vineyard was lost. In 1900 he headed off to the Klondike in search of gold. He soon returned empty-handed. On November 16 he collapsed and died in San Francisco while waiting for a cable car.

But now and then the Zinfandel question came up in academic circles. Scholars tended to say that the matter was still in doubt. In 1888 Professor George Husmann wrote that "the true origin and dissemination of this important variety is not yet clear." Some years later a German student of viticulture, Adolf Cluss, visited Professors Eugene Hilgard and Edward Wickson at the University of California. They apparently talked at length about the mystery of Zinfandel, the Haraszthy story, and the vine's possible European origins. From these conversations, Cluss concluded that at that moment (1908) it was not possible to be sure either about the origins of the variety in California or about its counterpart in Europe. But he was intrigued by the possibility that it might have come from Austria. So am I. As noted earlier, the powerful evidence suggesting the Austrian Empire as a source is far more than a possibility.[22]

The Haraszthy legend was now locked into the accepted popular record. Arpad Haraszthy's claims were generally repeated by leaders of the industry in the years after his death. Wine writers and other journalists could not be expected to go behind the story. I suppose even amateur historians should not be expected to go back and examine the sources from the 1850s and 1860s.[23] Wasn't the truth of the matter set out in the manuscript on file at the Bancroft Library, available to all interested parties? Astonishing as it may seem, not one twentieth-century wine writer or historian, amateur or professional, prior to the 1970s ever wrote a word about the heated debate of the 1880s from which the legend had been distilled.

CHAPTER SEVEN

THE STEALTH GRAPE, 1891–1918

THE AMOUNT OF SPACE I HAVE TAKEN TO EXPLAIN THE ORIGINS OF the Haraszthy legend and Zinfandel really misrepresents the importance of such concerns at the time. By 1887 the great boom of the 1880s was flattening out. Industry leaders and promoters, except for Arpad Haraszthy, had little real interest in the history or origins of grapes. Prices were falling, and by 1893 the bottom had fallen out of the wine market. During the depression that lasted through 1897, farmers of all commodities faced economic disaster. Thousands went under. This was the time of the great agrarian revolt we call the Populist movement.

The demand for wine plummeted. Dozens of winery owners in California were forced into bankruptcy. The most glaring fact about the state's vineyards was that there seemed to be too many of them. Some blamed the wine industry's ills on overproduction. Others blamed underconsumption, and those who did so pointed to the huge expanses of vineyard land created in California since 1878. Able wine pioneers such as Napa's Charles Krug and Sonoma's Emil Dresel argued that too many vines had been planted in the wrong places, resulting in poor wine that couldn't be sold except at rock-bottom prices. Such prices and such low quality drove down prices and demand for

WHOLESALE ZINFANDEL PRICES BY THE CASE, 1889

St. Helena	$5.00	Los Gatos	$3.50
Sonoma	$5.00	Napa City	$3.50
Oakville	$4.00	Rutherford	$3.50
Fresno	$3.60	San Jose	$3.50
Livermore	$3.50	Santa Rosa	$3.50

SOURCE: *Pacific Wine & Spirit Review*, April 26, 1889, p. 52.

even the best California wines. The same view was expressed by the professors in the university's Department of Agriculture. Eugene Hilgard also argued that massive dumping of bulk wine on the market was the primary reason for the low prices for all wine.[1]

When vineyards had expanded in Napa in the 1880s, no one could say enough about the excellence of the clarets made from the new Zinfandel vineyards around St. Helena. Now people who complained about the quality of California table wine in general began to focus on a major problem. The Central Valley was the source of most of the poorly flavored table wine being dumped by the thousands of gallons in eastern markets. And most of these wines were Zinfandel clarets. Glen Ellen and Los Gatos Zinfandels might still be delicious, but everyone in the industry by 1892 seemed convinced that Zinfandel was a major culprit in causing the wine industry's malaise.

Nevertheless, very little California wine was sold as a varietal. In fact, many of the best coastal valley Zinfandels ended up blended with Cabernet Sauvignon and labeled California Medoc, after the great red wine region of Bordeaux. And a large percentage of the best varietal Zinfandel was still being bottled with phony French labels and branded corks, a practice that did not become illegal until 1906. Thus, the typical consumer rarely saw a bottle labeled Zinfandel, except in Northern California, with its many experienced wine drinkers. The knock on Zinfandel came from within the industry itself, in trade journals and from the university. Hilgard almost demanded that no more Zinfandel be planted in California, and he didn't always distinguish between the Central Valley and the coastal valleys.[2] Gradually, growers began to develop a fairly common prejudice that Zinfandel was a "junk" grape. And to a certain extent this was true, as far as the thousands of acres planted in the Central Valley and Southern California were concerned.[3]

"Bah! I wouldn't crush a pound of Zinfandel," Paul Masson was supposed to have said around 1906.[4] But no matter how much poor, hot-valley, overcropped Zinfandel became a drug on the red table wine market in the 1890s, people who really knew wine were well aware of the excellent product that could come from a properly tended Zin grown on the hillsides or on the upper slopes of coastal valleys. Professor George Husmann understood the matter perfectly: "I have yet to see a red wine of any variety I would prefer to the best samples of Zinfandel produced in this state." But, he complained, such samples were as rare as "angels' visits."[5] He conceded that there was too much poor Zinfandel wine.

> But if planted on soils rich in iron, along our hillsides . . . it will develop an abundance of sugar and fine flavor. . . . Grown on rich valley lands, it is a wine of little color and character and becomes an indifferent beverage. . . . A Zinfandel claret from locations best adopted to it, carefully made, is good enough for anyone.[6]

A remarkable thing happened to Zinfandel between 1893 and 1914. There was virtually no mention of the variety in trade journals or wine country newspapers during these years. The occurrence of the word "Zinfandel" in print became almost as rare as an angel's visit. I have organized references to my research on California wine history in a computer database with about twenty-eight thousand entries. I've read and indexed almost all beverage journals and relevant agricultural publications of the nineteenth century. And I've read through and indexed most of the California wine country newspapers, including the big-city publications that have taken an interest in wine. (These articles include only those that I consider to be of real historical significance. I sometimes, but rarely, include wine writers' columns.)[7]

I have found a total of 627 articles on Zinfandel or in which our grape has an important part. These date from the 1850s. For the years before 1900, there are 257 entries for Zinfandel. From 1900 to 1919, we find 11; from 1920 to 1960, but 22. Then, from 1961 to 1997, there are 337.

What's going on here? Only 33 important references to Zinfandel over a period of 60 years?

I believe that this situation is what the German historian Oswald Spengler would call a matter of "form and actuality" or, as he wrote it, "Gestalt und Wirklichkeit." The form of the matter, what we perceive on the surface, shows us that Zinfandel after 1900 was not important in California. The actuality was just the opposite, partly as a result of the negative factors in people's minds from the 1890s:

—Too much wine was being produced.
—Much of this wine was poor to mediocre in quality.
—Overwhelmingly, the vine planted most in the period from 1878 to 1890 was Zinfandel.
—A large percentage of these grapes came from the hot Central Valley and contributed to the oversupply.

Therefore, the logic ran, it is not a good idea to plant Zinfandel. Time and again Zinfandel was associated in readers' minds with the woes of the California wine industry. Consequently, if you really knew the value of good Zinfandel, and if you wanted to plant it in places where it would make good wine, you didn't advertise the fact in the press or trade journals. Thus the 11 references in my database from 1900 to 1919, as compared to the 257 entries before 1900.

But Zinfandel was still almost as important to the California wine industry as it had been in the 1880s. When America began coming out of the great industrial depression of the 1890s, vineyard planting picked up, and Zinfandel was part of the story. The economy began its upturn in 1897, when agricultural prices began to rise. Soon credit became more readily available, and consumer buying power was taking off. More important for wine demand, the flow of immigration picked up again. All these factors pointed to a rise in the demand for California wine.

SELECTED ZINFANDEL AWARDS, PRE-PROHIBITION

ZINFANDEL AWARDS AT SAN FRANCISCO'S 1894 MIDWINTER FAIR

- J. L. Beard (Warm Springs/ Mission San Jose)
- Dresel & Company (Sonoma)
- Isaac De Turk (Santa Rosa)
- Beringer Brothers (St. Helena)
- A. R. Scott (Santa Clara)
- H. W. Crabb (To Kalon) (Oakville)

ZINFANDEL AWARDS AT THE 1895 ATLANTA EXPOSITION

- Inglenook (Rutherford)
- Ruby Hill (Livermore)
- Napa Valley Wine Company (Napa City)
- G. Migliavacca (Napa City)
- J. Thomann (St. Helena)

ZINFANDEL GOLD MEDALS AT THE 1909 ALASKA-YUKON EXPOSITION

- Italian Swiss Colony (Asti/Sonoma)
- George Bram (Santa Cruz Mountains)
- To Kalon (H. W. Crabb) (Oakville)
- Theodore Gier (Livermore)
- El Quito Olive and Wine Farm (Los Gatos)

ZINFANDEL GOLD MEDALS AT THE 1915 SAN FRANCISCO PANAMA-PACIFIC INTERNATIONAL EXPOSITION

- Brun & Chaix (Oakville)
- Theodore Gier (Livermore)
- Isaac De Turk (Santa Rosa)
- Inglenook (Rutherford)
- Italian Swiss Colony (Asti/Sonoma)
- Louis Kunde (Glen Ellen)
- Beringer Brothers (St. Helena)
- Larkmead (F. Salmina) (Napa Valley)
- C. Schilling (Napa Valley)

The Golden State's wine industry had been suffering from more than just an economic depression. The phylloxera root louse in the 1890s had practically wiped out some of California's finest vineyards. The pest produced its greatest devastation in the coastal valleys. The total bearing acreage in Napa Valley had fallen from about 21,000 in 1890 to little more than 3,000 in 1898. Napa's viticultural commissioner wrote as early as 1892, "Our vineyards are melting as the mist before the morning sun." By 1896 most of Napa Valley below St. Helena was a sea of blackened stumps. It was just as bad in the valleys of Sonoma, Santa Clara, and Livermore.[8]

It was clear to anyone who could work the figures in 1898 that California wine was going to be in short supply and that investing in planting wine grapevines was going to be a good way to make money. The result was an explosion in vineyard planting, all over the state. This explosion was facilitated by University of California experts and several Northern California vineyardists who, between 1894 and 1897, developed a satisfactory solution to the phylloxera problem. A native American vine, isolated by French scientists and named by them "Rupestris St. George," was identified as a universal rootstock, satisfactory for most California conditions. Onto this rootstock the tender vinifera wine varieties could be safely grafted. The St. George was completely resistant to attacks from the phylloxera. (Actually, better resistant rootstocks for specific conditions were identified in years to come.) Zinfandel did particularly well when grafted onto St. George stock, and still does today.[9]

The deep spirit of gloom that had been hanging over California's premium winegrowing regions began to evaporate after 1897. By the end of the century, a new planting binge in established winegrowing areas had struck the California wine country. But new areas began to open as well. Much of this new expansion was large scale and industrial, the result of massive investment by capitalists with their eyes on rising wine prices. The southern Santa Clara Valley, Mendocino County, the Lodi-Woodbridge area, even the Cucamonga area of Southern California, all became the home of huge new vineyards largely devoted to red table wine production. Thousands of acres were also planted in the San Joaquin and Sacramento Valleys, but there, and in many parts of Southern California, the emphasis was on sweet wine production.

This new planting was far more orderly than it had been twenty years earlier. Most of the vines planted were varieties with good yields and proven reputations for sound quality. (There was no significant growth in what we today call world-class varietals, such as Cabernet Sauvignon and Pinot noir. There was virtually no Chardonnay.) Zinfandel still had an important role but was nowhere near as dominant as before. We have no good statistics on varieties planted between 1898 and 1915, but acreage reports at the beginning of Prohibition give us a fairly accurate picture of which varieties were most numerous. They were Zinfandel, Carignane, Mataro (Mourvèdre), Grenache, and Durif, which Californians were by then calling "Petite Sirah," as they continue to do today. In some areas in Sonoma and Napa Counties, this variety became the red wine leader. But, overall, probably more Zinfandel was planted in the Northern California coastal counties than any other variety. And hardly a word about it appeared even in trade and farm journals.

Thus it was that our "very" old-vine Zinfandel, which survives here and

13. An ancient Amador County Zinfandel vine is measured against Rosslyn Sullivan's five feet eight inches in 1982.

there today, was planted. I prefer to call "old-vine" the Zin planted during Prohibition, about three-quarters of a century ago. And there is a bit of "extremely" old-vine Zinfandel that survived the phylloxera devastation of the 1890s and lives today. Some of it is in Amador County, in the Sierra Foothills, where phylloxera arrived late or not at all. Other vines were planted on good, resistant rootstock before 1900 and still live. An example is a patch of Zinfandel vines on the Kunde Estate near Sonoma's Glen Ellen. "Old Vine" is an expression found on many Zinfandel labels today, but as yet there is no agreement on—and no government regulation of—the use of that term. I will discuss this minor controversy later, in chapter 11.

From 1900 to 1918 Zinfandel was just another variety that was part of most producers' clarets. People who wanted a truly fine California claret, in what they thought was a European style, bought wine made from red Bordeaux varieties, particularly Cabernet Sauvignon. Such California wine almost always traveled under labels (legal at the time) that bore the generic term "Medoc." But the yields on such red Bordeaux varieties were low; and many wine houses, when making their blends, knew that a healthy shot of good Zinfandel made their house Medoc more profitable and didn't hurt the quality appreciably. But you can be sure that the labels of such wines made no mention of Zinfandel. When people did speak about such matters, it was always on the q.t. And, as noted earlier, there was virtually no mention of Zinfandel in the press.

We get a revealing statistical picture of the Zinfandel/claret situation from a survey undertaken by the California State Agricultural Society that was published in 1907, right after the planting frenzy had cooled somewhat (see table 1). County production figures were recorded for several types of wine, mostly for 1905. The stats for most counties were recorded for generic wines such as sauterne, burgundy, and claret. But some counties did report a few varietal numbers, Zinfandel and Riesling the only two of importance. The survey also recorded a few Cabernet gallons. If we accept the idea that almost all California claret was well laced with Zinfandel, we get a fair picture of the extent to which our stealth grape was lurking in California vineyards.

In constructing table 1, I have selected the information I thought most interesting, so the statistics cannot be taken too seriously, particularly those for Riesling, which was fast becoming a generic term on California wine labels, with heaven knows what included. But we can see that Napa red table wine wanted to be called "claret," without mention of Zinfandel, for all the approximately 3,000 acres of that vine in the county. In Sonoma, Zinfandel was King of the Red Wine Grapes—and county officials reported it as such. (This

TABLE 1. GALLONS OF WINE PRODUCED, CA. 1905

Selected Counties, Selected Generics and Varietals

COUNTY	ZINFANDEL	CLARET	BURGUNDY	CABERNET	RIESLING
Alameda*	119,000	581,500	22,500	17,000	17,000
Contra Costa	0	900,000	3,000	4,500	8,000
Los Angeles	50,500	650,000	6,000	6,000	0
Napa	0	1,173,700	75,000	0	735,600
Sacramento	0	1,140,000	0	0	0
San Bernardino	115,000	1,150,000	1,000	0	5,800
San Joaquin	0	546,975	0	0	4,300
Santa Cruz	0	364,000	0	0	40,350
Sonoma	7,080,000	4,224,000	304,000	400,000	528,000

SOURCE: *Report of the California State Agricultural Society for the Year 1905*, in the *Appendix to the Journals of the California State Legislature*, 37th sess., vol. 3, 1907. This report was also printed separately.

* Livermore and East Bay.

predominance is part of the county's popular image even today, if not reflected in official statistics. The ratio of Cabernet Sauvignon to Zinfandel acres in Sonoma today is about 2.2 to 1.0.)

Zinfandels labeled as such were produced between 1900 and 1919, but most of these stayed on the West Coast.[10] A 1908 wine list from San Francisco's Old Poodle Dog Restaurant offers five Zinfandels: one under the restaurant's own label, the others from Linda Vista (Mission San Jose), Chateau Chevalier (Napa), Sutter Home (Napa), and the California Wine Association. Easterners were far more comfortable with labels that simply read "claret." But California wine drinkers knew what Zinfandel was, and they were happy to drink it under its varietal name.

Zinfandel finally made it into the press reports in 1915, when the people of the San Francisco Bay Area told the world that they had totally recovered from the 1906 earthquake by hosting the Panama-Pacific International Exposition (PPIE) in the city of San Francisco. Officially the month-long event, held

Booze has often been involved in tilting the scales of justice. But the annals of jurisprudence have never produced a more remarkable outcome, at least as far as winebibbing is concerned, than that in the case of *The People of California v. Lee Chuck,* argued on appeal before the California Supreme Court in 1889.

Lee had been convicted of first-degree murder. The evidence in the jury trial showed conclusively that the defendant had shot and killed a man on the street in San Francisco. The jury had taken some time coming to its verdict, but all finally agreed that Lee was guilty of first-degree murder. The judge sentenced him to be hanged. But Lee's observant lawyer spotted a possible error in the jury's verdict process and appealed the outcome on grounds that members of the panel had drunk an intoxicating beverage while deliberating.

The record showed that during the jury's deliberations, its members had not arrived at a verdict by dinner time. So the judge instructed the bailiff to take the twelve-men-good-and-true to dinner at the state's expense. The officer marched them down to one of the city's French restaurants, where each partook of the table d'hôte. The price of the meal bought each of the jurors a half bottle of claret wine. Affidavits collected by the defense from members of the restaurant staff vouched that the beverage was "a good quality California Zinfandel, four years of age." On receiving this shocking intelligence, the Supreme Court reversed Lee's conviction.

For followers of the grape, the specificity of the court's identification of the wine hints that however generic the attitude toward table wine in California might have been before Prohibition, there was at least one grape variety in the Golden State worthy of precise identification. The staff at the restaurant knew what they were serving, although they had probably been instructed to tell customers the wine was a fine red Bordeaux. And whoever collected the information for the defense thought it quite appropriate to make use of the varietal term. Why not simply describe it as California claret? It could not have made a difference in the outcome, for the information was of importance only in that it showed the jurors had partaken of an alcoholic beverage.

The answer is clear. The waiters at the restaurant and the attorney's investigator were perfectly at home with this rather difficult word, "Zinfandel." Had the wine been made from any other grape or grapes, one can be sure that the final court report would have been no more specific than "claret."

14. When Karl Louis Kunde, pictured here, bought James Shaw's Wildwood Ranch near Glen Ellen in 1904, he kept Shaw's old Zinfandel vines, grafted to resistant rootstock. Some of those gnarled antiquities are still producing. (Source: Kunde Estate.)

where today's Marina district stands, celebrated the opening of the Panama Canal.

July 14 was, of course, Bastille Day, but it was also Wine Day at the PPIE. An international jury had earlier been assembled to evaluate California wines. We don't know how many Zinfandels were exhibited as such, but ten from identifiable sources won gold medals, all but one from Sonoma or Napa. Three Zinfandel golds also went to producers whose wines might have come from several areas. Some of the names of these producers might sound familiar today: Inglenook (Napa), Italian Swiss Colony (Sonoma), Theodore Gier (Liv-

15. The Wildwood Vineyard, near Glen Ellen, in about 1915. It is still a part of the Kunde Estate, a leading Sonoma producer of Zinfandel today. (Source: Kunde Estate.)

ermore and Napa), Louis Kunde (Sonoma), Beringer Brothers (Napa), Larkmead (Napa), Claus Schilling (Napa).[11]

Thus did the stealth grape finally make it into print in twentieth-century California newspapers and trade journals in a significant way. Four golds were also awarded to wines labeled claret. How much Zinfandel was involved we cannot tell, but we can be secure in the idea that wines such as the Gundlach-Bundschu Huichica Table Claret had plenty of Zinfandel in their makeup.

CHAPTER EIGHT

PROHIBITION AND THE FRESH GRAPE DEAL, 1919–1933

WINE INDUSTRY LEADERS WERE TRYING TO SELL MORE THAN WINE AT the Panama-Pacific Exposition. By 1915 the threat of national legislation prohibiting commerce in alcoholic beverages was palpable. Before the exposition, industry leaders had sent a team of filmmakers around the state collecting material for a movie on California winegrowing. Shown to more than one hundred thousand visitors to the Expo's Wine Palace, the film depicted California wine as the product of happy, solid farmers and dedicated entrepreneurs whose tidy wineries placed a healthy beverage on the tables of ordinary Americans. There was almost nothing on the growing industrialization of California wine. There was nothing on the grape brandy and fortified ports and sherries commonly sold in American saloons.

But this and other attempts by Californians to resist the threat of prohibition were useless in the face of Anti-Saloon League propaganda and a wave of patriotic fervor after America entered World War I in 1917. Most Americans knew nothing about wine, except that immigrants and rich people drank lots of it. The Eighteenth Amendment, outlawing the manufacture, sale, and transportation of alcoholic beverages, was ratified in 1919 and went into effect January 16, 1920. Congress could have ruled table wine exempt from this prohibition; many thought this would be the case. But leaders of the dry forces in Congress would not permit it. Wine could be produced commercially for medical and religious purposes, but not as a beverage.

Before the new amendment went into effect, Congress set up its enforcement apparatus through the Volstead Act. Apparently wine was to be illegal, since the line defining an alcoholic beverage was drawn at an alcohol content of one-half of 1 percent. But heads of households were still permitted to produce "un-intoxicating" cider and fruit juices in their homes. However, the one-half percent rule did not apply to such beverages. Congress decided that enforcement officials were required to prove in court that a homemade beverage in question was *in fact* intoxicating. Thus was the California wine grape industry saved. Every attempt in the 1920s by puritanical or legalistic enforcement officials to challenge homemade wine in the courts was defeated. And very few cases were brought.

The fact that table wine was a natural product—unlike beer, whiskey, and fortified wines such as port—had a powerful effect on public opinion. Even though most Americans never drank wine in any form, they were not inclined to fine or imprison their neighbors for allowing a barrel or four of crushed fruit to ferment.

Why four? Because the old federal rule had allowed the head of a household to make up to two hundred gallons of wine per year (four fifty-gallon barrels). All a person had to do then and in 1920 was to apply for a free permit. The resulting wine could not be sold or given away, but a family had about one thousand bottles per year, almost three bottles per day.

In fact, Prohibition Bureau officials didn't give a hoot about homemade wine. They had serious problems of enforcement to fill their working hours. The country was awash in illegal booze and beer for more than thirteen years while Americans legally consumed between four and six billion bottles of homemade wine.

To produce these billions of bottles, Americans had to have access to grapes, preferably good vinifera wine grapes. California was virtually the only source. The result was a massive movement by rail of fresh vinifera grapes to eastern and midwestern metropolitan areas, particularly those with sizeable immigrant populations. This commercial traffic came to be called the "fresh grape deal."

The size of this enterprise took almost everyone in the California wine and grape industry by surprise, but the nature of the bonanza was soon understood. For almost half a century, Central Valley and Southern California grape growers had been shipping fresh table grapes to eastern markets beyond the Sierras. But the idea of shipping fresh wine grapes to potential home winemakers was fairly new.

The first recorded shipment east was a 1910 load of Zinfandel sent to Chicago from Lodi in lug boxes.[1] By 1915 a few San Joaquin County shippers had developed a real trade to several eastern cities, amounting to about 750 boxcars, each car loaded with lugs totaling about fifteen tons of grapes. Hardly anyone paid any attention to this commerce at first, since a large percentage of these shipments were to eastern wineries that used California grapes in their wines.[2]

But when America went to war in 1917, talk of taxes on wine, threats of prohibition, and actual wine shortages changed matters dramatically. In addition, immigrant families in the Midwest and along the East Coast were catching on to home winemaking in a powerful way. In the past, some had made wine from eastern grape varieties, particularly from Concords. But such wine never had a wide appeal among people who knew what wine from good vinifera grapes tasted like. By 1917 the home winemaking fad was becoming increasingly popular, particularly when tasty red varieties arrived in good condition in refrigerated cars just a few days after they had been picked.[3]

In 1917 about four thousand carloads went east, followed by almost six thousand in 1918. By far most of these loadings took place in Fresno and San Joaquin Counties. But no one, at least publicly, was talking yet about eastern markets as the salvation of California's wine grape vineyards. At this moment, wine industry leaders were proclaiming that grape growers would be ruined if the Eighteenth Amendment passed. They had no interest in broadcasting logical solutions to the grape growers' plight if prohibition became a national reality.

All this changed in 1919. By then the war was over, but national prohibition by January of the next year was a certainty. In May California wine and grape producers got a look at the Volstead Act, which, if passed as submitted to Congress, would not spare wine for the table. Congress finally passed the bill October 28. President Woodrow Wilson immediately vetoed the measure, citing it as an unwarranted intrusion into Americans' private lives. Two hours later a cheering Congress overrode the veto. The gloom around California wineries was oppressive.

But local fruit jobbers and eastern wholesale marketers had already sensed what was going to happen to California wine grapes if the winemaking industry was shut down. Even some of the larger California vineyard interests had been lining up eastern wholesale wine grape buyers since the summer of 1919. By vintage time the word was out everywhere in the country: commercial wine was a dead item, but you could buy grapes and make your own. Also during the summer the railroads had been posted concerning a potentially larger demand for boxcars in the fall. It was essential that refrigerated cars be ready to handle the fragile wine grapes as soon as they were picked. Almost ten thousand carloads of wine grapes headed east out of the Central Valley and Southern California in 1919. About two thousand more were distributed in the California market itself, mostly in the San Francisco Bay Area.

In 1910 the first wine grapes sent east had been Zinfandel, but between 1915 and 1919 the market shifted. By 1919 the Alicante Bouschet was the leader in eastern shipments. Home winemakers liked it for two reasons. First, it looked good. Its thick skin allowed it to arrive at its destination in fairly good condition. Second, it was what wine people call a dyer grape (*teinturier*), which gave a wonderfully deep ruby color to a young wine. But the resulting wine from the Alicante was quite coarse and lacked any of the flavors we associate with really good red table wine. The market didn't seem to care. There were 293,834 lugs of Alicantes on the cars headed east in 1919. In close second place came Zinfandel, with 272,740 lugs.[4]

Other red wine grapes important in the fresh grape deal were Carignane, Petite Sirah (Durif), Mission, and Mourvèdre (Mataro). The only white wine grape of any importance was the Muscat of Alexandria, which some home winemakers used to tone down the Alicante and to give the resulting wine

ODE TO THE FRESH GRAPE DEAL

When Californians discovered that, despite Prohibition, they could still sell their grapes to home winemakers all over the country, they began calling that trade the "fresh grape deal." This poem, from the November 1921 issue of the *California Grape Grower,* is a tongue-in-cheek paean to that trade.

The season opened with a whiz,
From every angle looked like biz.
The yield was fair, quality grand,
Price established, bids on hand.
O Happy Day, O Happy Day,
When booze was banned and grapes held sway!

The East absorbed them like a sponge,
The Middle West made quite a plunge.
New York and Boston led the pack,
Chicago was not too far back.
O Gladsome Day, O Gladsome Day,
When "juice" grapes winged their vinous way.

The Alicantes packed in lugs,
Will color up some sturdy jugs.
The flavor champ, you know so well,
The awe-inspiring Zinfandel.
O Wondrous Day, O Wondrous Day,
When booze was banned and grapes held sway!

better flavor. But huge amounts of bargain-priced Central Valley Thompson Seedless grapes were also packed for sale to home winemakers. These cut the Alicante but added little to the wine's flavor. Home winemakers from coast to coast developed their own formulas.

The eastern demand in 1919 was a happy surprise to California vineyardists. The next two years proved that the fresh grape deal was no fluke. Leaders of the former wine industry couldn't understand it. Such a market simply could not continue, they believed. They were convinced that soon gallon cans of grape juice concentrate would surely replace the clumsy twenty-five-pound lugs. The economic advantages were obvious, but it never happened. Concentrates did become a part of home winemaking during Prohibition but never provided as much as 20 percent of the total juice fermented.

Obviously some kind of satisfying aesthetic was involved in looking over the different varieties available, determining their condition, and working out the formula for that vintage's *cuvée.* People discovered that wine grape varieties actually had names—and they learned them. Some of them also learned California geography, for certain varieties from one area seemed to make better wine than the same varieties from another. By 1922 only dullards and ignoramuses confused grapes from Sonoma with those from Fresno.

(Clever sellers, nevertheless, learned ways to expand apparent Sonoma production many times over.)

At the end of the 1919 season, California recorded about 170,000 acres of wine grapes, approximately 45 percent of them Zinfandel, four times as many acres as Alicante Bouschet. But the average lug price in the New York City market for the coarse, well-colored Alicante had been $2.45, almost fifty cents better than the Zinfandel or any other red wine variety. The acreage ratio soon began to change quickly, almost by the hour, through grafting and heavy planting of Alicantes.

The 1919 crop had hardly been harvested when the mad rush to plant wine grapevines began. The heaviest planting came in the Central Valley and in Southern California. But the frenzy was also observable in the coastal counties of Northern California. The economics were clear—plant Alicantes! At the University of California at Berkeley, the learned Professor Frederic Bioletti added his voice and warned against planting Zinfandel. The skin was too tender for shipping, he wrote, and the tight bunches tended to rot.[5] Those in the industry who had grown up listening to the knock on Zinfandel since the 1890s knew what he was talking about.

At first the planters listened, and Zinfandel acreage grew almost not at all. In fact, in some places such as Napa and Livermore large numbers of Zinfandel vines were grafted over to Alicante. More than 85 percent of the white wine varieties were grafted over or ripped up. One might wonder what happened to all the acres of world-class wine grapes that didn't ship well, such as the Cabernet Sauvignon and Riesling. Nonhistorian wine writers declaiming on the tragedy of Prohibition are always weeping about the disappearance of these vines. But, actually, they amounted to only about 2 percent of California's wine grape acreage in 1919. (And this percentage changed very little after the repeal of Prohibition. A large market for fine California wine did not exist until the 1960s.)

The prejudice against Zinfandel was short-lived, as far as shipping was concerned. It didn't take long for a sizeable number of eastern connoisseurs—though by no means a majority—to discover that Zinfandel packed a highly recognizable varietal flavor. And, unlike Carignane and Mourvèdre, it didn't

DANTE BAGNANI REMEMBERS THE FRESH GRAPE DEAL

The Bagnani family formerly owned the Geyser Peak Winery and developed the Four Monks brand of vinegar. In 1977 Dante Bagnani wrote down his recollections of the grape trade for home winemakers during Prohibition, which were eventually published in the January 1983 issue of *Wine West Magazine:*

> As grape buyers and shippers in San Francisco my father and uncles purchased grapes from Dry Creek, Alexander Valley and those vineyards north of Geyserville. Our buyer there would spend two or three months every year in Geyserville to look over the grapes and make his selections as the local vineyardists brought them in. Grapes meant for travel east had to be packed into what was known as the Los Angeles lug, with a lid, which held about 28 pounds of grapes. Grapes meant for San Francisco arrived at the produce district where the tracks were cleared to make room for the grape cars, six or seven tracks, each with ten to fifteen cars, filled with fragrant, juicy grapes. The scene was one of hectic activity.
>
> The grapes were shipped down in cattle cars because the open slatted sides provided ventilation for the grapes, which were shipped in the same boxes into which they were picked. Once the cars were on the tracks the grape commission men placed small step ladders at the doors so the buyers could step in to examine the grapes.
>
> The grapes from Sonoma were in great demand, principally Carignane, Zinfandel and Petite Sirah, with small lots of Burger. Occasionally when cars were brought in from Lodi and Stockton the less scrupulous grape merchants would connive with the depot agent to change the bill of lading to indicate that the grapes had come from the Sonoma towns Healdsburg, Geyserville or Cloverdale.
>
> When Repeal came most of the vineyards were planted with grapes intended for shipment to home winemakers. So the wineries had no choice but to crush these and produce a more or less standard red, dry wine, nondescript, but usually heavy in body and color. The average American consumer drank it only under duress. But the public's taste for wine slanted towards the sweet. It would be more than thirty years before dry wines had caught up to the sweet wines. But after 1967 there was no contest.

blend happily with the Alicante. Its flavors were simply lost when blended with that variety. For those who wanted that delicious raspberry fruit, Zinfandel did best when it stood alone, although it didn't suffer if blended a bit with Petite Sirah and/or Carignane.

By 1922, 30,767 acres of wine grapes had been added to the California total, which continued to grow until 1925. More than 60 percent of this expansion was in the Central Valley and Southern California. The 1922 planting frenzy also saw lots of Zinfandel added in Sonoma and Mendocino. But the added Zinfandel acreage around Lodi dwarfed the coastal counties' totals. By

ZINFANDEL ON THE TRACKS: SAN FRANCISCO, 1925

From the *California Grape Grower,* October 1925:

Nearly 1,000 [box]cars of grapes have arrived on the Drumm Street tracks in San Francisco already this season [October 1]. Much of the offerings have been grapes dumped on the local market after unwelcome rains made them unfit for Eastern shipment. Growers and shippers made an awful mistake in trying to salvage their rain-damaged grapes by sending them to San Francisco, for the Italian and other foreign buyers here are just as discriminating as those in the larger Eastern cities. They are willing to pay good prices for good grapes, as is evidenced by the fact that sound Sonoma Zinfandels have brought as high as $90 a ton, while some of the poorer stuff went for $30.

"Quality grapes," said one of the salesmen on the tracks, "can always command a good price. The San Francisco buyers are the most exacting of all, because they know good grapes when they see them."

The San Francisco trade favors Coast county grapes over those from the Central Valley. One of the amusing sights on the tracks are the names that are chalked on the doors of the boxcars. You see "Cloverdale," "Healdsburg," "Asti," and "Geyserville" on car after car that never came within a hundred miles of those places. Some foxy salesmen have no scruples. The most discriminating are not to be outwitted. They single out cars on the tracks of the Northwestern Pacific Railroad, whatever is chalked on the boxcars, and then can be assured that they can get good Sonoma or Mendocino Zinfandel. [The Northwestern Pacific was the rail connection from Sonoma to Sausalito and by barge to San Francisco.]

One of the novelties this season is a grape crusher located at the corner of Drumm and Green Streets where those who buy grapes on the tracks may have them crushed "while you wait." The sign in front of the building advertises Napa and Sonoma grapes, but Thompsons were being crushed when this writer visited the place. The big demand is for Zinfandel, Petite Sirah and Carignane grapes. Only a limited amount of Alicante Bouschet grapes can be sold in San Francisco. But a particularly fine car of Riesling brought $45 a ton.

the end of the 1920s Lodi Zinfandel shipments were about equal to those of all the rest of the state for that variety.[6]

A solid market for Zinfandel grapes in California and in certain East Coast markets had been developed by 1922. Through most of Prohibition, until 1928, Zinfandel kept its second-place out-of-state position behind the Alicante, but way behind. At its height, from 1925 to 1927, Zinfandel averaged only 40 percent of total Alicante eastern sales. Then Carignane took over second place in 1928, primarily because more and more Zinfandel was staying in the Golden State for the home market there. By 1932 Zinfandel was averaging only 27 percent of the Alicante shipments. In 1925 almost ten thousand carloads of Zin headed east; in 1932 the total was just over four thousand, overwhelmingly from San Joaquin (Lodi) and Fresno Counties.

The greater New York City area dominated the eastern market for California wine grapes throughout Prohibition, often accounting for as much as 60 percent of the total. Then came Boston (where Zinfandel was king), Chicago, Philadelphia, Newark, and Pittsburgh. But overall the San Francisco Bay Area ranked number two, and the city of San Francisco itself was just behind Chicago.[7]

The operation of the San Francisco Bay Area grape market during the dry years had a lasting impact on California wine—or, more precisely, on California Zinfandel. A small but important part of the fine Zinfandel we drink today comes to us as a result of what happened along the Drumm Street railroad tracks in San Francisco during Prohibition.

The city of San Francisco sits atop a peninsula and is largely inaccessible to direct railroad commerce from the east and the north. For years before and after the building of the bay's great bridges in the 1930s, freight cars coming from the north and east crossed the bay on huge barges pulled by tugboats.[8] The Drumm Street tracks lie close to the terminals where the cars came ashore. Here in September and October the railroad cars loaded with Sonoma, Mendocino, and Napa grapes were wheeled onto the huge piers and rolled out onto the Drumm Street tracks. There they were opened and the lugs of fresh wine grapes were placed on display for examination by the local wine cognoscenti.[9] It was the profitability of this trade in wine grapes along these tracks that encouraged so many small-scale North Coast vineyardists to plant, keep, or expand their vineyard holdings of Zinfandel. Names such as Seghesio, Pedroncelli, Foppiano, and Martinelli, today synonymous with good Sonoma Zinfandel, were closely associated with this aspect of the fresh grape deal.

We are still benefiting from what those North Coast folks, mostly Italian families, did to help pay off their mortgages between 1920 and 1925. That's when most of our surviving old-vine Zinfandel was planted. Of these ancient vines that remain, most are in Sonoma, although a few can also be found in Napa, Solano, Contra Costa, and Santa Clara Counties as well as farther

16. John Pedroncelli Jr. and his father, John Pedroncelli Sr., examine a Zinfandel vine in their Dry Creek Valley vineyard in 1964. Fifty-five years old then, many of the ancient vines there are still producing. (Source: Pedroncelli Winery.)

south, in the Central Coast and in the Sierra Foothills. In the Central Valley, where most Prohibition Zinfandel vines were planted, almost none survive—with one exception, around Lodi-Woodbridge, where a few families have saved some old vines and still make very good wines. I'll tell you about some of these gnarled aristocrats later.

A vintage drama similar to the one described in this chapter could be seen taking place all over the Bay Area. During the fall months huge tonnages of black grapes, mostly Zinfandel and Mourvèdre (Mataro), were sold here. In San Jose sellers cruised the neighborhoods in trucks, peddling from door to door. Livermore and Contra Costa grapes were trucked over the hills to Oakland and Hayward. The towns on the San Francisco Peninsula were all well supplied by local jobbers who brought grapes up from Mountain View and Cupertino. By the end of Prohibition very few grapes were heading east from the Santa Clara Valley, so strong was the local market.

But the center of it all, the place where the prices were set and the savviest buyers stroked their mustaches as they spotted the choicest loads in the Northwestern Pacific cars, was along the Drumm Street tracks in San Francisco.

Not everyone was a connoisseur. The first cars to arrive in the Bay Area were usually from the Central Valley and went cheaply. Sometimes, if there had been early rains, damaged fruit that would never have made the trip to the East Coast clogged the local market at giveaway prices. In fact, most of the trade in San Francisco was probably in Central Valley grapes. There the fruit jobbers sold 2,968 carloads to home winemakers in 1923, and only about 25 percent came from Sonoma/Mendocino/Napa. But those who bought the grapes from these three counties paid quite a bit more for them and were happy to do so.

These buyers were always on the lookout for freight cars bearing the name of the Northwestern Pacific (NWP), a little railroad that ran out of the redwoods above Ukiah, through Mendocino and Sonoma Counties to the Marin County piers at Tiburon and Sausalito. From there the cars were tugged on barges across the bay to the piers near Drumm Street. The grapes the experts were most interested in came from the Italian Swiss Colony vineyards south of Cloverdale. But buyers knew that towns such as Santa Rosa and Healdsburg were also trustworthy shipping points. Jobbers might chalk "Healdsburg" on a Southern Pacific car from Fresno, but the connoisseurs knew that the NWP cars probably held the precious Zinfandel, Carignane, and Petite Sirah from the better vineyards.

Each year the trade became more complex and competitive. In San Francisco crushers were set up near the point of sale; you could buy your grapes and pick them up crushed into an open-top barrel you could then use as a fermenter, free if you had cleaned and brought back last year's barrel. By 1925

17. The Italian Swiss Colony in northern Sonoma County was a leading Zinfandel producer. Visitors were always welcome. Here is the little whistle-stop station at Asti, built about 1900, where the Northwestern Pacific would drop off passengers. In the background is founder Andrea Sbarboro's country estate.

the barrel could be delivered to your home and lowered into the cellar. Sellers also began supplying buyers with packets of chemicals to help ensure a good fermentation, pure yeast cultures, and sulfite crystals.

A *New York Times* reporter told of walking through the North Beach section of San Francisco at the end of the 1928 vintage:

> A walk through the Italian quarter reveals wine presses drying in the sun in front of many houses. The air is heavy with the pungent odor of fermenting vats in garages and basements. Smiling policemen frequently help the owners of these presses to shoo away children who use them for improvised rocking horses.[10]

A similar picture might be seen in eastern and midwestern cities. But there the Zinfandel was less likely to arrive in first-class condition, whatever might

POLISH ZINFANDEL

In 1913 the great Polish pianist Ignace Jan Paderewski was concertizing in Portland when he lost the use of his left arm from an attack of rheumatism. He had to cancel his San Francisco concerts but headed south anyway, to visit the city. There a friend suggested he head farther south and take the hot mineral baths at Paso Robles. He did, and stayed two weeks. After he left, his arm soon recovered. During his stay in Paso Robles, he had decided to buy a 2,000-acre ranch west of town. He completed the purchase in February 1914 and named the huge expanse Rancho San Ignacio.

He was rarely able to visit the place and could not be there at all during World War I. But after serving as Poland's prime minister for a year after the war, he came back to California. It was March 1922, and Prohibition was upon the land. But the fresh grape deal caught his eye, and he decided to plant vines on his ranch. His advisor suggested that he invite Professor Frederic Bioletti, the viticultural expert at the University of California at Berkeley, to visit. Bioletti asked Horatio Stoll, the publisher of the *California Grape Grower,* to come along. The idea was to see whether planting wine grapes at San Ignacio made sense.

After the visitors arrived at the train station, they all rode out to the ranch in an old-fashioned surrey. Bioletti was entranced by the place and suggested a vineyard site and the vines to plant, Zinfandel and Petite Sirah.

By the time the vines were bearing, the fresh grape deal's profits had slimmed down somewhat, but Paderewski's superintendent found a ready market for the Zinfandel grapes in the Salinas Valley, where he sold them to Italian-Swiss dairymen at good prices. As the years passed, the Paderewski Zinfandels became famous. After repeal, he sold most of them to the nearby York Mountain Winery, which won awards for these wines.

In 1941, the year Paderewski died, Stoll noted that the vineyard was at its quality peak. But when San Ignacio was purchased in 1952, the new owner was unable to revive the old vines.

Today the memory of the famed Polish patriot and his Zinfandel vines is cherished by the winegrowing community around Paso Robles.

---

be chalked on the boxcars. Except in Boston, no special passion for Zinfandel developed east of the Rockies. Only in California, where "Zinfandel" was already a part of the wine drinker's vocabulary, did Zin make a truly lasting impression. The Bay Area boasted the "most discriminating buyers in the United States," according to wine industry leader E. A. Rossi. "They know the geography of the grape districts; they know their varieties."[11]

Shortly after the Great Crash in 1929 Horatio Stoll, founder of the industry trade journal *Wines & Vines,* concluded that the Zinfandel was the country's most popular wine grape, not because more were sold but because wine from the best of these grapes made the best wine. It was just too bad that the folks outside California rarely saw the best of them. In Northern California knowledgeable buyers were willing to find such grapes and to pay extra for them. (Average prices tell us nothing, for they always included an overwhelming number of grapes from the Central Valley.) Stoll wrote that these folks were "the best class of grape buyers, interested primarily in flavor." And we know that flavor is what Zinfandel is all about.[12]

In 1920 most Americans believed that national Prohibition might never end. No amendment to the U.S. Constitution had ever been repealed. Clarence Darrow remarked in 1921 that repeal was impossible: "One might as well talk about taking his summer vacation on Mars."[13]

But the Great Depression and a national revulsion at the social consequences of Prohibition did bring repeal in 1933. Unfortunately, the taste for good wines some Americans had had before 1920 had almost been lost. In the words of historian Thomas Pinney, the worst consequence of Prohibition was "the way in which it had warped American attitudes towards drinking. . . . If they were older Americans they had forgotten what the civilized use of wine was; if they were younger, they had never known."[14]

By the time that the siren blew atop San Francisco's Ferry Building on December 5, 1933, announcing the repeal of the Eighteenth Amendment, the small American interest in fine wine that had developed before the 1920s had all but vanished from the land. Luckily, one of the places where a hint of that interest remained was Northern California.

CHAPTER NINE

THE TWO FACES OF ZIN, 1934–1969

WHEN PROHIBITION ENDED, A LOT OF OLD RED TABLE WINE WAS sitting around under bond in California wineries. Just before the last Prohibition vintage, in 1933, twelve million gallons of dry wine were in storage, most of it red and, on average, of low quality, often oxidized and/or loaded with volatile acidity (read vinegar). Half of this table wine was listed as Zinfandel or claret. A large part of this poor stuff was blended into the 1933 wine and rushed onto the national market in 1934. The upshot was a great deal of wine on the shelves that was immediately an embarrassment to the California wine industry. And the large percentage of over-the-hill Zinfandel in this wine did nothing to raise the quality image of this grape inside the industry. Italian Swiss Colony's E. A. Rossi was a severe critic of the wine factories that sent this wine onto the market at a time when the industry needed to convince consumers of the solid quality of California wine. He growled that a large part of the dry wine shipped east was "not only inferior in quality, but in reality is not wine at all." [1]

Another lesson learned by the time the 1934 vintage got under way was that the only solid wine market in the United States was for fortified, mostly sweet, wines. And a third truth, which shocked many California producers, was the continued strong demand for fresh wine grapes in the East. Millions of people were now in the habit of making their own wine. In 1934 and 1935 Americans drank more California table wine of their own making than from the state's wineries. Finally, it was clear that almost no one except home winemakers gave a hoot about the names of wine grapes. Varietal designation on California wines was almost unheard of. The dry table wines coming out of California wineries were almost all labeled Burgundy, Claret, Sauterne, and such. Most fine lots of Cabernet Sauvignon, what little there was, and Zinfandel "went into the tank with the Alicantes." Thus spoke Louis Stralla, who owned the winemaking operation at the old Charles Krug place in the 1930s. "I wasn't in the wine business from the standpoint of romance." [2]

Most such wine ended up in tank cars hauled east to bottlers there. That was the fate of most California table wine before World War II. Only an elite few wineries such as Beaulieu, Wente, Inglenook, Fountaingrove, and Larkmead had established premium brands in the 1930s; and only a small part of their production carried a varietal label. Most of America never saw anything from California except cheap jug-quality wine in those days, and an overwhelming percentage of that was port, sherry, and muscatel.

Bill Dieppe, later president of Almaden Vineyards, lived on the East Coast in the 1930s and drank table wine with his meals as a regular part of his life. He told me in 1982 that before World War II he drank French wine and knew nothing about the California product. I asked whether he had ever heard of Zinfandel in those days. "Never, not until I came to California after the war," was his answer. If he had tried a bottle of California burgundy or claret then, he would probably have been drinking Zinfandel. But I am sure that he would not have loved it. Nor would I have.

Nevertheless, in California, some of the few who had tasted those great Zinfandels that won gold medals at the 1915 Panama-Pacific Exposition were still alive. Horatio Stoll, publisher of *Wines & Vines,* a trade journal out of San Francisco, made a point of reminding his readers how good Zinfandel had been and could be. When the State Fair wine competitions returned to Sacramento in 1934, Stoll and others made sure that Zinfandel was allotted one of the thirteen wine categories. The only other two varietals thus named were

STATE FAIR ZINFANDEL AWARDS

CALIFORNIA STATE FAIR, 1934–1941, ZINFANDEL AWARDS

1934 Cresta Blanca (Livermore Valley), Roma Winery (Lodi)
1935 Cal-Grape (Mendocino)
1936 Solano Winery, Inglenook, Cal-Grape (Mendocino)
1937 Larkmead (Napa Valley)
1938 Solano, Inglenook, Scatena (Sonoma)
1939 *No competition*
1940 Garatti (Livermore Valley), Italian Swiss Colony, Inglenook
1941 Simi (Sonoma), Solano Winery, Inglenook

State Fairs were not held between 1942 and 1946.

CALIFORNIA STATE FAIR, 1947–1956, ZINFANDEL AWARDS

G = gold medal, S = silver medal, B = bronze medal

1947 Glen Ellen Winery: G
Souverain Cellars (Napa Valley/Howell Mountain): S
L. Pocai (Napa Valley): B

1948 L. M. Martini (Napa Valley, Sonoma grapes): G
Souverain Cellars: S
Paul Rhodes (Castro Valley): B

1949 Los Amigos Winery (Mission San Jose, Santa Cruz Mountains grapes): G
Cadenasso Winery (Solano): S
Fountaingrove (Sonoma): B

1950 Roma (Fresno): G
Fountaingrove: S
L. M. Martini: S
Buena Vista Winery (Sonoma): B

1951 Almaden Vineyards (Santa Clara Valley): G
Garatti Winery (Livermore Valley): S
Novitiate of Los Gatos: S
Cucamonga Winery: B

1952 Almaden Vineyards: G
Charles Krug (Napa Valley): S
Roma: S
Italian Swiss Colony (Sonoma): B

1953 Concannon Vineyards (Livermore): G
Charles Krug: G
York Mountain Winery (Paso Robles): S
Souverain Cellars (Napa): B
Buena Vista: B

1954 Buena Vista: G
Souverain: S
Concannon: B
Freemark Abbey (Napa Valley): B

1955 Charles Krug: G
Souverain: G
Almaden: S
Buena Vista: B
Concannon: B

1956 Weibel Winery (Mission San Jose): S
Christian Brothers (Napa Valley): B
Signature (Fresno): B
Pedroncelli Vineyards (Sonoma): B
Almaden: B

From 1957 onward, most of the old premium producers no longer took part in the State Fair competitions.

Cabernet and Riesling, and the requirements of varietal purity for these two were almost nonexistent. The other eleven went to generics such as Moselle, Claret, Chianti, and Sauterne. The first award for Zinfandel in 1934 went to Cresta Blanca. In the following year six more categories were added to the competition, all generics. The top award for Zinfandel in 1935 went to the Cal-Grape Winery in Mendocino County.[3]

The wine in most of the bottles labeled Zinfandel in the years before World War II was made in a light and fruity style, ready for immediate consumption. If one were to see the face of Zinfandel in those days, that was its usual physiognomy. We might recognize today some of the medal winners in later years before the war: Inglenook, Larkmead of Napa Valley, Simi, Italian Swiss Colony, and the Solano Winery. Almost all of this wine was sold in California. The word "Zinfandel" was virtually unknown to America's few table wine drinkers east of the Rockies.

When the war came and European wine sources in France, Germany, and Italy dried up for Americans, the demand for fine California table wine shot up. Several premium wineries began to use varietal names on their labels. In 1943 New York's Waldorf Astoria Hotel listed thirty-one such California varietals on its wine list. You could buy Cabernets and Rieslings, and there was Petite Sirah, Semillon, Carignane, even Charbono and Folle Blanche. But there wasn't a bottle of Zinfandel. To whom would they have sold it? So it had been on the East Coast in the 1880s, while at the same time the Palace Hotel in San Francisco offered three Northern California Zinfandels on its wine list.

We can learn a lot about our wine drinking habits by studying what wine writers are focusing on at any particular time. We can often perceive the winds of change in the wine world from their books and columns. But the 1930s lacked any such newspaper columns, as far as California wine was concerned. (The first in California was by Los Amigos Winery's Robert Mayock in the 1940s, for the *San Jose News.* But it was years before a second appeared.) Occasionally a food writer would mention California wine in a magazine article. Such a person was Mary Frost Mabon of *Town & Country.* In 1942 she wrote the first systematic guide to California wine to be published in the twentieth

18. Louis P. Martini and Smokey examine the grapes on a venerable Zinfandel vine in the Martini family's Monte Rosso Vineyard, in the hills above the Sonoma Valley. (Source: Michael Martini.)

century, *ABC of America's Wines.*[4] She obviously liked Zinfandel at its best and gave special praise to the Zinfandels of Fountaingrove, Simi, Louis Martini, and Italian Swiss Colony.

But Zinfandel went nearly unnoticed in Harold Grossman's supposedly authoritative *Guide to Wine, Spirits, and Beers* (1940). Julian Street's *Wines*

(1933) quipped that Zinfandel wines "do not tempt one to linger and sip," but conceded that they could be "rugged, and friendly and invite proper drinking," whatever that means. On the other hand, John Melville's *Guide to California Wines* (1955) paid far more attention to Zinfandel than most earlier works, and for good reason. Like Mabon, he had gone into the field, moving through the state's wine districts, talking to the producers, and drinking their wines. He asserted that Zinfandel could be "a wine of peculiar charm, fruity, zestful and aromatic with a raspberry like flavor. . . . If price conscious and still wanting a fine varietal red table wine, a good Zinfandel is the wine to look for." Sounds a lot like George Husmann more than half a century earlier—"Good enough for anyone."[5]

Of all the wine writers in these early days, one stands out as a sort of hero. For years he was hated by the leaders of the California wine industry—that is, by the people in charge of the wine factories making millions of gallons of cheap, nondescript plonk, mostly sweet. But he was beloved by many of the small- and medium-scale producers who were attempting to reestablish the small premium sector of the industry that had come close to flourishing before Prohibition.

Frank Schoonmaker's editor at the *New Yorker* had assigned him to write a series on wine when it became clear that Prohibition's days were numbered. In 1934 Schoonmaker and Tom Marvel collected the series articles in *The Complete Wine Book,* aimed at the serious American reader interested in learning about the world of wine that had just been opened by repeal. For the next forty years Schoonmaker wrote about California wine, as a professional journalist and author, as a wine dealer, and finally as a part of the California wine industry he had helped to transform. (In the middle of this, he took off a few years to pretend to be a sherry broker in Spain during the war, in fact working for the U.S. Office of Strategic Services and spying on the Germans.)

Schoonmaker is most important in California wine history as the man who almost single-handedly led the state's producers to see the light on varietal labeling. Some, such as Louis M. Martini, Georges de Latour, the Wentes and Concannons, Martin Ray, and Inglenook's John Daniel, followed eagerly; a few others acceded grudgingly, and most came along kicking and

19. Frank Schoonmaker is pictured here pouring something other than Zinfandel. But between 1934 and 1970 his authoritative voice and pen became leading advocates for powerful Zinfandel made according to traditional Bordeaux methods. (Source: Unzelman Collection, Santa Rosa.)

whining.[6] But that is really not a direct part of my story, except for the fact that Schoonmaker became a wildly enthusiastic advocate of Louis Martini's Sonoma Zinfandel.

For this story, it is useful to follow Schoonmaker's words on Zinfandel from his first book until the years just before his death in 1976—for as his perception changed, so did that of others close to California's premium wines. It isn't that he alone caused people to modify their ideas about Zinfandel, or even that he was most important among many. It's that his ideas represent a sort of *Zeitgeist,* a spirit of his times.

Schoonmaker gave Zinfandel short shrift in his early articles and first book. As far as he was concerned, it was a "mediocre" wine grape, although it could produce a "wholesome, ordinary red wine when grown in the coastal valleys of Northern California."[7] Here was the first face of Zinfandel after the repeal of Prohibition.

During the next seven years Schoonmaker made several trips to California and drank lots of California wine. In San Francisco he contacted the leaders of Medical Friends of Wine and of the Wine and Food Society. Who was making really good wine in the Golden State? When he got his answers, he went out into the countryside and talked and drank. He was particularly interested in making some solid connections with the best producers in the late 1930s, as the war clouds in Europe were gathering. He knew that if war came, German, Italian, and probably French wine sources would disappear in the American market. He put together a marketing company and contracted with several of the state's finest producers to market their *varietal* wines east of the Rockies: Beaulieu, Wente, L. M. Martini, Inglenook, Larkmead, and Fountaingrove. In fact, he hired Inglenook's general manager, Carl Bundschu, to work for him in San Francisco. It was during these years that Schoonmaker discovered the Martini wines, which had heretofore not been marketed under their own labels. One of the Napa vintner's best wines, in Schoonmaker's mind, was his Mountain Zinfandel, grown at the Monte Rosso Vineyard in the hills above Sonoma Valley.[8]

Just before America entered the war, Schoonmaker published his *American Wines.* In it he wrote that "Zinfandels from the upland vineyards of Napa and

Sonoma Counties are among the pleasantest table wines of the world."[9] Schoonmaker had gotten a small glimpse of the other face of Zin.

In 1964 he published his authoritative *Encyclopedia of Wine.* It was the first book covering the entire world of wine that gave the best California wines their due. To this point, most of the Zinfandels Schoonmaker had encountered had been light and fruity, although the Martini wines were obviously an exception to his general experience. He praised the California Zinfandel as "about as pleasant a *vin ordinaire* as one could ask for." It was wine "unlike that of all other mass-production grapes." Zinfandel had an "easily recognizable varietal character, bouquet and flavor, especially when from hillside vineyards in a cool district." But he was clearly not thinking about the Martini 1941 Zinfandel when he added that Zinfandel "gains little by ageing."[10] When I last tasted that great wine, shortly before its fiftieth birthday, it was fading but still delicious.[11]

Soon Schoonmaker began to pick up on the muscled marvels being produced in the mid-1960s, and he modified the Zinfandel entry in the next edition of his encyclopedia to read that its wine "gains relatively little by ageing." Then, in the last edition before his death in 1976, he wrote, "Occasionally when made in the classic European manner it can have great body and a long life."[12] Frank Schoonmaker had come full circle in the previous forty years and now saw clearly the other face of Zinfandel, much closer, in all likelihood, to the one that you and I see on our dinner table today.[13]

One of the most important aspects of American wine drinking in the 1950s and into the 1960s was the gradual and steady rise of table wine consumption. Production of table wine in California between 1950 and 1960 more than doubled. Even more important was its rise in relation to sweet wine production. At the beginning of the decade, the ratio of sweet wine to table wine produced in the Golden State was about four to one. In 1960 it was a little less than two to one. One might reasonably suspect that if Americans were discovering California Cabernets and Rieslings in these years, they might also have learned to say "Zinfandel." But only a few premium producers brought out a varietal Zinfandel, and almost all of it was sold within the state. Looking back on the situation from the 1970s, wine expert Roy Brady thought that Zinfandel "seemed destined for oblivion except for *ordinaire*." [14]

The wine revolution that had been brewing in America in the 1950s finally exploded into the streets in the 1960s. And it was a true revolution, unlike the great wine boom of the 1880s. In the earlier century the growth in consumption had resulted from a change in population, as a new wave of wine-drinking immigrants poured into the country. The great change during the twentieth century's postwar years was a change of behavior: Americans were drinking more wine per capita, and the essential modification was coming in the table wine category.

By 1966 Americans were finally drinking more table wine than sweet wine. And a large portion of this table wine was coming from premium producers, some who had been around for a long time, others new to wine production. Since premium wines cost considerably more than *ordinaire,* it follows that a large percentage of the new market was made up of middle-class, well-educated professional people. They formed wine-tasting groups, took wine classes, read books on wine, visited wineries, and some even made wine themselves.

It is difficult to explain the rise of premium Zinfandel in Northern California out of this complex of variables, but rise it did. The old premium wineries had kept at it: Martini, Parducci, Krug, and Mirassou. There were a few newer producers, enthusiastic entrepreneurs, men and women, mostly with an eye on the European model where Zinfandel had no place—the owners of Hallcrest, for example, and those at Martin Ray and Freemark Abbey. But others of the same mold, such as Frank Bartholomew at Buena Vista and Lee Stewart at Souverain, enthusiastically produced powerful and elegant Zinfandels in the 1950s. Before 1966 it was the Zinfandels of Souverain that hooked me. They were a splurge at $1.89 per bottle, but those wines from Napa's Howell Mountain made me a believer. (Stewart won his first Zinfandel gold at the State Fair in 1955.)

Some members of this new class of wine drinkers drove out from their urban and suburban homes into the countryside with Melville's book as a guide and discovered small country establishments making excellent varietal Zinfandel, often in a delicious, well-aged rustic style: Foppiano (Healdsburg), Cadenasso (Fairfield), Gemello (Mountain View), Ruby Hill (Livermore Valley), Pedrizzetti (Morgan Hill), and Pesenti (near Paso Robles). I was fresh out of college and learning to drink wine when a former classmate, in 1959, directed me to Ruby Hill, near Pleasanton, where Ernesto Ferrario was selling tasty jugs of Zinfandel and Barbera. For the equivalent of about thirty-five cents a bottle, my wife and I were able to have delicious red wine on our table nightly.

The enthusiastic entrepreneurs of the 1960s made a juggernaut out of the fine Zinfandel phenomenon. Dave Bennion and his partners at Ridge Vineyards made their first Zin in 1964 from grapes grown on ancient vines at the Picchetti Ranch in the hills above what later came to be known as Silicon Valley. Then forgotten as a winegrowing district, the name Monte Bello soon became part of every serious California wine drinker's vocabulary, thanks to the work of Bennion and his successor, Paul Draper. By 1967 Bennion had also found old-vine fruit in Geyserville and at Templeton, outside Paso Robles. In 1969 he and Draper were even making vineyard-designated wines from Lodi grapes. Ridge produced twenty-one different Zinfandels in the 1960s.[15]

David Bruce, in the hills behind Los Gatos, also found old Zinfandel vines growing in the Santa Cruz Mountains and made some wine in 1965 at his new winery. The following year he made seven barrels and had two bottlings with the "cask" numbers on the label. In 1967 he made fourteen barrels. For all these wines he suggested extended bottle aging. Earlier he had even made a "white" Zinfandel, the first sold as such in California in the twentieth century.[16]

Perhaps the Zinfandel that received the most notice during the 1960s was Robert Mondavi's from the 1966 vintage. The San Francisco Wine Sampling Club featured it; and Walter Peterson, the club's president, wrote a lengthy description for the club's newsletter, with an excellent explication of what I have been calling the new face of Zinfandel. The wine was unfined and had been aged two years in French Nevers oak barrels. (Should we be

20. Paul Draper has been at the helm of winemaking at Ridge Vineyards for more than thirty years. Single-vineyard Zinfandels of powerful authority are his stock in trade. (Source: Ridge Vineyards; photo by Joel Simon.)

surprised that Walt's son, Joel, is the winemaker and one of the founders of Ravenswood?)

The way that some of this wine was sold gives a fair picture of what was happening with Zinfandel in the hands of some of the most knowledgeable retailers. Esquin Imports was one of San Francisco's top importers, with a newsletter that today is one of the best primary sources for the history of wine in Northern California in these years.[17] Esquin bought a barrel of the Mondavi wine and had it bottled for their customers. And in Sacramento wine merchant Darrell Corti bought three barrels for the wine-conscious clientele at his family's upscale grocery stores.

This was not a purely Northern California phenomenon. Interest in fine wine was also growing in the Los Angeles area. There, in 1968, Trader Joe's markets began putting out a regular "Insider's Wine Report," which covered all types of European and California wine. Trader Joe Colombe knew his Zinfandel and guided his customers to what he thought were the best bargains; Louis Martini and Parducci were always favorites in the early years. He also liked Ridge for Zinfandels with aging potential. The 1965 Ridge was the first of his recommendations in that category.

Bay Area and Southern California restaurants were also involved in promoting the new fine wines of California. A perfect example was Hank Rubin's Pot Luck in Berkeley, which had a vintage festival dinner during the fall. (Rubin also wrote a pioneer wine column for the *San Francisco Chronicle.*) In 1970 the Pot Luck had its seventh such event and featured the 1966 Mondavi Zinfandel with the $6.50 five-course dinner. One would naturally have drunk it with Le Boeuf Façon Sanglier. Rubin sold it for $6.00, a dollar more than he charged for the Beaulieu Private Reserve Cabernet Sauvignon. (If you had gone into the kitchen between courses, you would have found today's celebrated chef Narsai David hard at work.)

On the menu Rubin explained the two faces of California Zinfandel: "It is made in two styles; one a light, fruity wine to be drunk young, the other, like the one tonight from Robert Mondavi's Napa Valley winery, more like a Cabernet, full, heavy-bodied, improving with age."

I like to think of 1968 as a symbolic vintage for great California Zinfandel.

This was the year when late-harvest Zinfandel made its appearance, one at Mayacamas and a Zinfandel Essence at Ridge from Lodi grapes. But these wines were the beginnings of a fad that didn't last. For me, the symbolism comes instead from two 1968 wines, not necessarily better than other wines I've already discussed, but wines that seem to bring the rest of the decade into focus for the growing number of Zinfandel-made-like-great-Cabernet lovers.

The first was made from Amador County grapes at Napa's Sutter Home Winery. Through the offices of Sacramento home winemaker Charles Myers, Darrell Corti had discovered the old Zinfandel vines of Amador's Shenandoah Valley—specifically, the vines of the Deaver Ranch there. Corti had already caught the Zin bug from the 1966 Mondavi wine. Now he contacted Bob Trinchero of Sutter Home about the Deaver grapes, and 1968, a fine year for California wine generally, became the first vintage of the great Corti/ Sutter Home Zinfandels. I didn't buy this wine—I was too late. But it seemed that everyone in the world of Northern California fine wine, and in Southern California too, for that matter, was talking about it: "A wine for the next millennium!" It came out under the Sutter Home label. Corti's share was aged in French oak barrels and was sold under the Corti Brothers label.

When the 1969 became available from Corti, I got my case and am still waiting for the right situation to drink the last bottle. In 1974 I drank one of my first with Joe and June Swan. Joe had not tasted it yet and on first sniff remarked, "Sorry, Charles, it's corked." And it was. I raced off to the cellar and brought up another. I felt good watching the great master of Zinfandel smile as he sipped, and eventually say, "You'll have to be patient with this one. I'll have to get in touch with Darrell."

It was the 1968 Joseph Swan Zinfandel that lit the fuses not already sizzling on the powder keg. In retrospect, it and his subsequent 1969 Zin seemed to be the final blasts in the modern Zinfandel revolution.

Joe Swan had quit flying for Western Airlines and bought a spread near Forestville in the Russian River Valley. He wanted to grow Pinot noir and Chardonnay in that area's somewhat Burgundian climate. The old ranch he acquired had some ancient Zinfandel vines. In 1968, before he pulled them, he made some wine from their fruit. He didn't bond his place in time for that

CORTI BROTHERS
RESERVE SELECTION
ZINFANDEL
AMADOR COUNTY VINTAGE 1968

This Zinfandel was produced from grapes grown on the K. Deaver Ranch in the Shenandoah Valley just north of Plymouth, Amador County. This family ranch is situated on an east-west exposure and is the oldest established vineyard in Shenandoah Valley.

Climate and temperature make Amador County perfect for growing Zinfandel. Here these grapes produce a superior wine with great depth and fullness and more spicyness and richness than anywhere in California.

1968 was an extremely warm year with the grapes for this wine picked very ripe having an acidity of .85. This wine was bottled unfined and unfiltered in June of 1970.

Since this wine was bottled unfined and unfiltered, it will throw a deposit with time and should be decanted.

PRODUCED AND BOTTLED BY SUTTER HOME WINERY

ST. HELENA, CALIFORNIA ALCOHOL 13.5% BY VOLUME

21. Certainly one of the earliest heralds of Zinfandel's rebirth as a fine table wine was this 1968 wine. It was produced for Darrell Corti, to his specifications, by Bob Trinchero of Sutter Home Winery. The grapes were grown in Amador County on the Deaver Ranch. (Source: Darrell Corti.)

Zinfandel to be a commercial item. But the word certainly got around. Roy Brady claimed it was the greatest of those great Zinfandels of the 1960s. The following year Swan bought Zinfandel grapes at the Teldeschi Ranch in Dry Creek Valley. The rest is well known in the Zinfandel chronicles. There was soon a waiting list to get on the Joseph Swan mailing list, even before Brady's article appeared in *Wine World* magazine. There he wrote, "It was a classic example of the big spicy style of Zinfandel, which had become virtually extinct before Ridge Vineyards took the lead in its resurrection. . . . Joe Swan hit the target dead center on the first try."[18]

One might wonder what convinced the newborn winemasters of the 1960s that Zinfandel could be made in "the classic European manner . . . [to] have great body and a long life" (Schoonmaker's words), in the style of fine red Bordeaux. Robert Mondavi in 1966 and Bob Trinchero, who made the

22. Joseph Swan was a hands-on master of Zinfandel from 1968 to his last vintage in 1988. Here he is at his winery in Forestville, dumping Dry Creek Valley Zinfandel grapes into the crusher. These became his 1973 wine that won the Vintners Club Zinfandel Taste-Off in 1977. (Source: Lynn and Rod Berglund, Joseph Swan Vineyards.)

23. One of Joseph Swan's early Zinfandel triumphs was a blend of three wines from the 1969 and 1971 vintages.

1968 Amador wine, knew very well from their earlier experience that Zinfandel could be made with the proper flavors, structure, and chemistry to warrant long-term cellaring. It had been on their families' dinner tables since their youth. For others, perhaps new on the winemaking scene, certain wines that were still around in the 1950s persuaded them that Zinfandel could be made in the style of fine Cabernet Sauvignon. Three stand out in my mind, all Sonoma Zinfandels: the 1935 Simi, the 1937 Fountaingrove, and the 1941 Louis Martini. I have tasted the Simi and Martini wines in their old age, and I have talked to people who tasted the Fountaingrove. In my view these were great wines and obviously demonstrated Zinfandel's potential. And if a winemaker was looking at Bordeaux as a model, why not use French oak barrels? The Mondavi (1966), Corti (1968), Swan (1968), and Bruce (1968) wines were all given that treatment, which puts a special smile on the finer face of Zinfandel.

Another very important factor that encouraged new winemaking entrepreneurs to include Zinfandel in their fermenting tanks was the ready availability of Zinfandel grapes, all over the state. And the price! A ton of Sonoma Zinfandel in 1965 was about $95. Factored for price inflation in 2002, that would be about $650. During the 2001 vintage the average price for Sonoma Zinfandel grapes was $2,456.

By the end of the 1960s the story of California Zinfandel had entered modern times. In 1970 I saw some of these "hot" Zinfandels on the shelves of upscale bottle shops in New York City and Washington, D.C. But a lot of the story remains, including the swinging pendulum of approval and disdain and the meandering of stylistic fashion. In fact, the diversity of Zinfandel products almost defies analysis. Red table, white, blush, late-harvest, sparkling, and port-like have all become Zinfandel adjectives. And there are now fighting varietals, premiums, super-premiums, and ultra-premiums, but rarely real jug wines, and certainly not from the coastal valleys where Zinfandel grape prices have more than tripled since 1990.

CHAPTER TEN

OF PENDULUMS AND ROLLER COASTERS, 1970–1990

IF A WINE-LOVING RIP VAN WINKLE HAD TASTED THE "MAGIC FLAGON" in 1970 and awakened thirty, not twenty, years later, he certainly would not have been as confused as Irving's Rip, at least not about Zinfandel. Looking back three decades, he'd not be surprised to see the average price of a bottle at $20.00 (about $3.90 in 1970 dollars), nor would he blink at the large number of the highest-priced bottles with alcohol readings of more than 14 percent. But little could he tell from the condition of Zinfandel in the year 2000 about the marvelous swings in popularity and style that California's own varietal had undergone between 1970 and 2000.

The most important American wine facts of the 1970s were the rise in per capita consumption of wine in this country and the explosion of interest in fine table wine, whether from Europe or from California. Together these historic tendencies help to define the modern U.S. wine revolution in its simplest terms. California Zinfandel rode the crest of this revolutionary wave.

For an important segment of the American drinking public, wine was something of a fad in the '70s. Per capita consumption rose continuously throughout the decade but, to the concern of many in the wine industry,

peaked in 1985. Then, for the next ten years, consumption declined steadily, decreasing by 26 percent until it began turning around in 1996. For many, Zinfandel was also a fad, but a very popular one for more than ten years.

The Zinfandels that attracted the most attention in the 1970s were made like fine Cabernet Sauvignon: rich, brawny, and loaded with tannin/phenolics that told the consumer to lay down the bottle as if it were a 1970 Château Latour. These Zinfandels also had their own peppery/raspberry fruit that distinguished them from Cabernets. But I suspect that many drinkers in those years might have confused these varieties in a blind tasting, as I did on more than one occasion. A study done at the University of California at Davis in 1975 indicated that the scholars there regularly reversed the two wines when no labels were in view.[1] In 2001 I took part in an "old Cabernet" tasting among some Napa vintners that was won by a 1977 Napa Zinfandel.

Before we look at the Zinfandels of the 1970s, we should examine the statistics related to their production. Statewide acreage of the variety rose 29.7 percent for the decade, not much compared to that of the many other leading premium varietals (Cabernet Sauvignon rose 204 percent and Pinot noir 193 percent). But the low percentage increase is partly explained by the much larger early base enjoyed by Zinfandel. In all, there was a growth of about 2,000 acres in this ten-year period. In 1970 Zinfandel acres made up 13.6 percent of the state's wine grape total; in 1980 they were down to 8.6 percent. (In 2002 the Zinfandel acreage was 10.5 percent of the total.)[2]

The counties with the largest Zinfandel growth in total acres in the 1970s were, in order, San Joaquin (Lodi), Monterey, Napa, Sonoma, and Mendocino. The percentage growth leaders were Monterey (408 percent), Napa (172 percent), San Luis Obispo (138 percent), Amador (134 percent), and Mendocino (83 percent). The largest loser was San Bernardino, which lost 1,536 acres (40 percent). San Joaquin led throughout the period, with about 38 percent of the state's Zinfandel acres; in 2001 it had 39 percent of the total. San Bernardino was second in 1971 but was overtaken by Sonoma in 1972, with 18 percent. Sonoma still ranks second, but now has only 9 percent of the state's total Zinfandel acreage.

At the beginning of the 1970s the state's Zinfandel yield was very low, only about 2 tons per bearing acre. This was true in both the northern coastal counties and the Lodi area. By 1980 the yield in both areas had risen to about 3.5 tons per acre. (It is a remarkable fact that today the yield in the northern counties is still about 3 tons, while in the Lodi area it has risen to about 6 tons.)

In the 1960s the price for a ton of Zinfandel grapes rarely reached $100 anyplace in California. But by 1970–1972 the state average was $220 per ton (about $1,300 in adjusted 2002 dollars). In 1972 North Coast Zinfandel went for $473; Lodi grapes cost a winery $247 per ton. By 1980 really red, rather than white, Zinfandel was losing consumer favor. Nevertheless, Napa/Sonoma growers were getting about the same prices they had received in 1972. Their real income was much less, however, when corrected for price inflation. By 1980 Lodi prices had dropped to less than $200 per ton. Special demands in the late 1980s would drive these prices up, as the color of much bottled Zinfandel changed.

The average price of a bottle of premium Zinfandel from the vintages of the early 1970s was about $3.50 (close to $20.00 in 2002 dollars). I base this figure on my analysis of the annual Zinfandel evaluations conducted by the *Connoisseurs' Guide to California Wine* (*CGCW*), which began in 1974. By 1981 the average price had risen only to just over $6.00, an amount actually lower than the 1974 figure when corrected for price inflation. Most who lived through these years will not enjoy remembering the annual percentages of such price inflation between 1979 and 1982 (7.7 percent, 11.3 percent, 13.5 percent, and 10.4 percent). We'll return to the reason for this real price decline in a moment.

It would be nice to be able to objectively click off the best Zinfandels produced between 1971 and 1980. But I can convey only subjective opinions. Some opinions are better than others, however, particularly when the evaluator can't see the wine label. For this reason I find the results of the San Francisco Vintners Club blind tastings very useful. I have added up the results of all their Zinfandel tastings for the years 1974 to 1980 as if each event were a

TOP ZINFANDELS IN THE VINTNERS CLUB OF SAN FRANCISCO BLIND TASTINGS, 1974–2002

Since 1974 the Vintners Club of San Francisco has been holding blind tastings of Zinfandel, with several events held each year. Many of the members work in the wine industry, but some are regular, though very interested, consumers. These tastings have special value because of the time period they cover and because the tasters do not know the producers until after they have made their evaluations.

Vintners Club rankings for various spans of years are shown here, with 1 indicating the top-ranked wine during those years.

1974–1980

1. Joseph Swan Vineyards (Sonoma)
2. Ridge Vineyards (Santa Cruz Mountains)
3. Monteviña Vineyards (Amador)
4. Gemello Winery (Mountain View)
5. Rutherford Ranch Brand (Napa)
6. Chateau Montelena (Napa)
7. Clos du Val (Napa)
8. Wine & the People (Berkeley)
9. Lytton Springs Winery (Sonoma); Cuvaison (Napa) [tied]

1981–1985

1. Rosenblum Cellars (Alameda)
2. Montclair Winery (Alameda)
3. Ravenswood (Ravenswood)
4. Grgich Hills Cellar (Napa)
5. Ridge Vineyards; J. W. Morris (Napa); Joseph Phelps Vineyards (Napa) [tied]
8. Calera Wine Co. (San Benito); Hop Kiln Winery (Sonoma); Lytton Springs Winery; Raymond Vineyard (Napa) [tied]

1986–1992

1. Ravenswood
2. Rosenblum Cellars
3. Ridge Vineyards
4. Hop Kiln Winery
5. Nalle Winery (Napa)
6. Kendall-Jackson Winery (Lake)
7. Limerick Lane Winery (Sonoma)
8. Congress Springs Vineyards (Santa Cruz Mountains)
9. Grgich Hills Cellar
10. Franciscan Vineyards (Napa)

1993–1997

1. Ridge Vineyards
2. Limerick Lane
3. Ravenswood
4. St. Francis Vineyards (Sonoma)
5. Rosenblum Cellars
6. Green & Red Vineyard (Napa); Tobin James Winery (Paso Robles); Sherrer Vineyards (Sonoma); Eberle Winery (Paso Robles) [tied]
10. Norman Winery (Paso Robles)

1998–2002

1. St. Francis; Signorello Vineyards (Napa) [tied]
3. Ravenswood; Geyser Peak Winery (Sonoma); Domain Danica (Sonoma) [tied]
6. Saucelito Canyon Vineyard (Arroyo Grande)
7. Edmeades Winery (Mendocino)
8. Ridge Vineyards; Rabbit Ridge Winery (Sonoma); Mount Veeder Winery (Napa) [tied]

high school track meet, assigning points (five, three, or one) to the top three. The winner was Joseph Swan, with Ridge Vineyards a very close second. Well back came Monteviña, Gemello, and Rutherford Ranch.[3]

CGCW is also a good source for such opinions. Its tasting panels operate with the labels hidden and are usually made up of tasters from many elements of the wine industry. (I can attest to this, having been a member of the Zinfandel panels from 1975 to 1985.) For the 580 wines rated in the Zinfandel specials for these years, a count of the wines receiving two and three puffs ("distinctive" and "exceptional") reveals that Ridge and Swan were the top two producers, followed by Carneros Creek, Clos du Val, and David Bruce. Readers who may wonder at the exclusion of several noted producers of the 1990s are reminded that unless a winery was in the field twenty-five years ago, it is unlikely that its wines could have made either of these lists.[4]

Before Prohibition, a useful anecdotal way to identify the best California wine was to read the comments of European experts. Frederico Pohndorff and Charles Oldham, the most famous of these, did have commercial connections in California that might have colored their views. Such is not the case with Harry Waugh, who had been in the British wine trade thirty years before he came to California in 1964, shortly before retiring from the board of the Harvey's Group. Eventually he sat in on a Berkeley Wine and Food Society dinner, as the guest of William Dickerson, whose Napa Zinfandel vineyard became famous in the 1990s. Waugh visited Napa and became fascinated by what he saw happening at the premium end of the California wine industry. He began to visit the state regularly and included his observations, along with comments on the European wine scene, in a series of books that appeared between 1970 and 1987.

In *Pick of the Bunch* (1970), Waugh told of his reintroduction to Zinfandels. Those he had tasted earlier had been much lighter than those he tasted on this trip. He noted that those he appreciated most in the late 1960s would benefit from more time in the cellar. He loved the Louis Martini, Parducci, and Buena Vista Zinfandels from those early years. But his favorite in a blind tasting was a wine of historical importance, the 1966 Robert Mondavi (discussed in chapter 9). In *Diary of a Winetaster* (1972), Waugh related his dis-

24. The vines at Ridge Vineyards, perched on Monte Bello Ridge, look out on the Santa Clara Valley, two thousand feet below. Here Italian families began producing wine in the 1880s. A Cabernet Sauvignon from these vineyards won a gold medal at the Paris Exposition in 1900. (Source: Ridge Vineyards.)

covery of Ridge Zinfandels. His favorites were the 1968 Geyserville and the 1971 Occidental. But he reserved his strongest praise for the 1968 Mayacamas Late Harvest, "easily the richest unfortified wine I have ever tasted."[5]

Later he praised the Zinfandels of Sutter Home, Harbor, Chateau Montelena, Swan, Grand Cru, and Kenwood. In 1978 he was instrumental in founding the Zinfandel Club of London, an organization that was actually interested in California wine in general, rather than in the single variety. But in that same year, while summing up the remarkable gains of California wine over the previous ten years, he chose not to mention Zinfandel. In his later books he began complaining of a heavy style that he did not like, using terms such as "harsh," "rough," and "cumbersome." In his final book, in 1987, I can find only one mention of Zinfandel in the thirty-six pages devoted to his 1986 visit to California. This swing in favor, moreover, was in accord with a view held by many American wine consumers.

In the 1970s several California winegrowing areas had special Zinfandel stories. I have already alluded to the rediscovery of the Sierra Foothills as a premium grape source in the mid-1960s, beginning with Amador County's Shenandoah Valley. During the following decade El Dorado County also became important for its new vineyards, although El Dorado's winegrowing history stretches well back into the nineteenth century. In 1970 only 1 acre of wine grapes could be found there; in 1980 there were 360 acres, one-third of them Zinfandel.

At first, and until the late '70s, the greatest success came to premium wineries outside the area using Sierra Foothills grapes. The obvious exception was Monteviña under Cary Gott, whose briary heavyweights came on the market with the 1973 vintage. But by 1975 Ridge, Sutter Home, Carneros Creek, Mount Veeder, Gemello, Geyser Peak, ZD, and others were producing very good Amador Zinfandels. The success of the Sierra Foothills region as a winegrowing area is also reflected in acreage statistics: about 400 acres of Zinfandel in 1970, rising to 1,275 by 1980. In 2002 there were well over 2,000 acres of Zinfandel, accounting for about half the wine grape acreage for the region. Cabernet Sauvignon came in a distant second, with about 500 acres.

But before the '70s had ended, we could get a glimpse of ambivalence concerning Amador's success. As early as 1976, Norman Roby, writing for *Vintage* magazine, was concerned about some of the heavy, dark flavors in so many Amador Zinfandels. He correctly noted that these wines were not for everyone. He continued to be enthusiastic about Zinfandel as a fine claret grape but was more critical of "high alcohol monsters."[6]

The Zinfandel story in Monterey County during the years of the wine revolution is not as happy as that in the Sierra Foothills. Only 20 acres were planted there in 1968, rising to 475 in 1971 and then to 3,194 acres in 1974. The number peaked in 1978 and then plummeted. Over the next five years more than two square miles of Zinfandel vineyard disappeared from Mon-

25. The Lombardo Fossati winery in El Dorado County produced Zinfandel for the local market before Prohibition. Today the structure serves as a tasting room for the Boeger Winery, also one of the county's leading Zinfandel producers.

terey, mostly grafted to white varieties. This switchover was the necessary result of a general miscalculation by many new and inexperienced vineyardists, who had planted thousands of acres of vines in the wrong places all over California in the 1970s. What happened in Monterey's Salinas Valley was fairly typical: Zinfandel was planted too far to the north, where the maritime influence made it almost impossible for grapes to become properly ripe.

By 2002 fewer than 300 acres of Zinfandel were left in Monterey County, mostly planted in the southern portion or in the Carmel Valley, where the grapes can ripen properly. We can see the improvement in the quality of Monterey Zinfandel since the '70s by examining comparative grape prices. In 1980 growers in Monterey received only 44 percent of what their counterparts in the Sierra Foothills got for their Zinfandel. In 2001 the prices were almost the same.

To find the historic champion of Central Coast Zinfandel, we must look to the south, to San Luis Obispo County, and specifically to the Paso Robles area. There our famed variety has not suffered Monterey's roller coaster ride of the past thirty years. The county had about 500 Zinfandel acres before the 1960s, pushing the total to about 1,000 in the 1970s. Since 1994 the total has jumped to more than 2,000 acres. Grape prices in 2001 were similar to those in the Sierra Foothills, at a little more than $1,000 per ton. Thus, like the Zinfandels of the Sierra Foothills, those of the Paso Robles area are often seen as delicious bargains in today's market, in which wineries pay more than $2,000 per ton for Sonoma Zinfandel grapes.

By the late 1970s producers were beginning to note a decline in Zinfandel sales. By the early 1980s most agreed that the wine had become a "hard sell." This decline of California Zinfandel is not easily explained, at least not the decline of red Zinfandel in the style that made it famous in the early '70s. I believe that a combination of factors was involved, but I have no general theory that brings them together.

Many writers have suggested that the wide diversity of styles was nearly fatal. As early as 1973 Trader Joe's newsletter was concerned: "Tell us the mocking bird's song and we will tell you the Zinfandel's taste. After our blind tasting our panel could form no general conclusion as to what Zinfandel ought to taste like." [7] In 1977 Norman Roby devoted an entire article to the lack of focus in Zinfandel style, noting, "Everyone tinkers with the grape and shapes it into some different, often delightful, wine." And even though he declared his love for its many wines, "nobody can honestly say what it should smell and taste like." [8] Before long, more were joining the chorus, and the market began to move in a direction that rejected what writers were describing as confusion, even anarchy.

The most serious complaint that echoed across the country in the late '70s and early '80s came mostly from wine and food writers for newspapers and was centered on the high-alcohol "dark monsters." In later years accounts of

Zinfandel's decline, especially from wine writers, tended to rest on this facile explanation. But other data, which I trust, seem to belie this simplistic view.

In 1978 *CGCW* evaluated 246 wines in its Zinfandel review. The evaluators deemed 9 percent undrinkable. Of the satisfactory wines, they observed that 37 percent would benefit from cellaring. It is difficult to conclude from this that most of the varietal Zinfandels being offered to consumers then were "dark monsters." I don't believe that the bulk of the wine being offered to the public was the problem. Perhaps wine writers' complaints about some few specific wines were more to blame for the situation. *CGCW* noted in its Zinfandel review three years later "the falling prestige of Zinfandel at the premium end of the scale," evidenced by the widening gap between Zinfandel and Cabernet Sauvignon bottle prices. But *CGCW* went on to argue that "there are more attractive, well-made Zinfandels being offered now than ever before" and named Caymus and Grgich Hills, both from Napa, as the top choices. (We will encounter Mike Grgich's name when we come to the unraveling of the mysteries of Zinfandel's origins.)

The editors of *CGCW* had it right in noting that Zinfandel bottle prices had been flat or declining while Cabernet prices were soaring, the latter partially from a simple price inflation that was nationwide. (U.S. consumer prices rose 43 percent from 1979 to 1981.) It was a great time for Zinfandel consumers, but many producers were hurting. There was much talk of rising Zinfandel inventories and complaints that premium Zinfandel was simply not moving off the retail shelves. In a short time several important producers had left the field, most notably Robert Mondavi.

It is certainly true that laying down monster Zinfandels was a fad that ran out of steam in the early '80s. But consumer demand for red Zinfandel of all styles, light and heavy, was on the decline. In 1982 Kenwood's Robert Kozlowski organized a Zinfandel Guild. It was unsuccessful, according to the founder, primarily because it lacked industry support. At the same time, wine writer Jerry Mead began one of his media campaigns, this time to save Zinfandel. It too went nowhere, although I treasure my huge ZinFan button, a memento of the campaign.

Many serious Zinfandel producers stayed the course. They were able to continue producing these fine wines in part because of the remarkable development of White Zinfandel in these years. The idea of making a white or, better, a pink wine from Zinfandel grapes was not new. George West, near Lodi, had one such wine in the 1860s. Arpad Haraszthy had used a "white" Zinfandel in the first really successful *cuvées* of his Eclipse sparkling wine. Charles Wetmore had promoted the idea of making a pink wine from the free-run Zinfandel crush in the 1880s, specifically pointing to the Lodi area as the place where such a wine would be a success.

David Bruce had made a White Zinfandel in the 1960s, but Sutter Home under Bob Trinchero was the primary agent for that drink's modern success. It began on a small scale in 1972 with a small batch of dry pink wine that Trinchero labeled "Oeil de Perdrix [Eye of the Partridge], A White Zinfandel Wine." By 1980 production of a slightly sweeter and lower-alcohol product had risen to twenty-five thousand cases. By 1984 the total had reached 1.5 million cases, and the figure continued to go up for several years. Other producers, large and small, jumped aboard this Zinfandel express. Even Ridge produced about twenty thousand cases of White Zinfandel between 1982 and 1986.[9] Many writers later contended that a major key to Beringer's financial success in the '80s was its popular White Zinfandel.

One economic plus for producers of this style of wine was their ability to get it on the market only a few months after the harvest, thus generating an early cash flow not possible with most red Zinfandel. Not a few producers of powerful Zinfandels in the 1970s stayed the course in the next decade with a boost from their White Zinfandel cash flow. So many men and women have told me that they were able to keep producing small amounts of rich red Zinfandel because of dollars generated by White Zinfandel that I believe this was indeed a major factor in the survival of our muscled friend in the 1980s. It should be noted that Trinchero never gave up on red Zinfandel for a moment, producing about one hundred thousand cases in 1986. He also made his presence in the red Zinfandel field more noticeable by buying Monteviña in 1988.

We can locate the main source for this White Zinfandel flood by examin-

"Sutter Home"
CALIFORNIA
Oeil de Perdrix
A WHITE ZINFANDEL WINE
Produced and Bottled By
Sutter Home Winery,
St. Helena, California
Alcohol 13% By Volume

26. White Zinfandel was first produced in the Lodi area in the 1860s. But the origins of the wine's modern popularity can be traced to this small batch of Sutter Home wine in 1972. Within a few years the winery's sales of White Zinfandel were in the millions of cases.

ing Central Valley acreage statistics. In 1985, understandably, the Lodi area had 10,000 acres; it had always been Zinfandel country. But the unlikely desert counties of Kern, Fresno, Madera, and Stanislaus, which had but 510 acres in 1985, had 3,365 by 1990 and 8,800 by 1996. A large percentage of this growth went directly into the White Zinfandel market.

White Zinfandel has been pictured by some as a wine fad. But its rise and small decline was nothing like that of Cold Duck or wine coolers. Consumption did slip after 1989, but it is still in the millions of gallons. Wine industry analyst Jon Fredrikson wrote in 2002 that White Zinfandel was "still one of the best selling low priced wines." He predicted that the White Zinfandel segment of the market would continue to prosper.[10]

The renewed interest in red Zinfandel as a fine wine in the premium market dates roughly from 1986–1987. Earlier, in 1983, *CGCW* had lamented that "the bloom is off the Zinfandel market," although they found many North Coast Zinfandels to love. (Grgich Hills—again—and Rutherford Ranch were the most loved, again from Napa.) Sutter Home's Bob Trinchero admitted that Zinfandel "for the moment had lost its status as the darling of wine writers." Winery inventories were backing up; the number of producers was declining sharply. But *CGCW* nevertheless noted that "a few stalwart producers have hung on to their sources of grapes and have continued to offer a stream of well made wine."[11]

Soon wine writers were beginning to point to a greater emphasis on well-extracted Zinfandels with less harsh, softer (as opposed to hard) tannins and bright fruit flavors. Those could be drunk when young or could evolve in the cellar. And writers did not overlook the value that these fine wines offered. In 1986 you could easily buy a bottle of first-class Zinfandel, to drink or lay down, for $7.00 to $9.00. (*CGCW*'s three-puff wines in 1986 averaged $8.17 per bottle: Ridge, Rosenblum, and Quivira.)

In 1987, for the first time, Robert Parker gave Zinfandel a special section in his annual *Wine Advocate* review. (His favorites were Ridge, Ravenswood, and Lytton Springs.) By 1988 the *Los Angeles Times* was cheering the Zinfandel's comeback. *CGCW* reported that "all current signs indicate that red Zinfandel table wine has entered a new phase of popularity, after almost half a decade in the doldrums."[12]

Producers whose names began with *R* were becoming the darlings in this growing market: Rosenblum, Ravenswood, Ridge, and Rafanelli, for example. Hop Kiln won the 1987 Vintners Club taste-off. Nalle took second and third in 1988 and 1989. But the "Rs" took eleven of the eighteen top places in these three years. By the end of the '80s the best Zinfandels were still averaging under ten dollars per bottle, while Cabernet prices were still soaring. Writers were talking about Zinfandel as the affordable alternative to the higher-priced varietal.

The reason for the difference can be seen in grape prices. From 1988 to 1994 Sonoma Zinfandel was steady at $714 to $740 per ton. In 1988 Napa Cabernet Sauvignon went for $1,235, 73 percent more than that county's Zinfandel. Such numbers make it clear why *CGCW*'s top five Zinfandels in 1990 averaged only $11.30 per bottle, while its top Cabernets had a mean price of $30.03 (median price was only $17.00). It is also worth noting that now all five top Zinfandels came from Sonoma, whereas ten of the thirteen top Cabernets were from Napa. Throughout the '90s the perception of Sonoma as the premier Zinfandel country continued to rise, as did the prices for Zinfandel grapes there.

In 1994 the state's total Zinfandel acreage had reached 38,000, up 26 percent from 1988. But almost all this increase occurred in the Central Valley, where producers began taking advantage of Zinfandel's rising name recognition throughout the wine-drinking portions of the nation. For the most part the additional wine from this huge region became part of the White Zinfandel and "fighting varietal" markets. The latter are affordable, cork-finished wines, usually light and fruity, and ready to drink. The "fighting varietal" segment of the state's varietal wine market continued to grow as the country's per capita table wine consumption again rose in the late '80s and into the '90s.

In 2001 California boasted about 50,000 acres of Zinfandel. Two-thirds of this acreage was in the Central Valley, with almost 60 percent of this number in the Lodi area. Nearly 90 percent of the growth in Zinfandel acreage since 1990 has been in the Central Valley. What makes this growth remarkable is that the Zinfandel yield per acre in that huge region almost doubled in the 1990s, to about six tons per acre. In contrast, Sonoma/Napa yields have held fairly steady, at between three and four tons.

Going into vintage 2001, nearly 3,000 acres of Zinfandel vines were so young that they had not yet yielded a crop. The year before, that number had been almost double the 2001 figure. Most of these vines were in the Central Valley. As these new vines come to bear, they have the potential of adding more than 15 million bottles of Zinfandel to the state's total. We should not be surprised to hear complaints about overexpansion of Central Valley vineyard capacity in the years to come.

CHAPTER ELEVEN

FAT YEARS, 1991–2001

A glowing, freewheeling economy has allowed consumers to pursue luxury wines like never before.

JAMES LAUBE, *WINE SPECTATOR*, 2001

EXCEPT FOR THE WINES OF A FEW SMALL PRODUCERS IN THE LODI area, none of the rich and powerful Zinfandel wines that were the driving force of red Zinfandel's revival and boom in the 1990s came from the Central Valley. The beautiful and well-muscled red phoenix that rose up during that decade and continues its popularity in the new century comes overwhelmingly from the coastal valleys north of Santa Barbara and from the Sierra Foothills.

The interest in California Zinfandel in the 1990s took off like the stock market of those years. But the next decade has seen no bear market for producers and no slaking the thirst of Zinfandel consumers, many of whom (though a distinct minority) have been willing to pay as much for a bottle of old-vine Sonoma Zinfandel as for a Second Growth Grand Cru Bordeaux.

One of the most important Zinfandel events of the 1990s took place at San Francisco's Mandarin Hotel in 1992, where a certain producer/consumer group, organized the year before, held its first wine tasting. There were but twenty-two producers on hand, pouring young wine to about a hundred tasters. No fanfare preceded the event, and certainly no mob scenes marked it. The organization, Zinfandel Advocates and Producers, is known as ZAP.

27. Zinfandel Advocates and Producers (ZAP) is the largest and most successful varietal-specific wine advocacy group in the world. Here we see the group's annual tasting at San Francisco's Fort Mason, in 2001. (Source: ZAP; photo by Meg Smith.)

Now let us leap ten years hence to old Fort Mason on the San Francisco waterfront. Here on January 26, 2002, two gigantic Transportation Corps warehouses were converted into a pair of wine-tasting salons, either of which could hold two full-sized games of American football simultaneously, with room to spare. Almost nine thousand Zinfanatics paid thirty-five dollars (as ZAP members) or forty-five dollars (nonmembers) to taste the young wines of 267 Zinfandel producers. And they had seven hours to do it.

The human crush at this tasting event was challenging, particularly around tables of certain producers whose brands begin with *R.* (Years ago the alphabetical organization of tables was thrown out as a hazard to public safety.) I doubt if there is a happier purple-tongued group half this size elsewhere in the world. And I wouldn't miss it. I will return to some detailed observations on these tastings shortly.

Several organizations have formed in recent years to promote the consumption of wines from specific varieties (Pinot noir, Sauvignon blanc, and Cabernet Sauvignon, for example), with varying success, but none has come close to the influence of ZAP.

The Zinfandel Guild had worked to rebuild the flagging popularity of that wine in the early 1980s but failed to catch on with producers or consumers. ZAP was originally the 1991 brainchild of Napa's Jerry Seps, who has been making nothing but Zinfandel at his Storybook Mountain winery since 1979. At first ZAP was to be strictly a producers' marketing tool, aimed at raising the image of Zinfandel as a fine wine variety. But when *Sunset* magazine's Margaret Smith came aboard as executive director, the emphasis was modified to include the concerns of consumers (the "advocates" in the group's name).

The number of producer members has increased fivefold since the mid-1990s, when ZAP tastings started to really take off. But the ZAP producers are not concentrated in the Central Valley, where most of California's Zinfandel vines are planted. In 2002, 95 percent of the producers represented at the big tasting were located in the coastal valleys north of Santa Barbara to Mendocino, and in the Sierra Foothills.

When we look at the 2000 vintage, from which most producers were offering samples, some interesting numbers come to light. The total Zinfandel production of the premium areas that were overwhelmingly featured at the 2002 ZAP tasting represents a potential tonnage of grapes that can produce only about one in eight bottles (12.2 percent) of the California Zinfandel from that large vintage. In other words, the visible enthusiasm seen at Fort Mason was directed to a relatively small percentage of the Zinfandel that might be produced in the state in any given year.

The premium Zinfandel represented by this 12.2 percent actually comes from about the same tonnage as the Cabernet Sauvignon production of Fresno and Madera Counties in 2000, and it is little more than half of the Zinfandel production that year from those desert areas. Perhaps, then, there was not quite as much high-quality Zinfandel from the 2000 vintage as one might have thought. Still, there were enough Zinfandel grapes from the premium areas to produce about 31 million bottles of wine.

An additional factor involved in these numbers is difficult to quantify. Thirty-two of the 620 wines offered at the 2002 tasting came from the Lodi area of San Joaquin County. I tasted all of them (and spit out, as I did with all these wines), and to my taste they were all very good. Some, I thought, were really excellent. I have no way of knowing what percentage of San Joaquin County's almost 20,000 acres of Zinfandel is represented in these wines, some of which were actually made by producers from the coastal counties, such as Cosentino (Napa) and Laurel Glen (Sonoma). The number is likely quite small. Nevertheless, when we look at the Central Valley Zinfandel acreage and tonnage numbers, we always need to add a mental asterisk to remind us of the particularly high quality of a small percentage of the Lodi Zinfandels.

Also, several wines at the tasting simply carried a California appellation on their labels. These are more than likely from other parts of the Central Valley. I tasted a few and found that they represented what I have termed the older face of Zinfandel—light, fruity, and quaffable.

The catalogues of the annual ZAP tastings[1] show that the average price of the bottles offered at the 2002 extravaganza was a whopping $23.38. I counted 35 percent that were $25.00 or more. Four years earlier the average was $20.80, with 24 percent at or above $25.00. The 2002 ZAP numbers are not much different from those of the wines evaluated by *CGCW* in that year, with an average price of $24.20 per bottle.

Although these average prices seem high, we must keep in mind that about half of the wines cost less than the average. And at the ZAP tastings, producers are showing off what they consider to be their best efforts. Also, the prices listed in the catalogues are often well above those that consumers find on the same bottles at discount retail stores.

I personally like the big, rich, luscious style of Zinfandel that is so popular now, but that is not always the style of the wines I put in my cellar. I buy with an eye on the future, selecting wines for their structure, chemistry, varietal definition, and intensity. We are currently drinking our 1986s and 1987s, but we are finding a certain joy dabbling in more recent vintages. At Fort Mason in 2002, Roz and I tasted (and spit out) every wine under $20.00 that was bottled and ready for sale, mostly 1999s and 2000s. We found fourteen we would happily own, and I have bought four of them at an average price of $14.45 per bottle, all from discount retailers whose prices tend to be $3.00 to $4.00 below the listed prices, from which the high averages I have calculated were derived.

Although ZAP's beginnings at the first tasting in 1992 were modest, the organization's timing was perfect. Now the annual tasting is an important media event of international proportions. Today the group includes about 270 producer members, with an advocate membership of almost 7,000. The extent to which ZAP rode the wave of Zinfandel frenzy in the 1990s, or was in fact largely responsible for it, is debatable. In 1997 ZAP president Kent Rosenblum was asked, "Did ZAP create all this interest and energy?" His answer: "I think it was already there, but ZAP was responsible for organizing and channeling it into an effective force." [2]

Margaret Smith's newsletter, the *Zinfandel Express,* gave advocates a detailed program for enjoying Zinfandel all over the state. Advocates receive membership cards, which they display at member-producers' tasting rooms. A cordial reception and abundant hospitality are the almost invariable result. Most producers hold special ZAP events, always listed in the *Express.* This approach, plus the monster January tasting at Fort Mason, has done much to help the founders reach their original goal of promoting Zinfandel as a world-class wine.

One of ZAP's campaigns has been to secure national recognition of Zinfandel's special place in America's viticultural history. The first step was a tasting for Congressional representatives in Washington, D.C., in May 1994. There a resolution was read that proclaimed Zinfandel "a national treasure." [3] In July 1997 Kent Rosenblum made an official announcement of this "heritage" campaign. Two months later ZAP leaders met with representatives of the Smithsonian Institution at the Storybook winery to discuss the organization's possible association with the campaign.

Although much energy has been expended to have Zinfandel named America's "heritage grape," the resolution presented to the U.S. Senate in July 1999 (S.R. 132) by California's senators, Dianne Feinstein and Barbara Boxer, simply called for January 23–29, 2001, to be "Zinfandel Appreciation Week" and

ZINFANDEL SHOW-OFFS

The annual ZAP Zinfandel tastings are a place for producers to show off their best wines. Each producer is limited to three offerings. Many show a barrel sample of their newly fermented vintage. Others offer their new releases, while a few will have an older vintage. Some show only expensive, single-vineyard superstars, while others include a moderately priced wine under fifteen dollars. A very few who have a wide line show their least expensive wine. These are wines usually bearing a California appellation, from grapes grown in the Central Valley.

By looking at counties and regions represented and the number of participants from each, we get a fairly good picture of where the best Zinfandels are coming from. But it should be noted that many producers use grapes from outside their own region.

We also need to take a special look at the wines here from the Central Valley, where most Zinfandel grapes are grown. At the 2002 tasting, 267 producers poured 620 wines. Thirty-two of these wines were clearly identified as being made from grapes grown in the Lodi region of the Central Valley. Only 13 of the 620 were identified simply as "California." These were probably made from grapes grown in "Other Central Valley" areas.

The number of producer facilities represented at the 2002 ZAP tasting are listed here by region:

Sonoma County	94
Napa County	67
Central Coast (mostly San Luis Obispo County)	33
Sierra Foothills (mostly Amador and El Dorado Counties)	23
Mendocino County	15
Central Valley	12
Santa Cruz Mountains and Santa Clara Valley	11
East Bay (Alameda and Contra Costa Counties)	9
Lake County	2
Southern California	1

acknowledged that Zinfandel was a "national treasure." It is not clear to me how much grumbling occurred east of the Rockies by those who might have thought a native variety such as the Concord or Cynthiana more appropriate as a "heritage grape." But grumbling there was. And with the national political chaos during the last months of 2000 and the serious tone in Washington politics since the September 2001 terrorist attacks, the resolution has not come up for a vote.

At the state level, a similar move to honor the Zinfandel took the form of an assembly bill in 2002 (AB 2923) that would declare the grape California's "official state fruit." The idea supposedly came from a group of fourth-grade students in Elk Grove who wrote their assemblyman that Zinfandel deserved the honor "because of its long history in the state and because it is identified mainly as a California grape and is grown almost exclusively in California." As yet there has been no response from orange growers, but it should be noted that Elk Grove is in the northern portion of the Lodi-Woodbridge district, true Zinfandel country for at least a century.[4]

A more notable contribution by ZAP to the Zinfandel heritage has been a practical one. In 1995 work began at the Oakville Experiment Station to establish a Heritage Vineyard for California Zinfandel. The operation has been directed by James Wolpert, chair of the Department of Viticulture and Enology at the University of California at Davis, a man I consider perfect for the task, not only for his scholarly virtues but also for his steady devotion to Zinfandel, particularly to the preservation of the variety's old-vine heritage and to the improvement of its wine quality. Since 1998 ZAP has been the primary contributor to the project, with donations totaling $141,280 by 2002.

Wolpert and his associates were intrigued by the fact that the grape crops from some of the best old vineyards were quite different from one another, however fine the wine. Did this result from a genetic difference, cultural practices and the environment, or a combination of both? By rounding up vine selections from throughout the state, bringing them to one site, and farming them with uniform practices, perhaps some scientific answers to the old nature/nurture question could be answered for Zinfandel.[5]

Wolpert also wanted to preserve the biological heritage of the Zinfandel vines in these old vineyards. Zinfandel vines can live and produce for more than a hundred years, but they won't last forever. With the wide group of selections, wine could be produced from the Oakville site to determine which of the ancients could best be added to our young vineyards to help improve wine quality in years to come.

During the dormant season of 1995–1996 Wolpert and his crew of volunteers began scouring the state, collecting budwood from vineyards at least sixty years old. It was not difficult to locate many of them, for not a few names had become well known as the vineyard-designated specialties of many producers. At the 1995 ZAP tasting we had already seen and sipped from Aldo's

28. James Wolpert chairs the Department of Viticulture and Enology at the University of California at Davis. He also oversees the Oakville Experiment Station in the Napa Valley and its Zinfandel Heritage Vineyard. Here he checks out some Zinfandel grapes at Oakville. (Source: Department of Viticulture and Enology, UC Davis; photo by Debbie Aldridge.)

Vineyard (Biale/Napa), Bridgehead (Cline/Contra Costa), Monte Rosso (Ravenswood/Sonoma), Dusi Ranch (Peachy Canyon/Paso Robles), and Eschen (Terre Rouge/Amador), to name a few.

The Oakville Experiment Station is located between the Robert Mondavi and Far Niente wineries. In it a 0.76-acre plot was set aside for the Heritage Vineyard, and the budwood selections were grafted onto St. George resistant rootstock.[6] Later acquisitions brought an increase in the area devoted to Zinfandel. By the end of the next planting season Wolpert had fifty-seven selections from twenty-seven vineyards. By 1999 there were ninety selections. Seven vines were developed for each selection and planted on eight-by-nine-foot centers. They were head trained and spur pruned so that when they are about fifteen years old they will have the historic "goblet" look typical of many old California vineyards.[7]

Zinfandel is noted for giving a small crop on very young vines. In 1997 Wolpert's crew was able to harvest 1.26 tons at 26.3° Brix (sugar percentage) on September 8. He entrusted the crop to Nils Venge, whose Saddleback Cellars is near the station. Robert Biale Vineyards (Napa) made the 1998 wine, and Cline Cellars (Sonoma) produced the 1999. The 1998 vintage was good for 102 cases, most of it auctioned or sampled at the 2001 ZAP tasting. Some of each vintage is being kept as library samples so that the development of the wines can be followed over the years and viewed in relationship to the aging vines in the vineyard. In 2000 there were enough grapes for Rod Berglund of Joseph Swan Vineyards (Sonoma) to make several individual lots from specific field selections. This approach, in a few years, will be key to the eventual use of the best selections for the gradual improvement of Zinfandel. But it will take time for these research data to affect the source of budwood used to establish new vineyards. In Wolpert's words, "Ultimately this research will help us . . . preserve the specific qualities of the old vines for future generations."[8]

The matter of old-vine Zinfandel is not related solely to our viticultural heritage or to the quality of the vines in our vineyards years from now. One issue that arose during the 1990s concerned the term "old-vine" and its appropriate use on labels and in advertising. Currently no legal definition for the term exists.

One cannot avoid the notion that part of the mild enthusiasm for wines from ancient vines is the result of a marketing ploy. But there is some substance to the contention that grapes from very old Zinfandel vines make wines with particularly concentrated flavors. One explanation for such a phenomenon is obvious: older vines tend to have lower crop yields, a factor that definitely affects flavor intensity.

Occasionally I am asked to name the oldest stand of, let us say, Cabernet Sauvignon or Chardonnay vines in the state or in a region. My first mental reaction, beyond "That's an interesting question for a historian," is, why would anyone care? A Bordeaux grower would think someone daft to boast of having a Cabernet vineyard seventy-five or eighty years old. What could possibly be the advantage? But a Zinfandel vineyard, planted in the 1920s on upland soil, dry farmed, and head pruned, is a treasure today. Such vineyards help to account for the rather low yields Zinfandel vines have been averaging in the North Coast, but no one knows what percentage of the vines in any given place are of any particular old age.

It should not be thought that most producers are rushing to employ the "old-vine" term. Only thirty-seven of the wines offered at the 2002 ZAP tasting were identified on the label as coming from old vines. (Bonny Doon's entry read "Beastly Old Vines.") But dozens more there might have claimed old-vine status. And the number of such wines is growing every year. Many producers are concerned that some criterion should be established for using the term on labels. A few, such as Rodney Strong Vineyards and Dry Creek Vineyards, have backed away from using the "old-vine" term on their labels because of the imprecision of the expression. Rodney Strong is now using "Knotty Vine," and Dry Creek has typed its wine "Heritage Clone."

I am sure that a fair percentage of the Zinfandel vineyards whose wines bear claims of great venerability carry exaggerated birth dates. In the 1990s I winced to hear the numerous boasts about hundred-year-old stands in the North Coast. How did these vines survive the phylloxera blizzard that blackened the vineyards of Sonoma and Napa from the late 1880s well into the twentieth century? A few were planted on resistant rootstock by such prescient pioneers as Kenwood's James A. Shaw, who grafted his Zinfandel onto *V. riparia* stock in the 1880s. Such growers were able to buy riparia and rupestris rootstock directly from nurseries in Missouri in the early years. But, according to an 1891 state survey, few did the same. Some of Shaw's vines survive today on the Kunde Estate, as do some from the historic William McPherson Hill vineyard, now part of the Old Hill Vineyard, which supplies grapes for one of Ravenswood's famous Zinfandels. However, almost all the oldest Zinfandel vines in Napa and Sonoma date from 1897–1909, when serious replanting took place, mostly on St. George rootstock. Generally speaking, most of the truly old vines planted in the rest of the Bay Area and Lodi-Woodbridge are about seventy-five to eighty years old and date from the planting splurge of the early 1920s.

It is not possible to calculate precisely how many old vines of what age are still standing. But some of the available state statistics can lead to informed guesses. In 1970 Napa and Sonoma had almost 4,000 acres of Zinfandel vines that dated from 1959 or earlier. It seems reasonable to suggest that at least one-fourth of those vines forty years or older are still bearing. If so, with a typical yield of 1.5 tons per acre, we might expect from fifteen thousand to twenty thousand cases of old-vine Zinfandel from these two counties. Amador, Paso Robles, and Lodi also have their share of such vines. James Wolpert has estimated that slightly more than 5,000 acres of Zinfandel in California are thirty years old or more.

But how old is old? This question has sparked some debate among producers. And how do we know how old a parcel of vines is? And what about stands in which a large number of vines have been planted to replace those dead and dying? In 1999 the Bureau of Alcohol, Tobacco and Firearms, part of the U.S. Treasury Department, indicated that it planned to look into possible criteria to impose on labels that claimed old-vine status for their wines. Now, wisely I think, the bureau is looking the other way, as it did years ago on the question of what was a "mountain wine." But the debate has been lively since 1999 in the press and in wine publications.[9]

Most of those interviewed have expressed the opinion that forty years should be the absolute minimum age. But I have some trouble with failing to differentiate between vines planted in the 1960s and those in the 1920s. I prefer at least seventy-five years as a minimum age. Matt Cline has noted that old vines are no assurance of quality. He knows of ancient vines planted on deep soils that are pruned to yield five tons or more. Ravenswood's Joel Peterson claims that you can trick a young vine into giving old-vine quality grapes—head prune, short spurs, dry farm, St. George rootstock, small crops, reduced leaf cover, and—voilà! But he chooses his words carefully when he says that with such a careful regimen, "you do get *some* of the old-vine character" (my emphasis).

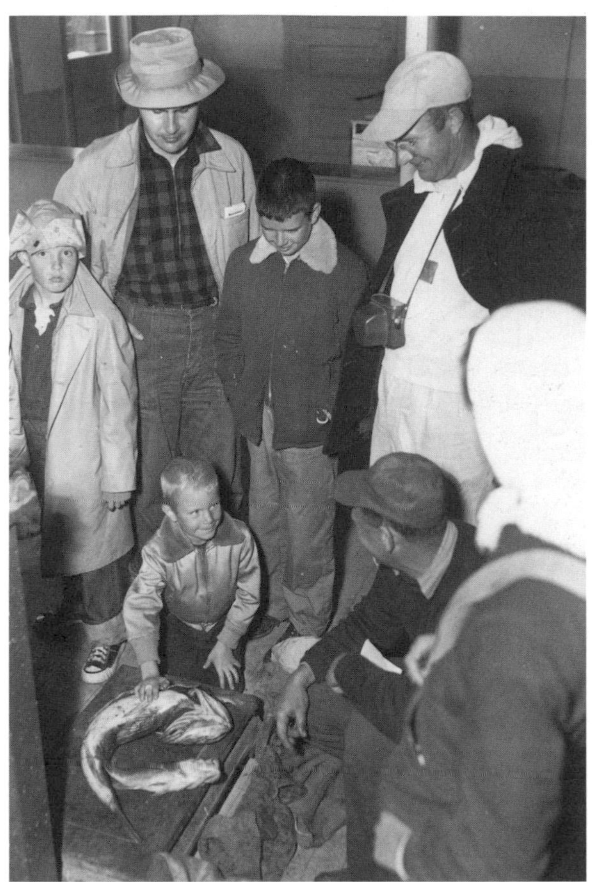

29. Shown with his fish is Ravenswood founder Joel Peterson, then a young boy but today a leading specialist in Zinfandel production. Looking on is his father, Walter Peterson (on the right, with his camera), founder of the San Francisco Wine Sampling Club and an early advocate of Zinfandel as a world-class variety. They are not talking about wine. (Source: Joel Peterson.)

One might think that serious blind tastings of old-vine versus young-vine Zinfandels would have been common, given the controversy. But I can find little notice of such events. Producers want the old-vine cachet on their label; they are not much interested in public demonstrations to prove the superiority of their wine, which might backfire if they lost. Strange things happen when tasters can't see the labels.

In March 2001 the San Francisco Vintners Club put on a well-balanced blind tasting of twelve Zinfandels from the 1998 vintage, six designated "old-vine," six not. Eight of the wines were appropriately from Sonoma, where old Zinfandel vineyards abound. The winner was a magnificent non-old-vine Sonoma wine that went on to win the club's Zinfandel taste-off a few months later. It was also my favorite. Overall the group favored wines not designated old-vine by 52 to 48, a very slim margin. My leaning toward to the younger vines was almost as close, 53 to 47.

In 2002, at ZAP's Zinposium in Sonoma, a similar public comparison was made, though it was designed only for evaluation by individuals, with no consensus taken. I thought the wines were wonderful. I rated them with the 100-point scale I have employed for over forty years. (Few schoolteachers misunderstand the difference between 89 and 90, or 82 and 83.) I gave the group of eight wines, which were from Napa, Sonoma, Contra Costa, and Southern California, an overall average score of 89.4. My average score for the old-vine wines was 89.9, and for the others 88.9. My favorite was from a "hundred-year-old" Contra Costa vineyard.

These data are far from definitive, and they are also fairly thin. I do consider the wines selected for both evaluations good representatives for their area and age. Many winemakers, particularly those with good access to old vines, are sure that these wines have uniquely concentrated flavors, and I respect these opinions. I am not so sure of the claim by *Wine News* that "it's indisputable that old vines produce more complex wines."[10] My data suggest that such an assumption is at least disputable. But I would be delighted to change my mind as the result of more carefully controlled evaluations.

In recent years old-vine Zinfandel has been involved in another lively viticultural story. In the 1980s a new phylloxera plague struck California vineyards, particularly those in Napa and Sonoma. The problem was the rootstock that most vineyardists had been using since the 1960s, the A x R No. 1; it was supposed to be resistant to the attacks of the voracious root louse, but it wasn't. Napa vineyards were devastated by the plague, and thousands of acres had to be replanted during the 1990s. Sonoma vineyards were also damaged, but there the effects of the new attack were not so hurtful.

The University of California had recommended the A x R No. 1 back in the 1950s. But foreign experience, particularly in France and South Africa, had previously shown that rootstock to be unreliable in the long run.[11] That it was not totally resistant is understandable, since it is a cross between a resistant American vine and a very nonresistant vinifera variety, the Aramon.

In some areas of the North Coast, particularly in Sonoma, a large percentage of the Zinfandel vineyards were unaffected by the new plague. In fact, virtually all really old-vine Zinfandel vineyards were unhurt. Here and there in northern California, and particularly in Sonoma, the St. George rootstock has had an almost universal following since the 1890s. At Ridge Vineyards, the founders, all scientists in their own right, used St. George for all their early plantings, wondering why anyone would use nonresistant stock.

Thus, almost all Zinfandel vineyards planted before the 1950s were untouched by the new phylloxera attack. The St. George is safe, because it is a pure American rupestris variety, which scorns the threat from phylloxera. Al though most North Coast old-vine vineyards have survived, Napa Zinfandel growers have not fared as well as their western neighbors, since many had followed the university's lead and planted on A x R No. 1. Well over 1,000 acres of Napa Zinfandel had to be ripped out. Since 1990 about 700 of those lost Napa acres have been replanted to Zinfandel. Sonoma has added about the same number during those years.

One might wonder why there was not a stronger surge in North Coast Zinfandel planting in the '90s, particularly in Sonoma, where the prices paid for that variety since 1990 have risen 337 percent to an almost unbelievable $2,456 per ton average in 2001. And yet Sonoma's Zinfandel land has grown only about 50 acres per year since 1990. The acres of Chardonnay in that county have grown at a rate of about 320 acres per year, yet Chardonnay prices have risen only 147 percent since 1990. In 2001 a ton of Sonoma Zinfandel was worth about $500 more than a ton of Chardonnay.[12]

Now let us look at the statistics from the areas where overwhelmingly our best Zinfandel grapes are grown and the finest wine made—that is, the coastal valleys from Santa Barbara to Mendocino and the Sierra Foothills, where 12.2 percent of the state's total Zinfandel wines are produced. From 1990 to 2002 the area devoted to Zinfandel vines here grew at an average annual rate of 0.8 percent. The average price per ton in this premium area rose from $616 to $1,760, or about 14 percent per year.

By comparison, Cabernet Sauvignon, whose quality is unchallenged in this premium region, has grown in acreage at a rate of 6.4 percent per year. Price per ton has risen by 5.2 percent per year. The 6,620 acres of Napa/Sonoma Zinfandel during the 2001 vintage brought growers an average of $2,340 per ton, about the same as Cabernet Sauvignon there in 1999, just two years earlier.

These data suggest that Napa/Sonoma Cabernet Sauvignon vineyardists have taken full advantage of rising grape prices in recent years by increasing acreage at a high rate. But Zinfandel growers all over the premium coastal area do not appear to have taken such advantage of the dramatic rise in their variety's price. Why not?

I am not sure of the answer. But perhaps it is partly related to the yield per acre of the two varieties. In 2001 Napa/Sonoma Cabernet acres yielded 3.86 tons per bearing acre. The two-county Zinfandel yield was 15 percent less. The previous year the Cabernet yield per acre had been 32 percent higher than Zinfandel for the two counties. Thus it appears there is more money to be made per acre from Cabernet than from Zinfandel. This helps to explain the more rapid advance of Cabernet acreage.

Another factor may be the long and steady character of Cabernet Sauvignon's excellent reputation over the past forty years. In contrast, Zinfandel has had its fads, its ups and downs. This somewhat shaky reputation may help to discourage the rapid growth of Zinfandel acreage. Ravenswood's Joel Peterson also believes that acreage expansion might have been affected by the limited availability in recent years of Zinfandel planting stock that fits the needs of the current premium market. He observes that too much of the clonal material available tends to be too vigorous, too productive, with too heavy clusters. The fruit quality is not what the premium market demands. It's fine for the quaffable "fighting varietal" Zinfandels, but it is not right for the rich and complex wines the market demands today at its higher end.[13]

We must also remember that, even though young Zinfandel vineyards will give a fairly good crop earlier than most other varieties, it takes about four to five years from the decision to plant Zinfandel to the production of a commercial vintage from that land. Some such decisions already have been made, probably as the result of soaring Zinfandel prices after the 1997 vintage. Since then, Zinfandel grape prices in the North Coast have gone up 85 percent. In contrast, Sierra Foothill and Central Coast Zinfandel prices have risen only about 20 percent in the same period. We can see decisions to plant in the nonbearing acreage statistics and changes in total acreage. Since 1997 North Coast Zinfandel area has risen by 541 acres, 96 percent of this total coming in Sonoma. Napa's Zinfandel acreage has actually declined. Another big jump has taken place in the Central Coast, notably in San Luis Obispo County, where the Paso Robles district is located. Bay Area and Sierra Foothill Zinfandel acreage has changed little since 1997.

Even though the Zinfandel acreage in the premium 12.2 percent of the state's total has risen since 1997, I would call this rise sluggish. And I think that soaring grape prices, particularly in the North Coast, are in large part the result of a shortage in what are perceived to be the very best Zinfandel grapes. Ravenswood paid almost $4,000 per ton for some of its best Sonoma fruit in 2001. And, of course, such high grape prices help to explain the high bottle prices for much of the North Coast product. State statistics don't suggest yet that vineyardists' future plans will do much to soften these price escalations. In the meantime we'll have to depend on the wisdom of comedian Mort Sahl, who often reminded us that "the future lies ahead."

My solution for now as a consumer is to be very cost- and quality-conscious when buying North Coast Zinfandel and to sharpen the focus of my tasting equipment on the Central Coast, the Sierra Foothills, and Lodi. Nevertheless, excellent wines and reasonable prices are still available from Napa, Sonoma, Mendocino, and Lake Counties, the North Coast. The day before I wrote this sentence, I bought two Zinfandels from the 2000 vintage, from the Napa and Alexander Valleys. I had given them an average score of 88.8 in blind tastings and bought them at a discount wine retail chain at an average price of $13.00 per bottle; their list price average was $17.25.

CHAPTER TWELVE

THE MYSTERY OF ORIGINS SOLVED—PROBABLY

IN THE INTRODUCTION TO THIS BOOK I DISCUSSED ZINFANDEL'S mysteries, and subsequent chapters told the story of the vine's transport from Austria to the New World (although there are still a few "smoking guns" I should like to discover). The Gold Rush voyage from New England to Northern California is fairly well settled, and Zinfandel's discovery as an excellent wine grape, its growth in popularity, and its subsequent ups and downs, including its recent and perhaps most brilliant comeback, are now in the chronicles of grape history. But what of the vine's European origins? Today most of the answer to that question is easily told. But the process by which we have come to know that answer is one of the most complex and exciting in viticultural history.

This discovery and its process have involved some practical economic questions. Lively controversy has swirled. Unsubstantiated and inaccurate claims have been put forward. Governments and governmental agencies have become embroiled in the battle. We might even argue that there was something of an international incident, highlighted by a rather good-natured journalistic outpouring of confused alarms. Not long ago I wrote that we might call this the "Second Zinfandel War." (The first took place in the press in the

1880s concerning Arpad Haraszthy's false claims, which I discussed in chapter 6.) At long last, however, science has given us a fairly clear answer to the puzzle, and the whole thing now looks like little more than a spirited skirmish.

The seeds of the discovery were planted in the autumn of 1967, when Austin Goheen, a plant pathologist for the U.S. Department of Agriculture, who was working out of the University of California at Davis, decided to visit Giovanni Martelli, a friend and plant pathologist then working on grapevine viruses.[1] The place was Bari, a town high on the heel of the Italian boot, on the Adriatic, in the province of Puglia (Apulia). His friend served him a red wine that tasted like Zinfandel, so Goheen asked to see some of the vineyards that produced the grapes for this rustic local wine. They drove from Bari to Taranto, more to the inside of the heel of the boot, and looked at several vineyards. Goheen was no ampelographer, but the vines looked very much like the Zinfandel vines he knew in California. He found that the growers and producers in Puglia called the vine the Primitivo, often adding a geographic term for greater specificity, such as Primitivo di Gioia, or di Turi.

Goheen arranged to have cuttings from these vines shipped to UC Davis, where they were planted in 1971 beside a row of California Zinfandel. Leon Adams picked up this information and was able to place a hint of the possible discovery in the first edition of *The Wines of America.* By the time the second edition appeared in 1978, Adams was able to report that Goheen's suspicions had been largely confirmed.[2]

The Italian vines growing at Davis did look like their fellows in the next row, and now a scientific procedure was available that would go beyond the ampelographer's observational approach. In 1975, using a technique developed in the 1960s, Wade Wolfe, a doctoral candidate at UC Davis, showed that California Zinfandel and Primitivo were probably the same variety. The technique, isozyme fingerprinting, is not as perfect a test as DNA fingerprinting, which did not yet exist.[3] California Zinfandel producers wondered at the "probably" in Wolfe's conclusions.

The discovery unlocked a torrent of viticultural nonsense, mostly from wine writers. Some announced that the *origin* of Zinfandel had been discovered. Others guessed that the vine had been brought to California by Italian immigrants. Or perhaps, wrote others, the Primitivo had been introduced to Italy from California.

In 1979 the Italian Trade Commission in California organized a tasting of Zinfandels and Primitivos. *Wines & Vines,* the influential trade journal, decided that "the Primitivo could well be Zinfandel" and could give our Zinfandel and other American wines "a run for the money."[4] The run began two years later, when an East Coast importer brought in a wine whose label announced it to be "imported Zinfandel," under the Mirafiore brand. Wine critic Norman Roby judged the wine to be "light, fruity, a little thin, but acceptable." At a similar tasting at the Italian Trade Center in New York, wine writer David Rosengarten found raspberry and cassis in the flavor, deeming the wine "a dead ringer for a California Zinfandel," but light and acidic, with a rather short finish.[5]

When Sonoma nurseryman Rich Kunde found a bottle of this wine in a mixed case of Zinfandel he had bought from a local merchant, he complained to the Bureau of Alcohol, Tobacco and Firearms (BATF), and the first major skirmish of the "war" was under way. In the process I was drawn into the fight, not for my explanation of how the Zinfandel got to California from the East Coast, but for my comments on some findings from my research at the National Agricultural Library in Maryland.

While there in 1983, I had looked through all the old Italian ampelographies in this great collection. Mind you, such items can't be very old, since Italy was not a united country until the 1860s. And before then it was highly unlikely that the benighted Kingdom of Two Sicilies, where Puglia was located, had done any such work.

I was asked to comment on the Zin/Prim question being examined by the BATF, and I suggested that the Primitivo might be sold in this country under a Zinfandel label after the Italians had successfully sold the wine as such in their country. I admitted "a chauvinistic pride in my state's wine."[6]

I also commented on the rumor abroad in this country that the Primitivo was actually a newcomer to Italy and had not appeared in Puglia until the 1880s. I showed this idea to be incorrect, citing Italian government publications from the 1870s that analyzed the Primitivo wines from vines certainly planted no later than the 1860s.[7] But I also noted that there was no official record of the vine's earlier presence in Italy. In other words, there was no documented evidence to show that the vine had been in Italy earlier than the 1860s. This was an error in communication that has haunted me ever since.

My statement that I could find no documented evidence of the vine was meant to imply that I could not tell how long the variety had been in Puglia. But, ever since, it has been reported in this country that I have written that the Primitivo was not in Italy before 1860. Thus, the vine was in America before it was in Italy. That is not a proper inference to draw from my statement. And for the past fifteen years Italians have been doing their best to knock down that inference, since California producers and their spokespersons were continually writing that the Primitivo had come to Italy after it came to America.

I do believe that the vine has been in Italy a long time, perhaps even brought there by Greek colonists when this southern land was known as Magna Graecia, or perhaps earlier by the Phoenicians from the Levant. But I still have seen no official or primary documentation of it before the dates implied in the early Italian ampelographies. (We will see this question pop up in a later skirmish.)

The Primitivo's length of stay in Italy had no bearing on the BATF's ruling in early 1985. The bureau simply disallowed the use of "Zinfandel" as a synonym for "Primitivo" on Italian imports to the United States. A letter to me from a BATF official explained that the decision was based on two factors: (1) it had not been proven that the Zinfandel and the Primitivo "are one and the same"; and (2) the European Union's list of Italian grapes did not include Zinfandel, which meant that it was not legal to sell Primitivo in Italy under a Zinfandel label. The official went on to write that the prohibition would stay in effect until both conditions had been reversed.[8]

Meanwhile a few Californians had acquired Italian Primitivo cuttings from one source or another. One "Samsonite" import was brought in by an eastern wine writer who passed on the cuttings to Joseph Swan. He grafted them and planted a plot in front of his porch in Forestville (Sonoma). There was no greater master of Zinfandel production in those days than Swan.

I think it was in 1984, before a dinner at Chez Swan, that he lined up four glasses of red wine and asked Roz and me to taste them. What did we think? They all tasted like high-quality Zinfandel. Then he announced that two of them had come from his Primitivo vines, and the others from two highly regarded Sonoma vineyards. Each had undergone the same viticultural regimen and cellar treatment. I was really excited after Joe let us know what we were drinking. I asked him what he was going to do now. "Graft them over to Pinot noir. I thought they might be something special here. But there is plenty of good Zinfandel around here. This is nothing special." Such was Swan's way.

About the same time another Sonoma producer brought out a wine from fifty-year-old Zinfandel vines and labeled it Primitivo, without reference to Italy. The BATF has also allowed the wines of several other California wineries to carry the term "Primitivo" on their labels.

By the late 1980s Italian viticultural specialists were becoming interested in the question. In 1987 Antonio Calo, then the director of the Experimental Institute for Viticulture in the Italian Agricultural Ministry, wrote an article whose English title was "Primitivo and Zinfandel: Two Names for the Same Vine." First he summarized Zinfandel's history in America. He cited my articles, which, he claimed, indicated that Agosto [*sic*] Haraszthy had brought the vine to California from New England around 1850. (Calo's English may be even worse than my Italian.)[9]

He did much better when he began looking into the documentary literature on the Primitivo in Puglia. He cited a 1919 work by an important viticultural expert in Bari who wrote, "I don't begin to pretend I can trace the origins of this excellent variety." But Calo had found secondary evidence that a certain Don Francisco Indellicatti at Gioia del Colle, near Bari, "noted that one vine was adapted, in preference to the others, to the red soil of the region." This was supposed to have been around 1800. He was said to have called the vine Primitivo "precisely because of the precocious maturation of the fruit."[10]

Calo properly calls this information a "glimmer of light" (*"Ecco davvero un barlume di luce"*), but nothing more than that, as far as Primitivo history was concerned. Since the early 1990s, however, this slender glimmer has become an Italian viticultural searchlight.

Now it has become a growing Italian passion to claim an early introduction of the Primitivo to Puglia. This interest can be understood partly as a counter to the Italian government report that the variety was introduced into the Taranto region of Puglia in 1890–1892. If true, such a finding does not preclude the vine's presence in other areas of the province in earlier years. There is no reason to believe absolutely that the vine was not there before 1860. We simply have no solid historical evidence. And I blush to read articles from American sources, based on my conclusion that I could find no evidence in official or primary sources, pooh-poohing the idea that the Primitivo was in southern Italy in the eighteenth century. My guess is that the vine was in Puglia in the eighteenth century, but it is not a very well-educated guess. However, I think that the 1919 sentence from the Italian writer I quoted above is a frail reed to grasp in order to claim "authoritative historical documentation" (a claim made by a Puglia producer, which I took off the Internet in 2000).

Wade Wolfe's powerful suggestion in 1976 that the Zinfandel and the Primitivo were the same variety was based on good science. But it wasn't a sure thing. The sure thing was delivered by Professor Carole Meredith and her UC Davis crew in the early 1990s. Her DNA fingerprinting indicated that the odds against the two vines being identical was in the millions-to-one. The expression "morphologically indistinguishable" sums it up and leaves no doubts.[11]

The Italians were quick to draw the logical commercial conclusion from these DNA findings. The two stated reasons given in the 1985 BATF ruling that kept "Zinfandel" off the labels of Italian wines entering the United States were (1) the lack of scientific evidence that the vines were identical; and (2) the fact that "Zinfandel" and "Primitivo" were not legal synonyms in Italy or under the rules of the European Union. The EU declared the second condition fulfilled after DNA research had settled the first.

A few Italian producers were quick to seize on the definitive DNA findings. By late 1997 reports of Primitivos with references to Zinfandel on the label began coming in from several U.S. markets. In Northern California we saw Mother Zin as the brand name for a five-dollar wine. Above the brand in small letters, the label read "Old Vines Primitivo." The back label reported that the Primitivo had been "transported to the United States by immigrants in the 19th century." The consumer was invited to discover the "mother of all Zinfandels." California producers sent up a howl, individually and through the Zinfandel Advocates and Producers (ZAP). Sightings of such wines in California soon ended. As far as the BATF was concerned, the 1985 ruling still held.

Of far more importance has been the mercurial leap in the quality of a few Primitivo wines coming from several producers in Puglia. I first perceived this leap in a bottle brought to me from Venice in 1999. It tasted like a fine young Zinfandel that might go for twenty-five dollars in California, if it had come from one of the state's top producers. I was sure that the grapes had been grown in northern Italy until I found that its production site was just up the road from Bari.

Overnight, it seemed, a small segment of wine production in Puglia had leaped into the premium category. In 1998 a consortium for the "Defense of Primitivo di Manduria" was formed, Manduria being an area southeast of Taranto. There the Perrucci family has led the way, backed by investment in stainless steel tanks, heat exchangers, and a jacketed rotary fermenter. At the gigantic ZAP tasting in San Francisco in 2000, Gregorio Perrucci was a guest of Darrell Corti.

Almost no reference to Zinfandel has been made in the recent promotion of these high-end Primitivos in the United States, at least not by the producers. But in Europe the connection has been made clear, since the EU has now accepted Zin/Prim as one variety. One can easily find these wines on the Internet; I did so by asking Google to search for the terms "Primitivo" + "Zinfandel."

Another related development that has surely caught the attention of California Zinfandel producers has been the meteoric appearance on the international wine scene of A-Mano ("by hand"), a brand of Primitivo introduced with the 1998 vintage. I first read about the 1999 vintage when it made *Wine Spectator*'s list of the world's best inexpensive red wine. I found it and bought a bottle listed in the monthly catalogue of a large-scale California discount house at $7.59. After drinking it, a friend and I wiped out the local store's inventory. Meanwhile, from London, a colleague sent me a two-page ad from the *Sunday Times* magazine announcing that the 1999 A-Mano had been named the "Red Wine of the Year" in *Wine Magazine*'s International Wine Challenge.

I understand why. In my opinion, this wine had all the character of a young $25.00 California Zinfandel that was worth the price. (In London it was selling for $8.47.) I recently searched the Internet for "Mano" + "Primitivo" and found almost three hundred entries for the 1999 and 2000 wines. They were on sale in the United States, Canada, New Zealand, Germany, the United Kingdom, Sweden, and The Netherlands. Many of the retailers with Web sites made direct reference to the California Zinfandel as the offspring of the Primitivo.

There is an unlikely star behind the A-Mano success. Mark Shannon came to Puglia in 1997 after making wine in California at Beringer and Bogle. He brought together grapes from several small growers with vineyards in the low hills east of Taranto. He also acquired the most modern production equipment and a load of new French oak barrels. To this, combined with his own technical experience with high-end Zinfandel, he has added the expertise of Elvezia Sbalchiero, a north Italy marketing specialist. The result has been three vintages of A-Mano Primitivo, with the 2000 vintage already receiving howls of critical approval.

In June 2000 wine writer and Italian wine expert Burton Anderson came out in praise of the Perrucci efforts with the Primitivo. He also referred to the yet undocumented antiquity of the Primitivo in Puglia. ZAP was quick to reply. Its press release insisted that the Zinfandel and the Primitivo "are not identical" and that the two names should not be considered synonymous. The release also indicated that ZAP officials had recently met with BATF officials to push a strong enforcement of the bureau's 1985 ruling.

In this matter the ZAP position should not be considered a purely ostrich-like denial of scientific reality. DNA identification of genetic identity does not differentiate between clonal differences in vine selection. Professor Meredith readily admitted that "most Italian Primitivo does not taste like California Zinfandel. . . . It is understandable that California producers want to differentiate their wine from that produced in Italy."

Many observers have given ampelographic notice of the differences between the growing and the fruiting patterns of the two vines. We can see such differences among Zinfandel clones in California. I have raised Zinfandel vines that tended to trail, while others stand tall. Some vines have grape clusters that are extremely tight, while others are looser. Some have huge cluster shoulders, and others are smaller. I take these to be clonal differences. We will learn more from James Wolpert's work at the Oakville Zinfandel Heritage Vineyard, where Italian Primitivo vines are neighbors to their Zinfandel twin sisters.

Between June 2000 and January 2001 the ZAP position seemed to be moving a bit closer to scientific reality. As evidence for this modification, the Perruccis had their own table to show off their wines at the 2001 ZAP tasting. Darrell Corti was there, introducing members of the Italian production team to some of the most illustrious California Zinfandel producers. All to whom I talked were convinced that the 1985 BATF ruling was dead or dying.

I wanted to hear what the BATF thought about the situation. My answer came from a supervisor of the Alcohol Labeling and Formulation Division (ALFD). Yes, the ruling was still in effect. Why should it not be? After voicing my necessary neutrality in the matter, I asked how the bureau was dealing with the UC Davis discovery that the two vines were the same variety. The supervisor's answer was that they had received no such information from UC Davis. I promised to send the ALFD the literature back to 1992, when Professor Meredith's findings first appeared. It was a sizeable package that included a tape of her talk at the 1997 conference of the American Society for Enology and Viticulture (ASEV), in which she had restated her well-circulated conclusions, none of which, somehow, had been picked up by the BATF.

I begged for a quick reply so that I could finish this chapter of my history.

After three months of silence, I wrote to the chief of the ALFD and included all the material I had sent earlier, plus my March 6, 1985, letter from the BATF.

That packet quickly elicited a phone call from the chief of the division. She said that the bureau would soon release a proposed ruling that American wines might now bear the term "Primitivo" on their labels. (I did not tell her that the bureau had been allowing this practice for years.) She stressed that this was only a proposal and that responses from the American wine industry would be encouraged.

I cautiously suggested that this was not the issue. Might Italian Primitivo be sold in the United States with a Zinfandel label? She responded very simply. If the EU and Italian law allowed the practice in Europe and Italy, it was legal in this country. The 1985 ruling, without fanfare, or even announcement, as far as I could learn, was dead.

In June 2001 ZAP published its current view of the battle in a press release stating that "California Zinfandel is genetically identical to Italian Primitivo." But ZAP also argued, correctly, I think, that no Zinfandel or Primitivo should be allowed in the United States whose label "states or implies that the origin of Zinfandel is Italian." I predict that the Italians will find that they don't need the word "Zinfandel" on their labels if they can sell a wine like A-Mano in this country for under ten dollars and make a profit.

But ZAP is certainly right in arguing that California is the home of Zinfandel wine. It is here that its potential was discovered. As the Zinfandel, the variety's grapes and its wine are as directly connected to California's history as Cabernet Sauvignon is to France's. How different California Zinfandel is from Italian Primitivo is a matter of taste. My experience is that some Primitivos can be close, but most are not. Paul Draper, the winemaker and CEO of Ridge Vineyards, believes that "unless the Italians are making wine of a quality that can compete with our own, there will forever be the distinction between the Italian Zinfandel and the California Zinfandel." [12]

Leon Adams in 1978 laid out a detailed history of Austin Goheen's discovery of the Primitivo-Zinfandel similarity. Adams also hinted at another discovery in the making. He had learned from Goheen of a grape growing on the islands and the mainland of the Dalmatian coast of Croatia, then part of Yugoslavia. Its description sounded like that of California Zinfandel.[13]

In 1979 Goheen began corresponding with Professor Ana Sarić at the University of Zagreb, who had been studying the Dalmatian wine grape varieties. He sent Sarić an import permit and asked her to send him some cuttings of the Plavac mali (PM). This plant material was analyzed using Wade Wolfe's isozyme fingerprinting process, but the results indicated that it was doubtful that the Plavac was Zinfandel.[14]

Leon Adams wanted to see for himself, particularly after talking to Mike (Miljenko) Grgich, a Napa winemaker and Zinfandel specialist. Grgich had been born and raised in Croatia and had come to the Napa Valley in 1958. Grgich was sure that the Zinfandel and the PM were either the same variety or very close relations. In 1983 Adams visited Croatia, taking along color photographs of Zinfandel leaves for comparison. "I found the leaves identical; and the Plavac wines I tasted could easily have been accepted as Zinfandel," he wrote.[15]

Later that year Adams and I talked a lot about Austrian imperial history and the historical geography of the Adriatic in general and the Dalmatian coast specifically. We drew a line on the map from Vienna through Croatia's Dalmatian coast to Puglia and Bari, which we jokingly called the "Zinfandel Axis."

In the early 1990s Professor Carole Meredith had begun her DNA research on grapevines, including her work on the Primitivo, discussed earlier. Later she discovered the parentage of several wine varieties, findings that truly turned the heads of all seriously interested in wine history. The Cabernet Sauvignon, for example, had been a chance result of a union between Cabernet franc and Sauvignon blanc; California's Petite Sirah, the French Durif, actually had the great French Syrah as one parent.[16] By the mid-1990s Meredith decided that the Plavac needed a closer look.

The PM material at UC Davis was, to her mind, not enough to guarantee a definitive judgment. One selection had come from a nursery in Zagreb, well removed from the Dalmatian coast, and the other from an Italian nursery.

Meredith later noted, "We had to be a little cautious about assuming that they were true examples."[17] But when she and her research team checked this Plavac material, even though it was not Zinfandel, it was quite similar. "The trail had grown warm again."[18]

Then, in 1996, the *Wine Enthusiast,* a consumer publication, announced: "Zinfandel—The Mystery Solved." The writer laid out "the true origin of America's Zinfandel grape. . . ." He based his argument partly on the idea that southern Italy was disqualified as a "home" because the Primitivo had arrived there after the "Zinfindal" arrived on Long Island.[19] Here was another instance of that tiresome and illogical inference being drawn from my statement that we had no official or primary documentation of the Italian vine's presence there before the 1850s.

The article "amassed an array of newfound evidence" that the Zinfandel "came from Croatia. It was the Plavac Mali." This was the evidence amassed:

—The Zinfandel and the PM have "virtually identical" flavor and character.
—A certain Croatian winemaker (not Mike Grgich) told the author that "Italians called it Primitivo because they know it was from thousand-year-old Croatian vineyards."
—PM and Zinfandel can both attain high levels of alcohol.
—A second-century Greek, Agarthchides, wrote of great wine on the island of Vis, where the PM has been the principal grape "for as long as anyone remembers."
—Mike Grgich is sure they are the same variety.

This is hardly a mass of evidence. Historically, it is little more than worthless. Meredith wrote to the *Wine Enthusiast* that she intended to acquire more PM material from Croatia very soon, but that as yet there was no proof of identity. As she remarked to a meeting of wine scholars, "We had a few more questions to answer."[20] But the article certainly helped to focus more public attention on the intriguing question.

Meanwhile Mike Grgich had bought land in Croatia near the coast and had begun producing wines, one a 1996 PM that he began marketing in the

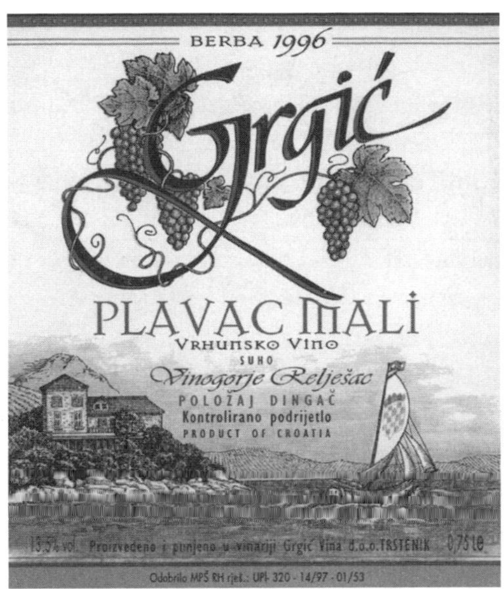

BERBA 1996
Grgić
PLAVAC MALI
VRHUNSKO VINO
SUHO
Vinogorje Pelješac
POLOŽAJ DINGAČ
Kontrolirano podrijetlo
PRODUCT OF CROATIA

30. Mike Grgich, Croatian by birth, is a specialist in Zinfandel production at his Napa winery. After Croatian independence, he returned to his native land, built a small winery, and in 1996 began producing Plavac Mali wine there. Grgich was an early believer in the idea that the Zinfandel and Plavac mali vines are related—as indeed they are. (Source: Mike Grgich.)

United States under his Grgić label. And he offered his services and good offices to help Professor Meredith in her effort to expand the examination of Croatian viticulture and its possible connection to California Zinfandel.[21]

What is this vine, the Plavac mali, that was attracting so much attention? It is a red wine variety that, according to local tradition, has grown along the Dalmatian coast for centuries. However, the first mention and written description we have of the vine appear—appropriately, given our interest in Vienna—in an Austrian publication of 1841 on the vines of Styria. This province of the Austrian Empire touched on what is today the northern borders of Slovenia, Croatia's neighbor to the north. The author of this 1841 piece noted that the variety was from Dalmatia and that "the vine yields very good table grapes, and does particularly well growing on a high wall." Given that George Gibbs thought he was importing table grape vines from Vienna in 1829, we cannot be surprised that an Austrian source praised the PM as such, with no mention of its potential as a wine grape.[22]

Today the PM is the leading red wine grape on the Dalmatian coast, growing on many of the 1,184 islands there. Dr. Edi Maletić, of the University of Zagreb, has identified several different PM clones, some with very distinct characteristics.

The PM finally came to California in great numbers in 1998 as the result of Professor Meredith's visit to Croatia. She had been in close contact with two members of the Faculty of Agriculture at the University of Zagreb, Edi Maletić and Ivan Pejić. Mike Grgich also helped to put the trip together. And Meredith had as an assistant Jasenka Piljać, a Croatian who had previously worked in her laboratory at Davis and now acted as her guide and translator on the trip. Meredith named the effort Zinquest. It was an exciting and fruitful adventure. "Some of those vineyards were so steep we climbed through them holding on to the vines to keep from falling into the Adriatic." They brought home 150 samples from forty vineyards. These were given the DNA treatment for comparison with the Zinfandel.

In November of that year Meredith announced that not one of her Croatian selections matched the California Zinfandel.[23] But it was clear that they did share a considerable family history. She thought that the Croatian and the Californian might have a parent-offspring relationship. She was not surprised, since she had written before the trip that "the current scientific evidence actually points to a common origin for Zinfandel and Primitivo in Croatia."[24] Her findings from this trip convinced her that the Zinfandel very likely had originated in Croatia. "But if it still exists there it must be tucked away in a remote location, perhaps on one of the many islands."

Pejić and Maletić continued their search, poking around more old Dalmatian vineyards. They gathered material from any variety they hadn't yet seen and sent it off to Davis. The result: again lots of close relatives, but no match.[25] Meredith and the Croatian scientists then began to plan a paper that would "put together a case for the Croatian origin of Zinfandel based on circumstantial evidence."[26] And they were now convinced that the Zinfandel was the likely parent of the PM.

31. Here is the team that discovered the perfect match between California's Zinfandel and Croatia's Crljenak Kaštelanski. Its members are (*foreground, left to right*) Dr. Edi Maletić, Professor Carole Meredith, and Dr. Ivan Pejić. Professor Meredith is from the University of California at Davis, and her two colleagues are members of the Faculty of Agriculture at the University of Zagreb. They are standing in the Croatian vineyard owned by Ivica Radunic (*background*), where the Crljenak Kaštelanski vines were rediscovered. (Source: Professor Carole Meredith, UC Davis; photo by Ante Vuletin.)

Late in the fall of 2001, as the project was about to run out of funds, the Croatian scientists went out on their final expedition. They found a vine near the town of Split on the Dalmatian coast that looked very promising. They had previously sent what they believed was a sample of this vine, which did not test to be Zinfandel. It turned out, however, that they had actually sampled a shoot growing from the vine next door. Now, with the correct sample, this selection really looked like Zinfandel.

Pejić's laboratory was now equipped to do limited DNA analysis. He ran the test—and it seemed to be a perfect match. His email to Meredith "was full of exclamation points." The sample arrived on the Davis campus in early December and was analyzed more extensively. On December 18 Meredith sent the Croatian scientists an early Christmas present: the sample was a perfect match to the California Zinfandel.[27]

The vine was Crljenak (pronounced Tzerl-yen'-ak) Kaštelanski (CK), which had once been widely grown in Dalmatia but had almost disappeared when the region was devastated by the phylloxera between 1897 and 1920.[28] The second word in the complete name refers to Kaštela, a little town just northwest of Split, on the coast. As of summer 2002 Pejić and Maletić had found only about nine CK vines. These were mixed with other varieties in a single vineyard. But some other possible candidates had been spotted.

In addition to the CK find, Meredith has used DNA typing to discover that the PM is the offspring of CK and another Dalmatian variety, Dobricić. Thus it appears that Mike Grgich was correct to insist that Croatia was probably the home of the Zinfandel. But it did not spring from the PM; the PM sprang from the Zinfandel/CK. As Grgich puts it, "They got to the Crljenak through the Plavac mali."

Can it be said with certainty that the Zinfandel *originated* in Croatia? Could it not have been brought up the Adriatic from Albania or Cyprus centuries ago by Venetian merchants or nurserymen? The answer is yes.

When Professor Meredith announces the results of her DNA findings, she often accompanies them with an indication of how statistically sure she is of the results. That certainty is usually expressed as odds, frequently in the millions to one. She cites such odds for the identity of the CK and the Zinfandel. She does not cite such odds for the site of the Zinfandel's origins. Rather, she stresses the word "probably" and admits that the vine's origins might be elsewhere.

Her belief in its probable origins rests on her discovery that so many of those suspect vines turned out to be close relatives of the Zinfandel. One of the principles of crop plant genetics posits the high probability that a center of genetic diversity in the form of close relatives is also the place of origin of the specific plant to which all appear related. Because the Zinfandel has numerous close relatives in Croatia, it is probable that Croatia is the place of origin or that Zinfandel has been in Croatia for a long time, long enough for

32. The Crljenak Kaštelanski of Croatia's Dalmatian coast, at Kaštel Novi. It, the Italian Primitivo, and the California Zinfandel are genetically identical. This single variety, with at least four historic names (remember the Black St. Peters), was likely born of a chance cross between two unknown vines on the Dalmatian coast many years ago. (Source: Professor Carole Meredith, UC Davis; photo by Edi Maletić.)

those related varieties to have descended from it. I believe that we should accept Meredith's millions-to-one conclusions as scientific facts. But there are numerous alternative explanations to the questions of origins—at least until the fates somehow place the parents of the Zinfandel/CK in scientific hands, and we discover those vines to be in or to have been in Croatia.

The Adriatic had been a Greek roadway since the early days of their massive Mediterranean colonizations. Greek colonies existed on the Dalmatian coast in 350 B.C., and the Greeks always brought their vines with them. From 168 B.C., this was part of the Roman domain. And during the early Christian era, the Greek Byzantine influence here was powerful.

Although most of the population has been Slavic since the eighth century, Dalmatia was ruled from 1420 until the Napoleonic period by the Republic of Venice, the great power in the Adriatic in those years, providing a steady Italian connection to Dalmatia. And the Greek island of Cyprus was also strongly connected to the Italians between the 1370s and 1573, for Venice owned Cyprus for almost half of that period.

If I were to suggest an alternative hypothesis to that of the Croatian origins, I would support the possible Venetian transport of viticultural material, perhaps including the CK, from Cyprus to the northern Adriatic between 1489 and 1573, when the Turks finally conquered the island. But I admit that this untested hypothesis is *probably* not correct, given the scientific evidence at hand.

Is there any real importance to the discovery of Croatia as the probable home of the Zinfandel? We have plenty of good scientific reasons for wanting to expand the biodiversity of a valued plant. This is why scientists recently have been looking for the possible forebears of the apple in central Asia. The search for more related vines in Croatia will go on, probably centered on the island of Solta, just across the water from Split. Out there, a lot of Dobricić is planted, one of the parents of the PM and CK's mate in the process. A good part of this further research is being funded by five Northern California wineries.

Another plus is the possibility that CK stock in California may give us a special Zinfandel. Selections from Croatia will soon be budded onto rupestris rootstock at the Heritage Vineyard in Oakville, next to their sisters and cousins, and now their identical twins.

As wine writer Rod Smith, who has followed the Zinfandel story closely, observes, "The discovery closes the genetic gap between modern California Zinfandel vines and their ancient forerunners. Who knows what sensory delights await Zin lovers once the old Croatian clones become part of the California vineyard mix?"[29] James Wolpert predicts an experimental California Crljenak wine from the Heritage Vineyard as early as 2007.

For me the discovery of the CK and its many relatives in Croatia provides a practical solution to a tantalizing historical puzzle. I don't believe that historical research will come up with a more precise explanation. The Croatian origin hypothesis is simply the explanation that best fits the available scientific and historical data. It is impractical to hope for a clearly precise historical explanation of any particular variety's movement in the ancient or medieval eras from the eastern Mediterranean to the north or west. Heretofore we have never seen developed a truly historically believable picture of such transport for any vinifera variety.

The Zinfandel/Crljenak is probably a chance cross between two unknown vinifera varieties in old Croatia. It became popular and was likely taken to other areas of the Adriatic, such as Italian Puglia. In the eighteenth century, it, like other plants in the Austrian realm, was collected and housed at the imperial garden and nursery in Vienna. From there, it and other named and unnamed vines were imported by George Gibbs of Long Island. In New England the vine somehow picked up the "Zinfindal" name and became a popular hothouse table grape, as it had been in southern Austria in the 1840s. In the 1850s it was brought to California by several nurserymen and gardeners, where its value as a wine grape was discovered, exploited, and extolled.

CHAPTER THIRTEEN

INTO THE NEW CENTURY

FROM 1999 TO 2002, THE SAN FRANCISCO VINTNERS CLUB HELD three Zinfandel taste-offs among the top wines in each previous year's preliminary competitions. Of the thirty-six wines represented, half were from Sonoma, eight were from Napa, and the rest, except for one, were scattered among the other premium Zinfandel districts: Paso Robles, Sierra Foothills, Mendocino, and the Santa Cruz Mountains. One old-vine preliminary winner was from Cucamonga.

There was no geographical shift in the club's findings in these recent years. In 1996 Sonoma had eight of the top twelve, Napa and Paso Robles two each. In 1994 the results were almost identical. But there was a shift in style. The alcohol levels in the 2002 finalists averaged 15.02 percent, and none was under 14 percent. In the early 1990s Zinfandels with over 14 percent alcohol were rare. But producers had not reverted to the tannic behemoth style of the 1970s. Fermentation techniques now could bring forth wines with more gentle tannins from quite ripe grapes, rich and tasty. Although high alcohol levels were to be expected from such grapes, the alcohol no longer seemed hot and abrasive.

Perhaps a more important change was seen in prices of the top wines in these tastings. From 1999 to 2002, the average price of a finalist's wine rose from $20.16 to $26.54. In 1996 the wines were mostly from the delicious 1993 vintage; then the average was only $16.25, with seven under $15.00.

We may ask, "Is most premium Zinfandel being priced at a level similar to that of *grand cru* Bordeaux?" As discussed earlier, recent Zinfandel grape prices in Sonoma and Napa suggest that the answer is "yes." Yet prices from other premium districts have not soared to anywhere near the level reached by those two counties. Since a bit less than half of the premium Zinfandel is produced in Napa and Sonoma, I would answer, "Perhaps not."

Other data and my personal experience make me drop the "perhaps" altogether. The summer 2002 Zinfandel listings for what is probably the leading retail discount house for wine in California, with stores in both the northern and southern parts of the state, offered eighty-eight Zinfandels whose mean price was $16.04; the median price was $14.99. Most of the very highly priced wines that were making the Vintners Club's finals were not listed—understandably, since the production of many of these wines is very small and distribution quite limited.

The data from the 2002 tasting organized by Zinfandel Advocates and Producers (ZAP) confirm that my "perhaps" would be overly cautious. There I found 194 wines that carried a suggested retail price of $20.00 or less. Typically, that means $17.95 or less at many retail stores. And of these, sixty-eight were from Sonoma and Napa grapes. A third of these "show-off" wines from the Sierra Foothills, Paso Robles, and Mendocino were listed at the tasting at $20.00 or less.

Earlier I employed the metaphor of "two faces" to describe the dual style of California Zinfandel after World War II. Today I would describe four "faces." The first is the small and costly visage, but one that is attractive enough to draw heavy coverage in the press. For example, an article in the *New York Times* in January 2002 concentrated on "cult producers" whose highly priced offerings are usually from single vineyards and often from very old vines. The average price of the wines recommended in this more-than-full-page article was $33.25.[1] Such wines have also been winning the Vintners Club's taste-offs, where the top three between 1999 and 2002 had an average retail tag of $29.25.

It is not possible to calculate accurately what percentage of California's Zinfandel product fits this "cult" profile. But the total Zinfandel tonnage of the premium areas in 2001 was just short of fifty thousand, which would make close to eight million gallons of wine. Many, perhaps most, of the "cult" wines come from production lots of under one thousand cases. I doubt that the Zinfandel selling for more than twenty-five dollars made up more than 2 percent of that large total. And that total would supply consumers with about thirty million bottles of very good wine at a reasonable price. These are the wines that will take up important space on retail shelves. They are the very familiar second face of Zinfandel today. A large portion of the "cult" wines rarely touch a retail shelf; instead, their small lots are often allocated to consumers on mailing lists.

Such contrasts in prices are not at all unusual. For example, Guigal, one of the great wine houses of France's Rhône region, sells some of its single-vineyard Côte Rotie wines for $125 to $200 per bottle. Robert Parker awarded such a wine, its 1999 La Landonne, a score of 99. But I can buy that house's delicious Côtes du Rhône just down the street from where I live for less than $10.

What of faces three and four? The third represents the now usually tasty and quaffable "fighting varietal" Zinfandels coming from the huge recent plantings in the Central Valley. Some of this wine actually flies higher in quality than the typical product in this $5.95-and-under market segment. This is particularly true of the red Zinfandel from the Lodi area. Much of that wine travels under labels of well-established premium wineries. The case production numbers from several of Sonoma's best Zinfandel producers reflect this trend: Ravenswood (400,000), De Loach (240,000), Cline (200,000), and Rabbit Ridge (150,000). The wines from these totals from the Central Valley usually bear labels with a California appellation. They are marketed nationally as varietal Zinfandel, attesting to the fact that America's wine-drinking community has definitely expanded its vocabulary by at least one important word in the past thirty years.

PARKER'S 90S

Robert Parker is a world-renowned and controversial wine critic whose *Wine Advocate* has been published since 1978. He began discovering outstanding California Zinfandels in the 1980s. He uses the 100-point system, as I do, and considers a score of 90 or higher an A grade. These are wines that he believes "are the very best of their type." I looked at the names of wineries whose Zinfandels received a 90 or better in each of Parker's ten annual summaries through 2002.

The following list includes the wineries that made the cut five times or more. The two winners made it every time.

1. Ravenswood (Sonoma); Ridge Vineyards (Santa Cruz Mountains) [tied]
3. Rosenblum Cellars (Alameda); Storybook Mountain Vineyards (Napa) [tied]
5. Turley Cellars (Napa)
6. Coturri Winery (Sonoma); Saddleback Cellars (Napa) [tied]
8. Hartford Court Winery (Sonoma); Martinelli Winery (Sonoma); Scherrer Winery (Sonoma) [tied]
11. Seghesio Vineyards (Sonoma); Edmeades Winery (Mendocino); St. Francis Winery (Sonoma); Cline Cellars (Sonoma) [tied]

One reason for this expansion in the Central Valley relates directly to the fourth face of Zin, White Zinfandel. Although some considered it a national fad in the 1980s, White Zinfandel has proven to have staying power. Sales of this wine did slip in the 1990s, but it is still very popular. Beringer's and Sutter Home's White Zinfandels in 2000 both ranked in the top ten brands for sales of a varietal wine. In fact, Beringer was number one.[2]

To understand more fully the place of Zinfandel in California winegrowing today, as well as the four faces I have described, let us look at two recent vintages, the last of the old century and the first of the new, 2000 and 2001.

First let's go to where most Zinfandel vines are planted, the Central Valley. Here almost all Zinfandel production consists of inexpensive red and pink (blush) table wine from that variety. In 2002 there were more than fifty-three square miles of Zinfandel vines in this giant area, 35,000 acres stretching from Redding to the desert south of Bakersfield. These acres held 70 percent of all the Zinfandel vines in California and produced 84 percent of all the Zinfandel wine.

PUFFS FROM *CGCW*, 1998–2002

In 1974 *Connoisseurs' Guide to California Wine* began a regular series of Zinfandel evaluations, which its editors have continued into the new century. In 2002 *CGCW* brought out a compilation of its evaluations since 1998, which covered about 1,500 Zinfandels. The publication offers a fairly straightforward explanation of this commitment: "We started our newsletter with special attention to Zinfandel, and our love of the grape and the wines it produces is unchanged and unwavering."

During these five years, about one in eight of the Zinfandels rated received two puffs (as "distinctive, memorable") or three puffs ("exceptional"). This is my compilation of the leading wineries in this extraordinary evaluation:

1. Rosenblum Cellars (Alameda)
2. Ridge Vineyards (Santa Cruz Mountains)
3. Seghesio Vineyards (Sonoma)
4. Ravenswood (Sonoma);
   Rabbit Ridge Vineyards (Sonoma) [tied]
6. Robert Biale Vineyards (Napa);
   Cline Cellars (Sonoma);
   De Loach Vineyards (Sonoma) [tied]
9. Storybook Mountain Vineyards (Napa);
   Marietta Cellars (Sonoma);
   Lolonis Winery (Mendocino) [tied]

We need to see these figures in proper perspective. These vines amounted to just over one-tenth of all the wine grapevines planted in the great valley. Together, Cabernet Sauvignon and Merlot account for far more acres, with about the same quantity of Chardonnay. Fresno County has 2,600 acres of Zinfandel, but it has even more of six other wine grape varieties. And in Lodi, where Zinfandel is first in wine grape acreage, that number is but 29 percent of the area's total. Zinfandel is no more than a small—yet important—segment of the Central Valley's wine grape industry.

Since the mid-1980s analysts of the California wine industry have cautioned against overplanting Zinfandel in the great valley. Plantings right after 1984 added about 10,000 new acres for White Zinfandel. Then the rise in Zinfandel's national popularity in all forms after 1992 added another 15,000 acres. With the higher yields being produced, these acres have doubled the Zinfandel tonnage in the Central Valley.

As vintage 2000 approached, analysts held their breath. It was obviously going to be a whopper. And it was: the valley Zinfandel crush totaled almost 330,000 tons, 81.5 percent of the state's Zinfandel and more than the entire

Years ago one regularly heard that vintages did not matter in California. "All vintages are excellent" was the wine industry's watchword. It is true that the state's vintages do not exhibit quality variations anywhere near as dramatic as those of Bordeaux or Burgundy. But vary they do, in both quality and quantity.

Weather is the variable that keeps California's winegrowers on their toes throughout the year. Spring frosts can cut the crop, but they rarely hurt grape quality. The same is true of late spring showers, which can inhibit berry set when the vines are flowering. Such rains rarely hurt quality as long as steps are taken to eliminate the mildew that might result.

From June to October the weather becomes a matter of powerful concern for Zinfandel growers—and consumers. We want warm weather, but long stretches of hundred-degree days can desiccate bunches and increase raisining on the vine. Such conditions promote off flavors in the resulting wine. We want warm weather to continue steadily through September, and perhaps October. And we don't want rain, since Zinfandel is particularly susceptible to the bunch rot that usually follows.

Since 1990 the weather in our best Zinfandel districts—that is, the coastal counties from Santa Barbara to Mendocino, and the Sierra Foothills—has regularly favored the production of very good to great Zinfandel wines.

1990—Three May storms and September drizzles produced much worry among growers but little injury to the crop. The summer was warm, but the few heat spikes did not desiccate. Warm fall weather lingered until the end of October. For Zinfandel the result was a wonderful vintage of highly flavored, long-lasting wines. One needs to have patience with the best of them—or have wine collector friends with patience.

1991—An ugly 1990–1991 winter of terrible downpours and numbing frosts did nothing to hurt Zinfandel quality. The summer was warm, with few heat spikes. Mid-September to mid-October was as hot as most of August. Thus, almost all the Zinfandel was in before the skies opened on October 25. The resulting wines were rich and tasty, with excellent chemistry and structure. This was a vintage whose finest Zinfandels were numerous and could be enjoyed soon after release or a decade later.

1992—The weather wasn't perfect, but in the end California could count three fine vintages in a row for Zinfandel. A late June downpour caused some mildew, and the summer was very hot. Napa had twenty-one days with highs of 95°F or more. The crop came in early and was large. The Zinfandels had excellent flavors and helped to feed the growing national interest in these wines. This vintage included many cellar treasures, but I suspect that relatively few bottles made it to the cellar.

1993—The huge June downpour during flowering cut back yields for many varieties, but Zinfandel came through almost unscathed. The harvest was early, after a sizzling August. Zinfandel quality in the coastal counties slipped somewhat from previous years, but there were numerous delicious wines nonetheless. Many might have been used to illustrate perfect Zinfandel varietal flavors. Those with a long-term future require patience, which should start to be rewarded after 2005.

1994—If excellent weather can sculpt an almost perfect vintage, 1994 could be a good example. A long and mild growing season allowed fruit to develop wonderful flavors and chemistry. An unexplained shortness of the Zinfandel crop in some areas helped to increase flavor intensity. Only the Paso Robles area had a full crop. Some were concerned about mildew on unharvested vines when a gully-washer hit Northern California October 4. But mild to warm weather followed, and there was little damage. Cellar treasures from this vintage abound.

1995—This was a year when bizarre weather had producers on edge until the grapes were in at the end of October. California was hit with floods, frosts, and hail. Portions of the summer were searing. Napa had fifteen days with highs in the hundreds. The wine grape crop almost everywhere was short, except for Zinfandel. The tonnage in Sonoma and the Sierra Foothills was huge. We were astonished at the uniform excellence of the Zinfandel wines. Great flavors were combined with excellent chemistry and structure. The only factor that held down my purchases of '95s was my overcommitment to the '94s.

1996—If the previous six Zinfandel vintages all rate a grade of A or A-, with perhaps one B+, in 1996 we finally have a crop to which we can assign an honest B. Although low yields were reported for most varieties, Zinfandel was steady in the coastal valleys and up in the Sierra Foothills. Zinfandel prices soared in the premium districts. But the summer was torrid. The average high at St. Helena in July was 95.4°. And the vintage had to come to a quick halt in late September as fall storms began coming in. There were plenty of tasty Zinfandels but not many with the depth and structure of previous years.

1997—"Tumultuous" best describes the Zinfandel story of 1997. The huge crop came along nicely until the upper edges of Tropical Storm Ignacio dumped a rare August deluge on Northern California. More good weather was interrupted in mid-September by the remains of Hurricane Linda. A bit more warm weather was followed by the coolest October in fifteen years. In many areas the huge crop ripened irregularly. Mendocino growers had to cut off so many rotted clusters that the crop there actually declined from 1996. And yet excellent wines were produced throughout the premium districts. But it was definitely a vintage calling for consumer caution.

1998—This was the year of El Niño for California vineyardists. It was the coolest year of the 1990s. There have rarely been wetter years. Northern California had fourteen rainy days in May, and it was still drizzling in June. The crop was late, and not much Zinfandel was in the fermenters when the skies opened up in late September. Then it wouldn't warm up. Napa had only three days over 80° between September 21 and October 20, a situation that occurs perhaps once a century. That so many tasty Zins were produced this year was a miracle. But those with much of a future were rare.

continued on page 174

ZINFANDEL VINTAGES, 1990–2002 *(continued)*

1999—After a very chilly spring, Zinfandel growers could smile all the way to harvest in 1999. (April 9 saw a 29° reading in Carneros.) The summer was warm, with no severe heat spikes. This year the growers and producers made their harvest decisions without worrying about the weather. Dry Creek Valley growers had their Zinfandel in the fermenters three weeks before the deluge on October 28. The Zinfandels from the coastal valleys and the Sierra Foothills were rich and concentrated; many will live for years. Coastal conditions in the Lodi area made it possible for some wineries to produce small lots of first-rate Zinfandel.

2000—This was a strange year for Zinfandel, and a roller coaster ride for most growers. The weather after mid-May swung from mild to torrid and back again—and again. It was the kind of weather that confuses the Zinfandel vine and tends to produce too many unripe grapes among the ripe ones. The Zinfandel crop was large, except in Napa and Mendocino. The vintage came to a soggy conclusion on October 9, when the rainy season set in. There were many delicious wines made, but it was certainly a consumer-take-care year.

2001—Several unusual weather situations occurred in 2001, but none hurt the Zinfandel crop. Although the North Coast had two terrible frosts in April, Zinfandel seemed not to care; Sonoma had an excellent crop. In many areas June was warmer than July. The harvest was early; Dry Creek was picking Zinfandel in early September, well before a storm came through on September 24. Growers and producers have been praising 2001 Zinfandels to the sky. At the January 2002 Zinfandel Advocates and Producers tasting, wineries were proud to offer barrel samples from 2001. To my taste, there were scores of outstanding wines from the coastal valleys, the Sierra Foothills, and the Lodi area.

2002—Weather conditions were close to perfect throughout the coastal counties and the Sierra Foothills, although a May 21 storm worried some growers. The warm weather was steady from June to mid-October, and there were no severe heat spikes. The vintage was orderly, and all reports indicate another fine year for Zinfandel. The large crop and declining grape prices may prove a boon for consumers when the wines hit the shelves.

state total for that variety in 1999. But the predicted crash in Zinfandel grape prices did not take place. At Lodi prices slipped about 4 percent from 1998, while for the rest of the valley they were off about 11 percent.[3]

With storage facilities still loaded with wine to be sold in the spring of 2001, many eyes were on the coming vintage. Surely, as in days of old, a large Central Valley crop would leave many vineyards unpicked in the wake of collapsing prices. And the harvest was big, bigger than any but the 2000 crop.

Still, Zinfandel grape prices held and in some places rose slightly. It was clear that consumer demand for the inexpensive Zinfandel wines of the great valley was holding steady, even in the face of a national recession.

The craze for White Zinfandel in the late '90s may have cooled somewhat, but not much. The important fact was the national wine-drinking public's growing acceptance of inexpensive varietal red Zinfandel with a California appellation.

Statistical verification of this acceptance is somewhat camouflaged in state crushing statistics. We know it is better to crush grapes at a low sugar reading if White Zinfandel is the product. Well under 20° Brix is perfectly acceptable. This is not the case for red table wine, which wants a number somewhat higher.

In the five vintages before 1999, the Central Valley, not counting Lodi, crushed its Zinfandel at an average Brix of 18.1°. In the next three vintages the number jumped to 19.5°. For Lodi the advance was from 19.5° to 20.9°. The change here does not indicate higher sugars from global warming. Rather, producers are using more of the Zinfandel crop throughout the valley to make bright red varietal table wine.

Historians are supposedly precluded by their training from predicting the future. But the present, as of the summer of 2002, looks stable for the often unstable Central Valley Zinfandel industry. And growers are being far more cautious than they were five years earlier. We can tell this by looking at non-bearing acreage, which reveals the number of newly planted vines not yet in production. In 1997 there were more than 4,000 nonbearing acres of Zinfandel in the Lodi area, whereas in 2002 there were only about 400.

Far less drama accompanied the 2000 and 2001 Zinfandel vintages in the state's premium districts. In Napa and Sonoma, the scarcity of Zinfandel grapes caused their prices to skyrocket above those of 1999; Napa Zinfandel prices, in particular, soared 66 percent. Zinfandel production had not kept up with demand, creating a sellers' market. This was mainly a result of growers' attraction to the marvelous prices for Cabernet Sauvignon in the 1990s. Napa/Sonoma Zinfandel production dropped 35 percent from 1997 to 1999. In 2000 and 2001 Sonoma production began to climb, as did the Zinfandel acres. In 2002 Sonoma had 690 acres of nonbearing Zinfandel vines, a sign of rising production to come. Napa, however, continued its decline in Zinfandel acreage and tonnage.

In the Sierra Foothills, vintage 2001 set a regional record for Zinfandel. But the total production has not varied much in recent years. Zinfandel averaged about 55 percent of the region's total wine grape production during the 1990s. In 2000 and 2001 the average was 47 percent, down because of the growth and diversification of other varieties there. Zinfandel prices have more than doubled since 1990, but the price lure to other varieties has not been strong. Cabernet Sauvignon brought about $200 more per ton in 2001, while Napa Cabernet brought the grower $1,637 more. The region has a solid reputation for high quality at reasonable prices. But these factors have not led to expansion in recent years.

To the south, the Paso Robles area is the premium Zinfandel leader. There, almost half the Zinfandel vines were planted between 1995 and 1998. When these vines came to full bearing in vintages 2000 and 2001, the region's tonnage jumped almost 50 percent. This new record makes San Luis Obispo County's Zinfandel production equal to that of Mendocino and Lake Counties combined. A good part of this weight comes from the high yields here, the highest of any premium area. The result is lower average grape prices that wineries pay growers, less than half what Napa and Sonoma wineries pay.

There is no shortage of Paso Robles Zinfandel grapes, nor are the moderate grape prices reflected in consumer perception of lower wine quality. It will be far easier to find land suitable for future expansion here than in the North Coast. But such expansion for now is not going to Zinfandel. In 2002 nonbearing Cabernet Sauvignon acres here led Zinfandel by more than ten to one, reflecting the much higher profits from that variety.[4]

Earlier I asked rhetorically, Who else but California grows Zinfandel? I left it with the question, but Zinfandel under that name is indeed growing outside California. According to ZAP, thirteen states claim at least a few vines. I have found ten that produce and market a commercial Zinfandel. That vine in Oregon dates from the nineteenth century. Arizona, New Mexico, Nevada, and Texas have some locations where the climate suggests possible commercial success. I also believe there might be a few places in eastern Washington. Less likely are Illinois and Ohio. I discovered that the North Carolina winery that produces Zinfandel does so with imported California grapes.

Outside the United States, we find some Zinfandel vines in Baja California, some of them quite old. Australia has a Zinfandel vineyard that dates from 1980. I have also heard of a small patch in Bordeaux. And recently Italians have planted a vineyard of Zinfandel using budwood from a famous Sonoma vineyard. In 1990, at the Society of Wine Educators conference, a member of the audience at a Zinfandel session came forth with a bottle of commercial South African Zinfandel. I thought it tasted like Zinfandel. Nevertheless, I doubt that there would be much sense in having an international Zinfandel competition now, even if Italian Primitivo were included.

In 1976 in Paris, California winemakers had a chance to test some of their best wines against those of French producers whose wines were recognized around the world for their superior quality. The tasting was on French ground, the evaluation by well-known French wine authorities. Unfortunately for the French, the identity of the wines was hidden until after the ratings were collected. The evaluators had picked a California Cabernet Sauvignon and a California Chardonnay as the top wines.

I doubt that any book on California wine since then has failed to mention this event. It was symbolic and has become historic because of the symbolism, not because it proved that California wines were superior to the French.

There is little likelihood such an event could take place in the foreseeable future with Zinfandel as an object of evaluation. What is lacking to produce a "Paris 1976" in San Francisco is an established Zinfandel industry elsewhere in the world. It would be silly to think that great Zinfandel could be raised only in California's coastal valleys and the Sierra Foothills. A similar Mediterranean climate can be found in Chile, Australia, and South Africa. And many spots in the Mediterranean world have climates and soils similar to California's. But to have a "San Francisco 2025" we first must see Japanese consumers pondering price differentials between Sonoma and Australian *grand cru* Zinfandels. And California consumers will have to be at odds over whether wines from certain old-vine clones can stand up to the challenge from the hot new California Primitivo and Crljenak wines on the market.

I would delight in such a future.

APPENDIX

REGIONAL SUMMARIES

This appendix attempts to focus more precisely on the role of Zinfandel in specific California regions and counties in recent years. I suggest that the reader also consult the statistical charts that accompany the following summaries.

SAN JOAQUIN COUNTY—LODI AREA

The Lodi area of San Joaquin County has been an important winegrowing district since the turn of the twentieth century. In 1986 the Bureau of Alcohol, Tobacco and Firearms (BATF) created the Lodi American Viticultural Area (AVA), which includes a piece of southern Sacramento County, just to the north. Statistics for the Lodi area in this study also include those Sacramento County grapes.

Zinfandel has always been important in the area's statistics. In 2002 San Joaquin County led the state in Zinfandel acres, as it did half a century ago. It also led in total wine grape acreage. It was second in Cabernet Sauvignon production and third in Chardonnay. In that same year Zinfandel accounted for 29 percent of the county's wine crop.

Statistics for the Lodi area make it clear that dry table wine is the major thrust of the area's winegrowing efforts. The Lodi AVA is cooled by maritime air that comes through from the San Francisco Bay Area, which makes the production of good table wine grapes possible.

White Zinfandel is an important product here and accounts for a good part of the acreage growth in the 1980s. In 1993 the expansion of Zinfandel acreage in this area began to accelerate, growing by about 7,500 acres (59 percent) in the next five years. A substantial part of this new acreage went into the production of moderately priced table wine in the five- to eight-dollar per bottle range. Several well-known producers in the coastal valleys—for example, Ravenswood and Cline Cellars—have been able to expand their sales of such wine by utilizing this growth of production.

Recent years have seen an increase in the number of small producers, many with old-vine acreage, who previously had simply sold their grape production to larger producers. Such Lodi Zinfandels have enjoyed a quickly rising reputation. We can see this increase in prestige by examining the 2001 vintage prices for the top-quality grapes in the area. Twenty-four lots of Zinfandel sold for more than $1,000 per ton, in the face of a district average of only $440. Most of these lots were of moderate size, under fifty tons. But three of them weighed out at more than two hundred tons.

From 1996 to 2002 Lodi Zinfandel prices have declined at an average of about 6 percent per year. There has also been a small decline in Zinfandel acreage from its 1999 high point. Such a tendency suggests that, at least in 2002, the Zinfandel planting and production boom of earlier years has peaked.

CENTRAL VALLEY

California's Central Valley is about 450 miles long and covers about 25,000 square miles. Except for the Lodi area, it is a dry and hot desert region that depends on irrigation to produce its huge crops.

In 2002 seven of the valley's counties (other than San Joaquin) had at least 1,000 acres of Zinfandel vines: from north to south, there were 1,141 acres in Colusa, 1,077 in Sacramento, 1,104 in Stanislaus, 1,237 in Merced, 3,104 in Madera, 2,637 in Fresno, and 2,012 in Kern. Since 1992 the Zinfandel acreage in these counties has doubled. But since 1999 about 1,300 acres of that variety have disappeared in this region. This decline has been greatly influenced by the 39 percent decline in Zinfandel grape prices here since 1996.

Yields are huge, with Zinfandel averaging more than ten tons per acre. Heavy irrigation and generous pruning account for these large crops. Together, since 1996, these counties have regularly produced more than ten times as much Zinfandel as Sonoma. The grapes go toward the production of White Zinfandel and low-priced varietal and generic red wine. Invariably these wines carry a California appellation on their labels, but all wines so labeled do not necessarily come from the Central Valley.

SIERRA FOOTHILLS

The Sierra Foothills AVA includes portions of eight counties, from Yuba in the north to Mariposa in the south. But 98 percent of the Zinfandel vines are in Amador, El Dorado, and Calaveras Counties. (The statistics compiled for this region include numbers for only those counties.) For the entire AVA, Zinfandel is the leading wine grape variety, with 2,136 acres, 41 percent of the total wine grape acreage.

When the modern American wine revolution began in the late 1960s, Zinfandel was by far the leading variety in this region; by 2002 five times as much Zinfandel had been planted here as in 1968.

Almost every one of the fifty-five wineries in the AVA produces a varietal Zinfandel. They tend to aim at the high-end premium product, whose labels often bear the names of local AVAs such as Shenandoah Valley, Fiddletown, and El Dorado.

Yields here are quite comparable to those of Sonoma, Napa, and Mendocino Counties, but grape prices are not. Foothills wineries pay only about half the price for Zinfandel grapes that North Coast producers had to meet in 2001. In that year the highest price for any lot of Foothills Zinfandel (15.6 tons at $2,000) was less than the average price paid in Sonoma for that variety.

In the early 1980s all premium Zinfandel producers suffered from the complaints that their wines were hot and harsh, with an excess of alcohol and hard tannins. Foothills producers began reacting to these complaints by picking earlier, to reduce sugar content and thus lower the alcohol. From the late 1970s to the 1981 vintage, growers were picking their grapes at an average Brix (sugar measurement) of 23.7°, which would make a wine with an alcohol content of about 13.3 percent. For the next fifteen years, their Brix readings often did not hit an average of 22°. But by the late 1980s fermentation techniques for red wines were being modified throughout the industry so that rich flavors were retained while harsh tannins were subdued. Wineries began producing the rich, flavorful Zinfandel so popular today, which still had high alcohols but seemed far less harsh. Since 1998 the average Foothills Zinfandel Brix has never been below 23.5°, and many growers pick at 25° and 26°, producing quite drinkable wines with alcohol levels well above 14 percent.

MONTEREY—SAN BENITO

Historically these two Central Coast counties were one; they separated in 1874. San Benito had about 300 acres of Zinfandel coming out of Prohibition; Monterey had fewer than 100. But in the late 1950s and early 1960s, as urbanization placed increasing pressure on vineyard land in the Santa Clara Valley (which is today almost always referred to as Silicon Valley), the wine industry there began looking south for vineyard land.

San Benito's total wine grape acreage rose from 1,650 to almost 5,000 between 1961 and 1971. But Zinfandel was never an important part of the total. Throughout the 1970s and into the 1980s, its acreage held at about 200. In recent years the county has had fewer than 100 acres.

Monterey's story is quite different, but the recent acreage numbers indicate similar grower sentiment about the Zinfandel's ability to ripen here. From 1964 to 1974 the county's total wine grape acreage rose from 69 to about 25,000. Zinfandel acreage rose from 15 to 3,200, with most of these new vines planted where ripening would be difficult. In 2002 the county had almost 42,000 acres of wine grapes but only about 300 of them were Zinfandel, most in the warmer southern portions of the county and in the Carmel Valley.

The Zinfandel grown now in the two counties is of good quality and fetches as much as that variety does in the Sierra Foothills. In 2001 the Zinfandel Brix here was a hefty 23.1°. Twenty years earlier growers had been lucky to get average readings of 20°.

SAN LUIS OBISPO

Zinfandel has been a favorite in San Luis Obispo County since before Prohibition, particularly in the Paso Robles area and on the low foothills and valleys east of town, and to the south around the village of Templeton. In 2002 Cabernet Sauvignon was king here, with half of the wine grape acreage in the county. But among red wine grapes, Zinfandel was a solid second, with 2,200 acres.

Coming out of the 1960s, the county had about 500 Zinfandel acres, and acreage has risen steadily, even in the troublesome 1980s. Because yields are generally more than five tons per acre, well ahead of Sonoma and Napa, the county Zinfandel tonnage here is not far behind that of Sonoma. But average grape prices are quite moderate, usually a bit below those of the Sierra Foothills. This fact helps make many Zinfandels from the Paso Robles AVA good bargains in the new century. Nevertheless, individual vineyards with reputations for high quality receive top dollar. Twenty-nine vineyard lots sold for $1,500 per ton or more in 2001.

Neighboring Santa Barbara County to the south is fine wine country but mostly too cool for Zinfandel. In 2002 this county had 54 Zinfandel acres, 40 of them planted in one warm spot in 1998.

SOUTHERN CALIFORNIA

After 1901 the Cucamonga area of San Bernardino County became a very important viticultural area, with about 15,000 acres of wine grapes planted before World War I. About one-third of those were Zinfandel, whose grapes were used to produce table wine and sweet wine. Winegrowing also developed next door, in the Mira Loma area of Riverside County, with about 200 acres of Zinfandel.

During Prohibition this region was involved in the "fresh grape deal," and Zinfandel acreage grew to about 7,000. After the repeal of Prohibition, Zinfandel acreage held steady until 1962, at about 6,000 acres. Then the expansion of suburbia and the decline of the local wine industry brought about a steady contraction of acreage. By 1987 only 950 acres of Zinfandel were left, about a third of the San Bernardino County wine grape total.

From 1990 to the new century, wine grape acreage remained at about 6,500 acres. Some grapes went to White Zinfandel; some were sold to Central Valley producers. But after the 1994 vintage, the price of Cucamonga Zinfandel from a few older vineyards began to soar. By 2001 the average price had more than doubled, to $969 per ton. Some of these grapes were purchased by premium wineries in the north. In 1997 Sonoma's Geyser Peak Winery made a wine from Cucamonga's old D'Ambrogio Vineyard. It won the Vintners Club's first-round Zinfandel tasting in 1999. The runners-up included wines from Ravenswood, Beringer, and Signorello. I was at that tasting and had not an inkling that a Southern California wine had been included. Along with the other tasters, I gasped when the labels were exposed, having given the wine a very good rating. In 2001 a photo of these vines showed them to be on their last legs. In 2002 they were ripped out.

SAN FRANCISCO BAY AREA

Before World War II the counties that surrounded the southern portion of the San Francisco Bay—Contra Costa, Alameda, Santa Clara, San Mateo, and Santa Cruz—

had a fairly large winegrowing culture. (Santa Cruz County looks down on the inland water but does not touch it.) There were about 15,000 acres of wine grapes in the region; of these, about 4,500 were planted to Zinfandel. Suburbanization took its toll on these vines after the war: by 1961 the total was cut in two, and Zinfandel had fallen to 1,700 acres.

In 1999 the BATF was moved to grant a San Francisco Bay AVA to much of this area. Producers in Alameda County's Livermore Valley supplied the force behind the petition for this move. (Because of its cooler climate and distinct soils, the Santa Cruz Mountains AVA was not included in the new designation.) By 2002 wine grape acreage had slipped to 5,000 acres; only 684 of these were planted to Zinfandel. And 63 percent of these were in the eastern portions of Contra Costa County, sufficiently removed from the bay to have plenty of warm days to ripen Zinfandel.

Zinfandel acreage in Contra Costa declined fairly steadily until 1994. In the years just preceding, however, several old vineyards had been discovered by premium producers, Rosenblum Cellars and Cline Cellars chief among them. Since then, Zinfandel acres have grown steadily in the face of advancing housing developments. In 2001 Zinfandel prices for the entire area averaged $1,235 per ton, well above those of the Central Coast and the Sierra Foothills.

MENDOCINO AND LAKE COUNTIES

The winegrowing areas of Mendocino and Lake Counties make up the northern portion of the North Coast AVA. Lake County had a sizeable acreage in the 1890s, more than 1,000 acres. But those numbers were not achieved again until the 1970s. Mendocino winegrowing on a large scale dates from 1901–1909. In both counties Zinfandel made up a larger percentage of the total wine grape acreage before Prohibition than it does today.

Lake County came out of Prohibition with about 500 acres of wine grapes. This number declined until the 1970s, when the county's total grew to almost 3,000. Then, between 1999 and 2001, the total doubled. Throughout these years Zinfandel has accounted for about 10 percent of the county's total (9 percent in 2002). Lake County Zinfandel grapes in recent years were sold for about the same price as those from the Paso Robles area.

Mendocino entered Prohibition with 2,800 total acres and had almost 8,000 at repeal, almost 3,000 of which were Zinfandel. By 1964 Zinfandel acreage accounted for 16 percent of the total 5,000. In 1996 it was still 15 percent but had declined to

12 percent by 2002. We should note, however, that this percentage is higher than that of any other North Coast county, including Sonoma.

The quality of Mendocino Zinfandels has been well established since the 1970s. This fact is reflected in the grape prices of the 1990s, when Napa's Zinfandel grapes regularly sold for a price 5 to 8 percent cheaper than the price fetched by Mendocino grapes. There are quite a few very old Zinfandel vineyards that date from the planting boom of the 1920s. Grapes from these places bring prices similar to those found in Sonoma. In 2001 fourteen vineyard lots sold for $2,500 per ton or higher. These expensive grapes made up an important part of the county's Zinfandel production, enough to produce more than thirty thousand cases of wine.

NAPA COUNTY

Napa's nineteenth-century reputation for fine wine rested on its Zinfandel, by far the most numerous vine after the 1880s. After the phylloxera epidemic and the valley's replanting between 1898 and 1910, Zinfandel was still number one, but as a plurality, not a majority.

During the Prohibition years, the Petite Sirah (Durif) took over as the leading grape, though it had only about 25 percent of the total wine grape acreage; Zinfandel had about 10 percent. When Napa began to feel the great boom of the 1970s, total acreage soared, and Zinfandel more than doubled to about 2,000 acres, finally passing Petite Sirah in 1973. But at that point Zinfandel stood in sixth place among all varieties.

Through the 1980s and into the 1990s, Napa Zinfandel acreage held at about 2,000, or about 6 percent of total acres. Through all these years, the reputation of the county's Zinfandel wines remained solid, as can be seen by the puffs from *Connoisseurs' Guide to California Wine* and from the Vintners Club competitions. Nevertheless, between 1993 and 2000, Napa Zinfandel acreage declined slowly but steadily by a total of 17 percent. The reason was clearly economic. From 1993 to 2001 the Napa Zinfandel growers' price per ton averaged slightly less than half that received for Cabernet Sauvignon. And at the same time the yield per bearing acre of Cabernet averaged 15 to 29 percent more than Zinfandel. Clearly, with 2001 Napa Cabernet prices averaging $1,700 per ton more than Zinfandel, the lure to graft over to the more precious fruit was powerful.

Still, much Napa Zinfandel fruit brought excellent prices. Fifty-one vineyard lots sold in 2001 at $2,500 per ton or higher. Two lots totaling 112 tons both sold for

$3,800 per ton. A bottle of Zinfandel from such prized grapes would not go for $12.99 retail.

SONOMA COUNTY

Several environmental factors contribute to Sonoma's leadership in the world of California Zinfandel. There are the fine red soils of Dry Creek Valley, and the almost perfect weather at Geyserville. There are also historic and cultural factors. Modern Sonoma inherited a huge stand of old-vine Zinfandel in the 1970s. In 1980 more than half the county's acreage dated back to the 1960s and earlier. And a sizeable number of Sonoma growers might be said to have a powerful emotional attachment to the variety and to the almost universal St. George rootstock on which most of it has traditionally been planted for more than a century. And there is an economic factor, particularly in recent years. In 2001 Sonoma Zinfandel grapes brought more dollars per ton than Napa growers had received for their Cabernet Sauvignon three years earlier. Still, in 2002, four other varieties had more acreage in Sonoma than Zinfandel (Merlot, Pinot noir, Cabernet Sauvignon, and Chardonnay).

Sonoma came out of Prohibition with about 10,000 acres of Zinfandel vines. This number declined to fewer than 4,000 in the 1960s. The total has yet to top 5,000 acres, but there has been a steady rise in acreage since 1996, which accompanied the rise in prices for that variety of almost 100 percent since that year. The sauntering pace of this acreage growth has been the result of economic factors. As was the case in Napa, Zinfandel prices in Sonoma were less than half those of Cabernet Sauvignon in the mid-1990s. But the results of the 2001 vintage may accelerate the expansion of Sonoma Zinfandel. In that vintage, Sonoma Zinfandel prices jumped up to 91 percent of the county average for Cabernet Sauvignon. As in Napa, the most valuable Zinfandel grapes here fetch remarkable prices. In 2001 forty-two vineyard lots sold for $3,000 per ton or more. This was more than $5 million worth of grapes, a number that may help speed up the lazy growth of Sonoma's Zinfandel acreage.

TABLE 2. ZINFANDEL TONS CRUSHED, 1974–2002

Selected Counties and Regions, Selected Years

YEAR	SONOMA	NAPA	BAY AREA*	SAN LUIS OBISPO	SIERRA FOOTHILLS	LODI	OTHER CENTRAL VALLEY	TOTAL CALIFORNIA
1974	9,964	2,544	—	—	—	58,930	4,400	89,300
1976	7,947	1,982	668	—	—	35,468	16,066	73,096
1978	9,879	4,187	548	—	—	40,170	16,022	93,087
1982	11,323	5,702	838	3,017	2,545	35,801	6,698	83,253
1984	11,348	6,197	789	3,282	3,762	34,719	11,783	93,584
1986	13,271	8,578	1,203	7,486	4,277	61,505	22,587	143,401
1988	15,034	8,427	1,713	6,877	4,694	72,576	33,846	170,091
1990	15,314	9,145	1,353	6,787	5,067	71,584	50,185	185,491
1992	17,900	11,343	1,385	7,691	6,759	78,675	66,378	228,165
1994	14,581	8,046	1,155	7,592	5,340	78,031	74,391	223,670
1996	14,135	8,213	1,304	7,877	7,154	94,947	130,221	249,843
1998	12,230	5,880	1,300	7,338	5,315	117,338	149,989	339,712
2000	13,322	5,688	2,034	10,731	6,591	165,659	163,754	404,167
2001	14,286	5,214	1,790	10,811	7,781	133,614	134,378	336,546
2002	13,360	6,081	2,189	9,193	7,765	140,822	173,886	370,300

SOURCE: California Agricultural Statistics Service, "Grape Crush Report," annual publications.

*The San Francisco Bay Viticultural District includes Alameda and Contra Costa Counties and parts of Santa Clara County.

TABLE 3. ZINFANDEL ACRES, 1936–2001

Selected Counties, Selected Years

YEAR	SONOMA*	NAPA*	MENDOCINO*	SAN JOAQUIN (LODI)	AMADOR	SAN LUIS OBISPO	FRESNO/ MADERA	SAN BERNARDINO
1936	8,623	1,668	2,970	16,113	391	344	3,283	6,418
1961	3,964	949	1,062	6,588	404	472	301	6,411
1968	4,032	899	648	7,167	408	512	236	4,517
1972	3,874	832	749	9,218	424	469	319	3,627
1976	3,962	1,925	1,222	11,720	755	1,042	363	2,666
1980	4,664	2,136	1,336	11,147	898	1,008	280	2,348
1984	4,532	2,031	1,341	10,193	1,049	989	232	1,718
1988	4,424	2,110	1,719	11,733	1,114	1,268	1,013	667
1990	4,130	1,993	1,849	12,723	1,186	1,367	1,379	642
1992	3,963	2,139	1,823	12,782	1,248	1,224	1,620	636
1994	4,062	2,041	1,773	14,829	1,245	1,205	2,038	—
1996	4,069	2,030	1,937	17,334	1,602	1,861	5,507	665
1998	4,310	1,917	1,874	19,842	1,677	1,706	5,958	641
1999	4,533	1,958	1,892	20,289	1,996	2,192	6,190	702
2000	4,611	1,885	1,953	20,192	1,717	2,173	5,853	700
2001	4,871	1,749	1,898	19,930	1,706	2,211	5,741	671

SOURCE: California Agricultural Statistics Service, "California Grape Acreage," annual publications.

*These three counties, plus Lake and a small portion of Solano, make up the North Coast Viticultural District.

TABLE 4. ZINFANDEL PRICE PER TON, 1972–2002

Selected Counties and Regions, Selected Years

YEAR	SONOMA	NAPA	BAY AREA*	SAN LUIS OBISPO	SIERRA FOOTHILLS	LODI	OTHER CENTRAL VALLEY	CALIFORNIA AVERAGE
1972	$472	$472	—	—	—	$247	$227	$315
1974	307	307	—	—	—	165	92	185
1976	371	398	283	—	—	162	98	204
1978	441	468	369	318	—	202	124	285
1980	451	485	436	382	445	171	130	290
1982	485	505	455	395	437	174	119	298
1984	426	425	374	315	404	188	126	253
1986	446	425	366	308	382	317	286	340
1988	715	618	756	565	685	962	756	817
1990	727	683	604	486	473	345	263	391
1992	678	625	549	446	531	435	327	434
1994	741	638	627	483	577	459	375	463
1996	1,221	877	1,054	613	808	588	425	564
1998	1,724	1,080	1,084	757	831	457	294	460
2000	2,143	1,499	1,234	891	980	404	255	464
2001	2,456	2,064	1,235	888	1,044	441	261	520
2002	2,493	1,934	1,305	856	977	403	239	476

SOURCE: California Agricultural Statistics Service, "Grape Crush Report," annual publications.

*The San Francisco Bay Viticultural District includes Alameda and Contra Costa Counties and parts of Santa Clara County.

TABLE 5. ZINFANDEL ACRES, 1919–2001

Selected Regions, Selected Years

YEAR	"PREMIUM" REGION*	LODI-WOODBRIDGE	OTHER CENTRAL VALLEY	SOUTHERN CALIFORNIA	TOTAL**
1919	—	—	—	—	ca. 70,000
1936	14,180	16,113	23,050	7,290	61,643
1961	8,119	6,588	1,015	6,843	23,016
1968	7,199	7,167	1,058	4,882	21,189
1972	8,540	9,218	1,866	3,856	23,786
1976	13,277	11,720	2,554	2,867	30,588
1980	13,780	11,147	1,625	2,501	29,148
1984	12,313	10,103	1,141	1,824	25,454
1988	14,010	11,733	4,309	816	30,735
1990	13,521	12,733	6,373	762	34,379
1992	13,102	12,782	7,406	724	34,738
1994	12,880	13,515	7,722	635	35,337
1996	13,174	17,334	14,303	755	46,588
1998	14,344	19,842	15,207	713	50,268
1999	15,026	20,289	15,588	767	51,811
2000	14,525	20,192	14,571	757	50,200
2001***	14,617	19,930	14,279	728	49,700

SOURCE: California Agricultural Statistics Service, "California Grape Acreage," annual publications; *California Grape Grower,* April 1920 (1919 data); U.S. Agricultural Adjustment Administration survey of California fruit and nut acreage, published in *Wine Review,* March 1938, pp. 18–19 (1936 data).

* "Premium" region: North Coast, Bay Area, Central Coast, and Sierra Foothills.

** Because scattered plantings are not included here, totals are not equivalent to the numbers listed.

*** Note that "premium" areas had 29 percent of the Zinfandel acreage in 2001 but produced only 12.2 percent of the wine.

TABLE 6. ZINFANDEL TONS PER BEARING ACRE, 1982–2001

Selected Counties and Regions, Selected Years

YEAR	SONOMA	NAPA	BAY AREA*	SAN LUIS OBISPO	SIERRA FOOTHILLS	LODI	OTHER CENTRAL VALLEY	CALIFORNIA AVERAGE
1982	2.7	2.9	1.4	3.3	2.6	3.3	5.0	3.1
1984	2.7	3.1	1.6	3.7	3.2	3.4	10.9	3.8
1986	3.2	4.3	2.4	6.8	3.5	6.3	20.2	5.9
1988	3.6	4.3	3.8	5.7	3.8	7.3	23.8	6.8
1990	3.9	4.9	2.9	5.3	3.9	6.5	15.5	6.6
1992	4.8	6.0	3.1	6.4	5.0	6.4	9.3	7.0
1994	3.8	4.0	2.7	6.5	4.4	6.2	10.7	6.8
1996	3.8	4.3	3.4	6.2	4.3	6.9	14.8	8.3
1998	3.3	3.4	3.0	5.7	2.9	6.8	11.8	7.8
1999	2.8	3.5	3.3	5.3	3.1	6.1	11.1	7.0
2000	3.3	3.4	3.6	5.6	3.6	8.3	11.5	8.5
2001	3.4	3.2	2.7	5.1	4.0	6.7	11.1	7.1

SOURCE: These statistics have been calculated based on data available in two annual publications of the California Agricultural Statistics Service: "California Grape Acreage" and "Grape Crush Report."

NOTE: The tons-per-bearing-acre figure is extremely important to vineyardists and wine producers. The grower's gross income can be calculated by combining these figures with the average price per ton for a given area. Thus, in 1994, it apparently was as profitable to grow Zinfandel in the Lodi area (6.2 T/A × \$459 = \$2,845) as it was in Sonoma (3.8 T/A × \$741 = \$2,815).

*The San Francisco Bay Viticultural District includes Alameda and Contra Costa Counties and parts of Santa Clara County.

NOTES

CHAPTER ONE. HOW I SOLVED THE HISTORICAL MYSTERIES SURROUNDING ZINFANDEL—SORT OF

1. John Melville, *Guide to California Wines* (Garden City, N.Y.: Doubleday, 1955).
2. Vincent P. Carosso, *The California Wine Industry, 1830–1895* (Berkeley: University of California Press, 1951). My nose for historical accuracy was continually tweaked by the uniform spelling of a great German grape as "Reisling."
3. Robert A. Thompson had a good reputation for historical sleuthing. His article in the *San Francisco Evening Post* (May 1, 1885) was the result of extensive research.
4. "An Historian's View of Zinfandel in California," *Wines & Vines,* February 1977, pp. 18–20; "A Viticultural Mystery Solved," *California History* (the quarterly of the California Historical Society), Summer 1978, pp. 114–129; "The Historical Origins of Zinfandel in California," *Vintage,* April 1979, pp. 42–47, and May 1979, pp. 19–25. This work was expanded and later published in "Zinfandel: A True Vinifera," *Vinifera Wine Growers Journal,* Summer 1982, pp. 71–86.
5. Thomas Pinney, *A History of Wine in America: From the Beginnings to Prohibition* (Berkeley: University of California Press, 1989), pp. 188–190; William Robert Prince, *A Treatise on the Vine* (New York: T. & J. Swords, 1830), p. 343.
6. *The Prince Family Manuscript Collection,* Library List 101 (Beltsville, Md.: Na-

tional Agricultural Library, 1978) is a very detailed 37-page catalogue of the materials in this important source, including many nursery catalogues.

CHAPTER TWO. SOJOURN IN THE EAST

1. For the best history of this early viticulture, see Pinney, *History of Wine in America,* pp. 55–229. For a less thorough, but delightful, history, see Ulysses Prentice Hedrick, *The Grapes of New York* (Albany: New York Agricultural Experiment Station, 1908).
2. B. Philip Miller, *The Gardeners and Florists Dictionary, or a Complete System of Horticulture* (London, 1724); W. Wilson, *Treatise on Forcing Early Fruit* (London, 1777); George W. Johnson, *The Grape Vine . . .* (London, 1847), pp. 18–19.
3. J. Fisk Allen, *Practical Treatise in the Culture and Treatment of the Grape Vine,* 3d ed. (New York: C. M. Saxton, 1855), pp. 24, 135–139. This edition is more often available and is more complete than the earlier two (1847 and 1848).
4. Ibid., pp. 93–97.
5. Daniel Denison Slade, *The Evolution of Horticulture in New England* (New York, 1895), pp. 174–176; Marshall Pinckney Wilder, "The Horticulture of Boston and Vicinity," in *The Memorial History of Boston,* vol. 4, ed. Justin Winson (Boston, 1881), pp. 607–640.
6. See, for example, Miller, *Gardeners and Florists Dictionary;* William Speechley, *A Treatise on the Culture of the Vine* (York: G. Peacock, 1790).
7. T. V. Munson, *Foundations of American Grape Culture* (Denison, Tex., 1909), p. 166. The Isabella was a chance vinifera/native hybrid found by a certain I. G. Swift of Dorchester, South Carolina, later a neighbor of the Gibbs family in Brooklyn. See also *The American Farmer* (Baltimore), March 22, 1822, p. 415.
8. *The American Farmer,* November 15, 1822, p. 267. Gibbs began his Long Island work "after witnessing the excellence of the fruit under the care of the skillful Horticulturists of Boston."
9. Pinney, *History of Wine in America,* pp. 188–190.
10. The National Agricultural Library publication *The Prince Family Manuscript Collection* includes a large number of the nursery catalogues.
11. W. R. Prince's "American Fruit Book, 1829–1837," p. 168. This is actually a letter book with miscellaneous notes, in the *Prince Family Manuscript Collection,* National Agricultural Library, Beltsville, Md.
12. Prince, *Treatise on the Vine,* p. 468.

13. *New England Farmer* (Boston), October 15, 1830, p. 102.
14. Ibid., November 2, 1831, p. 99. Perkins was also selling cuttings of the "Frankendalt" and the Black St. Peters.
15. *Transactions of the Massachusetts Horticultural Society,* 1833, p. 28; 1834, p. 21.
16. *American Gardener's Magazine* (Boston), December 1835, p. 459. In the following year the name of Hovey's journal was changed to *Magazine of Horticulture,* the name under which it is usually filed.
17. *Transactions of the Massachusetts Horticultural Society,* 1840, p. 29; 1844, p. 62; 1845, p. 90. See also *Magazine of Horticulture,* 1842, p. 200.
18. William Chorlton, *The American Grape Growers' Guide* (New York: A. O. Moore, 1859), pp. 30–36.
19. *New England Farmer,* January 7, 1825, p. 190; *Yankee Farmer* (Portland, Maine), May 15, 1841.
20. Hedrick, *Grapes of New York,* pp. 56–57.
21. Allen's article appeared in the *Magazine of Horticulture,* 1847, vol. 13, p. 43.
22. "Notebook on greenhouse plants and notebook on grapes," p. 407, Prince Family Manuscript Collection. Prince also wrote that he was growing the native *V. californica* vine from seeds he had brought back.
23. "Annual Descriptive Catalogue of Fruit and Ornamental Trees, Grape-Vines . . . ," for Warren's Garden and Nurseries (Brighton, Mass., 1844), pp. 15–16.
24. *Transactions of the Massachusetts Horticultural Society,* 1865, vol. 10, p. 39.
25. Ibid., 1876, vol. 16, pt. 2, p. 9.

CHAPTER THREE. HO! FOR CALIFORNIA!

1. I am indebted to Professor William P. Marchione of the Art Institute of Boston for his research paper "James L. L. F. Warren: 'Father of California Agriculture'" (1999) and for his copy of Warren's nursery catalogue of 1844, which lists the "Zinfendel" (see figure 3 in chapter 2). For information about Warren's years in California, see Walton Bean, "James Warren and the Beginnings of Agricultural Institutions in California," *California Historical Society Quarterly* 13, no. 4 (1944), pp. 362–375.
2. Ernest S. Falbo, "State of California in 1856," *California Historical Society Quarterly* 42, no. 4 (December 1963), pp. 311–330.

3. Hubert Howe Bancroft, *History of California,* vol. 4 (San Francisco: History Co., 1886–1890), p. 727.
4. On the significance of New Englanders in the opening of California to foreign commerce before 1846, see John Walton Caughey, *California* (New York: Prentice-Hall, 1940), pp. 206–208, 214–215.
5. *California Farmer,* March 5, 1858; *San Francisco Bulletin,* May 1 and 5, 1885; *Napa County Reporter,* July 4, 1884; *St. Helena Star,* June 18, 1885.
6. *Transactions of the California State Agricultural Society... 1858* (Sacramento, 1859), pp. 98–99, 123 (hereafter cited as *Transactions*); *California Farmer,* June 15, 1854; *Alta California,* October 12, 1856; *Sacramento Bee,* September 29, 1857, and August 31, 1858.
7. *California Farmer,* November 30, 1860.
8. Ibid., October 10, 1856.
9. *San Jose Telegraph,* October 14, 1857; *Alta California,* September 28, 1858.
10. *San Jose Telegraph,* October 14, 1857, and October 26, 1859; *Pacific Rural Press,* September 30, 1882; *San Francisco Merchant* (later the *Pacific Wine & Spirit Review*), July 31, 1885.
11. Thomas Hart Hyatt, *Hyatt's Hand-Book of Grape Culture* (San Francisco: H. H. Bancroft, 1867), pp. 157, 162.

CHAPTER FOUR. PLANT YOUR VINEYARDS! BEGIN NOW!

1. *Alta California,* August 11, 1860. Macondray sold the Baywood estate to John Parrott in 1860. John was the father of Tiburcio Parrott, whose Miravalle winery on Napa's Spring Mountain produced one of California's greatest pre-Prohibition Cabernet Sauvignons. Today it is the site of Spring Mountain Vineyards.
2. *California Farmer,* January 11, 1855.
3. Ibid., October 5, 1855.
4. Ibid., September 18, 1857.
5. *California Wine, Wool, and Stock Journal,* June 1863, p. 107; *California Farmer,* May 17, 1855, and April 22, 1859; *Alta California,* September 29, 1861; *St. Helena Star,* June 8, 1885.
6. *San Francisco Evening Bulletin,* May 1, 1885.
7. *Napa County Reporter,* July 4, 1884; *St. Helena Star,* June 8, 1885.
8. *Transactions... 1858,* pp. 269, 303; *Alta California,* August 14, 1860.
9. *Transactions... 1858,* p. 213; *Transactions... 1860,* pp. 63, 64, 306, 315.

10. *California Farmer,* September 27, 1861.
11. The original catalogue of these vines was published in the *First Annual Report of the Board of State Viticultural Commissioners* (San Francisco: Edward Bosqui, 1881), pp. 184–188.
12. *Transactions . . . 1866,* pp. 535–540; *Alta California,* November 3, 1866.
13. *Alta California,* May 6, 1867. The editor noted here that the Zinfandel and Black St. Peters were now thought to be the same vine.
14. *Pacific Rural Press,* December 23, 1871.
15. *Alta California,* May 20, 1870.
16. *Report of the Commissioner of Agriculture . . . 1866* (Washington, D.C.: U.S. Department of Agriculture, 1867), p. 606.
17. *Alta California,* January 20 and 26, 1868.
18. *Transactions . . . 1870,* pp. 507–511.
19. *Alta California,* December 6, 1869.
20. Jancis Robinson, *Vines, Grapes, and Wines* (New York: Alfred A. Knopf, 1986), pp. 141–143.

CHAPTER FIVE. BOOM! 1872–1890

1. *First Annual Report of the Board of State Viticultural Commissioners,* 2d ed., rev. (Sacramento: J. D. Young, 1881), p. 65.
2. *St. Helena Star,* January 26, 1877, and October 26, 1877.
3. Ibid., March 4, 1876.
4. *Santa Rosa Democrat,* October 12, 1877.
5. Ibid., September 16, 1875.
6. *Second Annual Report of the Board of State Viticultural Commissioners* (Sacramento: J. D. Young, 1882); see pp. 28–30 for De Turk's report and pp. 43–45 for Krug's report.
7. *San Jose Herald,* July 2, 1885, and September 16, 1885.
8. *San Jose Mercury,* December 1, 1881, and August 27, 1882; *San Jose Herald,* August 27, 1885.
9. *Livermore Herald,* May 27, 1886.
10. *Pacific Wine & Spirit Review* (*San Francisco Merchant*), June 6, 1884, and May 22, 1885; *Livermore Herald,* August 18, 1881.
11. *Pacific Wine & Spirit Review,* February 12, 1886.
12. *Second Annual Report of the Chief Executive Officer to the Board of State Viticultural*

Commissioners for the Years 1882–1883 and 1883–1884 (Sacramento: James J. Ayers, 1884), p. 118.

13. *Alta California,* June 6, 1866; November 24, 1866; August 9, 1867; January 14, 1869.
14. *Pacific Wine & Spirit Review,* November 20, 1885.

CHAPTER SIX. THE HARASZTHY MYTH

1. For the details of Agoston Haraszthy's life, the best source is a volume written by his great-great-grandson, Brian McGinty; see McGinty, *Strong Wine: The Life and Legend of Agoston Haraszthy* (Stanford, Calif.: Stanford University Press, 1998). An excellent analysis of Haraszthy's life, his contributions to California wine, and the numerous flaws in how he has been perceived historically are found in Pinney, *History of Wine in America,* pp. 269–284.
2. *Transactions . . . 1858,* pp. 242–246.
3. *Alta California,* July 2, 1869.
4. For information about Arpad Haraszthy's early years, I have drawn from the biographical essay by Ruth Teiser and Catherine Harroun written as an introduction to Haraszthy's *Wine-Making in California* (San Francisco: Book Club of California, 1978), a limited edition that collected articles originally written by Haraszthy for the *Overland Monthly* in 1871–1872. I have also depended on Ernest P. Peninou's work *A History of the Orleans Hill Vineyard and Winery of Arpad Haraszthy and Company* (Winters, Calif.: Winters Express, 1983).
5. Peninou, *History of the Orleans Hill Vineyard,* pp. 12–17.
6. *Sonoma Democrat,* May 28, 1870; *Alta California,* May 20, 1870.
7. *San Francisco Bulletin,* January 20, 1877.
8. *First Annual Report of the Board of State Viticultural Commissioners,* pp. 45, 54, 65.
9. *Second Annual Report of the Chief Executive Officer to the BVSC,* pp. 114, 117–119. For information about Charles Kohler, see Charles L. Sullivan, *A Companion to California Wine: An Encyclopedia of Wine and Winemaking from the Mission Period to the Present* (Berkeley: University of California Press, 1998), pp. 171–173.
10. *San Francisco Evening Bulletin,* May 5, 1885.
11. *St. Helena Star,* June 8, 1885. Some of the information had appeared earlier in the *Napa County Reporter,* July 4, 1884.
12. *San Jose Herald,* May 28, 1885; *Pacific Wine & Spirit Review,* July 3, 1885.
13. *Napa Register,* July 10, 1885; *Pacific Wine & Spirit Review,* July 3, 1885.

14. Both Arpad's manuscript and the H. H. Bancroft typescript are in the Bancroft Library, University of California at Berkeley.
15. Pinney, *History of Wine in America,* p. 483.
16. Arpad Haraszthy, "Early Viticulture in Sonoma," *Sonoma County and Russian River Valley, Illustrated* (San Francisco, 1888), pp. 77–79.
17. See particularly Arpad Haraszthy's articles from April to June 1864 in the *California Wine, Wool, and Stock Journal.*
18. *Alta California,* March 9, 1869. Arpad Haraszthy and Isador Landsberger were using free-run "white Zinfandel" as the basic wine in the successful *cuvée* they were developing, later to be Eclipse champagne.
19. Arpad Haraszthy's series of articles ran from December 1871 to May 1872; see *Overland Monthly,* vol. 7, pp. 489–497; vol. 8, pp. 34–41, 105–109, 393–398.
20. California State Vinicultural Association, *Grapes and Grape Vines of California* (San Francisco: Edward Bosqui, 1877; reprint, New York: Harcourt Brace Jovanovich, 1980). In a historical note written for the 1980 reprint of the Bosqui volume, Leon Adams warned that the author was "in error" on the introduction of the Zinfandel to California, adding that research had proved otherwise. Adams had recently gone over my findings, and in 1978 he had written that my research "into the introduction of the Zinfandel grape to California was an important contribution to the wine history of the United States."
21. *Pacific Wine & Spirit Review,* February 17, 1888; *Scientific American,* March 18, 1899. The *New York Tribune* article is cited in *Pacific Wine & Spirit Review,* July 20, 1888.
22. George Husmann, *American Grape Growing and Wine Making,* 4th ed. (New York: Orange Judd, 1902), pp. 201–202; Adolf Cluss, "Kalifornien als Weinland," *Allgemeine Wein Zeitung,* nos. 32, 33, 37 (1908).
23. For examples, see Theodore Schoenman, *Father of California Wine: Agoston Haraszthy* (Santa Barbara: Capra Press, 1979); Paul Fredericksen, "The Authentic Haraszthy Story," written for the Wine Advisory Board of the Wine Institute and printed by *Wines & Vines* in 1947. Some professors at the University of California, however, continued to be skeptical about the myth. M. A. Amerine and A. J. Winkler wrote in 1944 that the Zinfandel "was brought in with earlier importations, but when, whence and *by whom* remain a mystery" (my emphasis) ("Composition and Quality of Musts and Wines of California Grapes," *Hilgardia* 15, no. 6 [February 1944], p. 604).

CHAPTER SEVEN. THE STEALTH GRAPE, 1891–1918

1. For examples of some of these opinions, see *Pacific Wine & Spirit Review*, December 20, 1890; and *San Jose Mercury*, August 8, 1889.
2. Since the early 1880s Hilgard had emphasized that fine Zinfandel was grown in the upper portions of the coastal valleys and the foothills; see *San Jose Herald*, July 2, 1885. Later Frederic Bioletti was another university critic of what he called "lowland Zinfandel"; see *San Jose Mercury*, August 16, 1908.
3. The university was voicing the same caution against such planting practices fifty years later; see, for example, Amerine and Winkler, "Composition and Quality of Musts and Wines of California Grapes," pp. 604–605.
4. Nevertheless in 1893 Masson was praised for making one of California's best Zinfandels; see *Pacific Wine & Spirit Review*, November 6, 1894.
5. This expression serves as the title of a popular and very interesting book on Zinfandel, David Darlington's *Angels' Visits* (New York: Henry Holt, 1991). It was reissued as *Zin: The History and Mystery of Zinfandel*, with a new epilogue, by Da Capo Press in 2001.
6. Husmann, *American Grape Growing and Wine Making*, pp. 201–202.
7. This history database can be accessed on the Internet at *www.winefiles.org*, a service provided by the Sonoma County Wine Library and the California State Library.
8. Board of State Viticultural Commissioners, *The Vineyards of Napa County* (Sacramento, 1893), pp. 9–12. For the Napa story in this dismal decade, see Charles L. Sullivan, *Napa Wine: A History from Mission Days to the Present* (San Francisco: Wine Appreciation Guild, 1994), pp. 101–122. For the Santa Clara Valley story, see Charles L. Sullivan, *Like Modern Edens: Winegrowing in Santa Clara Valley and Santa Cruz Mountains, 1798–1981* (Cupertino, Calif.: California History Center, De Anza College, 1982), pp. 85–87.
9. Sullivan, *A Companion to California Wine*, pp. 262–263, 289–290.
10. Canadian wine and food historian Gilles Dupré reports that he has spotted California Zinfandel on the wine lists of the Canadian Pacific Railroad from as early as the 1890s (personal correspondence to the author, May 18, 2002).
11. *Pacific Wine & Spirit Review*, June 30, 1915. The awards were published before the July 14 Wine Day. Other Zinfandel award winners were J. L. Da Roza, A. Finke's Widow (San Francisco), Lachman & Jacobi, A. Mattei, and A. Repsold.

CHAPTER EIGHT. PROHIBITION AND THE FRESH GRAPE DEAL, 1919–1933

1. *San Jose Mercury,* September 25, 1910.
2. *Pacific Wine & Spirit Review,* December 31, 1915, and December 31, 1916.
3. *American Wine Press and Mineral Spirit News,* April 1917, October 1917; *San Jose Mercury,* September 7, 1917.
4. *California Grape Grower* (later *Wines & Vines*), March 1920.
5. Frederic T. Bioletti, "Propagation of Vines," California Agricultural Experiment Station, Circular 225, 1920.
6. Horatio Stoll's *California Grape Grower,* later *Wines & Vines,* provided excellent wine grape planting and acreage statistics throughout the Prohibition years (and is the only good source for California wine grape statistics before the 1960s). For the Prohibition years, the best issues in which to find these scattered numbers are April 1920, September 1921, April 1923, April 1924, September 1927, and December 1930.
7. The *California Grape Grower* ran articles on the wine grape operations in individual cities, such as New York (January 1925), Boston (February 1925), and Chicago (March 1925).
8. *California Grape Grower,* October 1927.
9. Ibid., October 1926.
10. *New York Times,* April 28, 1929.
11. *California Grape Grower,* October 1928.
12. Ibid., December 1930.
13. John Kobler, *Ardent Spirits: The Rise and Fall of Prohibition* (New York: G. P. Putnam's Sons, 1973), p. 341.
14. Pinney, *History of Wine in America,* p. 441.

CHAPTER NINE. THE TWO FACES OF ZIN, 1934–1969

1. *American Wine and Liquor Journal,* June 1934, p. 39; *Wines & Vines,* January 1936 and June 1936.
2. Napa Valley Wine Library, "Napa Valley Wine History," an oral history collection, in the St. Helena Public Library, vol. 2, pp. 313–314.
3. *Wines & Vines,* October 1934 and October 1935. Today Mendocino County tops all others in the North Coast region for the percentage of Zinfandel in its

vineyards, with 12.4 percent. Sonoma has 8.8 percent, and Napa has 4.1 percent. The highest percentage in the state is Lodi's San Joaquin County, at 30.2 percent.

4. Mary Frost Mabon, *ABC of America's Wines* (New York: Alfred A. Knopf, 1942).
5. Harold J. Grossman, *Grossman's Guide to Wines, Spirits, and Beers* (New York: Sherman and Spoerer, 1940); Julian Street, *Wines: Their Selection, Care, and Service* (New York: Alfred A. Knopf, 1933), p. 216; Melville, *Guide to California Wines,* pp. 12–13; Husmann, *American Grape Growing and Wine Making,* p. 202.
6. In 1949 a Wine Institute official wrote to wine writer Idwal Jones that Schoonmaker thought of wine "as a beverage to be appreciated only by a small fraternity of high priests" (Idwal Jones Papers, Bancroft Library, University of California at Berkeley). Louis M. Martini would have chuckled at being taken for a high priest of wine.
7. Frank Schoonmaker and Tom Marvel, *The Complete Wine Book* (New York: Simon & Schuster, 1934), pp. 30, 38.
8. Zoltan Csavas, *The Louis M. Martini Winery* (St. Helena, Calif.: Louis Martini Corporation, 1983), pp. 78–79. The Zinfandel vines there were old when Martini bought the vineyard in 1938. In 1983 they had "the appearance of small trees, with gnarled branches extending several feet from the trunk" (ibid.).
9. Frank Schoonmaker and Tom Marvel, *American Wines* (New York: Duell, Sloan and Pearce, 1941), pp. 145–146.
10. Frank Schoonmaker, *Encyclopedia of Wine* (New York: Hastings House, 1964), p. 353.
11. For a delightful account of this truly great Zinfandel tasting, see Darlington, *Angels' Visits,* pp. 261–275.
12. Schoonmaker, *Encyclopedia of Wine,* 1973 ed., p. 363; 1975 ed., p. 379.
13. By the 1960s Professors Maynard Amerine and A. J. Winkler at the University of California at Davis had softened their cautionary 1944 words on Zinfandel. In 1963 they even recommended bottle aging to improve its quality; see Amerine and Winkler, *California Wine Grapes: Composition and Quality of Their Musts and Wines,* California Agricultural Experiment Station Bulletin 794 (Davis, Calif., 1963), pp. 47–48.
14. Roy Brady, "Super Zin," *Wine World,* August/September 1973, pp. 18–20.

15. For a complete list of Ridge wines from 1962 to 1992, see Charles L. Sullivan, *Wines and Winemakers of the Santa Cruz Mountains: An Oral History* (Cupertino, Calif.: D. R. Bennion Trust, 1994), pp. 696–705. This volume also contains an extensive series of interviews with Ridge leaders; see pp. 563–695.
16. For the David Bruce Zinfandel story, see ibid., pp. 341–369. For a complete list of Bruce wines through 1982, see pp. 371–375.
17. The Shields Library at the University of California at Davis has a good collection of Esquin newsletters.
18. Brady, "Super Zin," pp. 18–20. For more on Swan and his wines, see Charles L. Sullivan, "Some Notes on Joseph Swan," *Connoisseurs' Guide to California Wine,* March 1989, p. 65; *Los Angeles Times,* April 17, 1988; *San Francisco Chronicle,* January 17, 1989.

CHAPTER TEN. OF PENDULUMS AND ROLLER COASTERS, 1970–1990

1. C. S. Ough and W. A. Winton, "An Evaluation of the Davis Wine-Score Card and Individual Expert Panel Members," *American Journal for Viticulture and Enology* 27, no. 3 (1976), pp. 136–144.
2. Acreage and price statistics cited in this chapter are taken from two annual publications of the California Agricultural Statistics Service, "California Grape Acreage" and "Final Grape Crush Report." They can be ordered by phone at (916) 498-5161 or by writing to the service at 1220 N Street, Sacramento, California 94271.
3. The results of the club's tastings for the early years can be found in Mary Ellen McNeil-Draper, ed., *Vintners Club: Fourteen Years of Wine Tasting, 1973–1987* (San Francisco: Vintners Press, 1988).
4. It is difficult to find old copies of *Connoisseurs' Guide to California Wine.* The most likely sources are any of the libraries with special wine interests that I have listed in an earlier work; see Sullivan, *A Companion to California Wine,* pp. 188–189.
5. Harry Waugh, *Pick of the Bunch* (London: Wine & Spirits Publications, 1970); Waugh, *Diary of a Winetaster* (New York: Quadrangle, 1972), esp. p. 136. Waugh's books covering his California wine visits are listed in the bibliography of this book.
6. Norman Roby, "Amador County Zinfandel," *Vintage,* June 1976, pp. 39–44.

7. The Shields Library at the University of California at Davis has a good collection of Trader Joe's newsletters.
8. Norman Roby, "California Zinfandel: Almost Anything Goes," *Vintage,* August/September 1977, pp. 42–46.
9. Sullivan, *Wines and Winemakers of the Santa Cruz Mountains,* pp. 701–703.
10. *St. Helena Star,* February 7, 2002.
11. *Connoisseurs' Guide to California Wine,* April 2, 1983, pp. 69–70; August 21, 1983, pp. 113–114.
12. *Los Angeles Times,* June 30, 1988; *Connoisseurs' Guide to California Wine,* July 1988, pp. 109–110.

CHAPTER ELEVEN. FAT YEARS, 1991–2001

1. These catalogues are useful historical documents, but mine is the only collection of which I am aware, other than the one available at the ZAP office. The ZAP office address is P.O. Box 1487 in Rough and Ready, California 95975; the phone number is (530) 274-4900. The same is true for the *Zinfandel Express,* which by 1995 had attained the size of a small magazine.
2. *Zinfandel Express,* July 1997, p. 2.
3. See *Zinfandel Express,* June 1994, p. 81, for the text of the resolution and those in attendance at the Washington, D.C., tasting.
4. "A Grape Revival," *San Jose Mercury News,* April 11, 2002, p. 15A.
5. Rod Smith, "Saving California History," *Los Angeles Times,* February 14, 2001.
6. For information about the special reasons for using this stock for Zinfandel, see "St. George and the Phylloxera," in Sullivan, *Napa Wine,* pp. 116–118.
7. *Zinfandel Express,* October 1997, p. 11.
8. Ibid., July 1998, p. 2.
9. See, for example, Larry Walker, "The Zins of the Father," *Wines & Vines,* November 1999, p. 18; *Quarterly Review of Wine,* December 1999, p. 89; *Practical Winery and Vineyard,* February 2001, p. 29; Gerald D. Boyd, "The Lure of Ancient Vines," *San Francisco Chronicle,* January 17, 2001; Lyn Farmer, "The Old Vine Character Dispute," *Wine News,* April/May 2001, pp. 7–8.
10. Farmer, "The Old Vine Character Dispute," p. 8.
11. *San Francisco Examiner,* July 19, 1992; *San Francisco Chronicle,* August 3, 1992; Kim Marcus, "Phylloxera, California's Billion Dollar Nightmare," *Wine Spectator,* August 31, 1992, pp. 28–33; Arthur Lubow, "What's Killing the Grapevines

in Napa?" *New York Times Magazine,* October 17, 1993, pp. 26–28, 59–63, reproduced by the *San Francisco Chronicle's This World* magazine, October 31, 1993, pp. 8–9, 14–16.

12. Prices by area, variety, and vintage can be found in the annual "Grape Crush Report" of the California Agricultural Statistics Service; acreage statistics are contained in this agency's annual report "California Grape Acreage."
13. Interview with the author, August 3, 2002.

CHAPTER TWELVE. THE MYSTERY OF ORIGINS SOLVED—PROBABLY

1. Carole Meredith, "Zinfandel Origins?" oral presentation at the annual conference of the American Society for Enology and Viticulture (ASEV), San Diego, June 27, 1997. This and my talk "Zinfandel and Its Histories" are available on audiotape from Tree Farm Communications, 23703 Northeast Fourth St., Sammamish, Washington 98074.
2. Leon D. Adams, *The Wines of America,* 1st ed. (Boston: Houghton Mifflin, 1973), pp. 403–404; 2d ed. (New York: McGraw-Hill, 1978), pp. 554–556.
3. Wade H. Wolfe, "Identification of Grape Varieties by Isozyme Banding," *Journal of the American Society of Enology and Viticulture* 27, no. 2 (1976), pp. 68–73.
4. *Wines & Vines,* April 1979, p. 18.
5. Norman S. Roby, "Recent Zinfandels," *Vintage,* November 1979, pp. 13–14; David Rosengarten, "Zinfandel from the Heel of the Boot," *Wine Spectator,* January 1985, p. 18.
6. My complete response can be found in Charles L. Sullivan, "The 'Zinfandel' or 'Primitivo' Question," *Vinifera Wine Growers Journal,* Spring 1985, pp. 23–26.
7. Direzione Agricoltura di Italia, *Bulletino Ampelografica, Anno 1878* (Rome: Eredi Botta, 1878), pp. 1033–1043; ibid., *Anno 1879,* pp. 480–481.
8. Letter to the author from Betsey Bradford, Chief, Product Compliance, March 6, 1985.
9. Antonio Calo, "Primitivo e Zinfandel: Due Nomi per un Solo Vitigno," *L'Enotecnico,* May 1987, pp. 71–74. Later Calo told Professor Carole Meredith that he thought the vine had probably come from Croatia to Puglia.
10. G. Musci, *Il Primitivo di Gioia* (Bari, 1919).
11. Carole Meredith, "DNA Fingerprinting," *Practical Winery and Vineyard,* November 1992, pp. 29–30; Carole Meredith et al., "DNA Fingerprint Characteriza-

tion of Some Wine Grape Cultivars," *Journal of the American Society of Enology and Viticulture* 44, no. 3 (1993), pp. 266–274.

12. Lynn Alley, "A Zin by Any Other Name . . . ," *San Francisco Chronicle*, July 31, 2002. This long article includes numerous comments by California Zinfandel producers on the new stance of the BATF. It also lists California producers that are now making wine from Primitivo grapes grown in the state. One winery, for instance, sells Prindello, a blend of Zinfandel and California Primitivo. The article also lists Northern California retailers who are selling the Italian product.
13. Adams, *Wines of America*, 2d ed., pp. 555–556.
14. N. Mirosević and Carole P. Meredith, "A Review of Research and Literature Related to the Origin and Identity of the Cultivars Plavac mali, Zinfandel and Primitivo," *Agriculturæ Conspectus Scientificus* 65, no. 1 (2000), pp. 47–48.
15. Leon D. Adams, *The Wines of America*, 3d ed. (New York: McGraw-Hill, 1985), p. 548.
16. James Ruby, "Who Were the Parents?" *Wines & Vines*, August 1997, p. 46; *San Jose Mercury News*, April 29, 1997; Nicholas Wade, "Vintage Genetics," *New York Times*, November 23, 1999.
17. Meredith, "Zinfandel Origins?" ASEV Conference, June 1997.
18. Carole Meredith, letter to the editor, *Wine Enthusiast*, October 1996, p. 28.
19. Terry Robards, "Zinfandel—The Mystery Solved," *Wine Enthusiast*, August 1996, pp. 44–48.
20. Meredith, letter to the editor, *Wine Enthusiast*, October 1996; Meredith, "Zinfandel Origins?" ASEV Conference, June 1997.
21. Richard Paul Hinkle, "Mike Grgich: You Can Go Home Again," *Wines & Vines*, May 1999, pp. 30–32.
22. Franz Trummer, *Systematische Classification und Beschreibung der im Herzogthume Steiermark vorkommenden Rebensorten* (Graz [Austria], 1841), pp. 182–184.
23. Ivan Pejić, Carole Meredith, et al., "Relatedness of Cultivars Plavac mali, Zinfandel and Primitivo," *Agriculturæ Conspectus Scientificus* 65, no. 1 (2000), pp. 21–25. "We judged that the Plavac mali cannot be of the same genotype as cv. Primitivo or Zinfandel . . . ," but they "probably are related as parent and progeny." The paper was published in Croatian, and there is a short English summary.
24. Meredith to ZAP, December 22, 1997.

25. See "Looking for Zinfandel in Croatia," *Zinfandel Express,* January 2002, p. 9, where Meredith tells the whole story of the discovery process.
26. Author's notes from an oral presentation by Carole Meredith, Zinposium, Santa Rosa, California, June 2002.
27. Rod Smith, "Solved: The Great Zinfandel Mystery," *Los Angeles Times,* July 10, 2002, which presents the best journalistic rendition of the story that I have seen.
28. George Ordish, *The Great Wine Blight* (New York: Scribner, 1972), pp. 178–179.
29. Smith, "Solved: The Great Zinfandel Mystery."

CHAPTER THIRTEEN. INTO THE NEW CENTURY

1. Eric Asimov, "Zinfandel Muscles In on the Big Boys," *New York Times,* January 9, 2002, p. B1.
2. Gerald D. Boyd, *San Francisco Chronicle,* July 10, 2002.
3. Acreage and price statistics included in this chapter are based on California Agricultural Statistics Service, "California Grape Acreage" and "Grape Crush Report," annual reports.
4. Larry Walker, ". . . Zinfandel: To Grow or Not to Grow," *Wines & Vines,* September 2002, pp. 56–57.

SELECT BIBLIOGRAPHY

The chapter notes serve as the research bibliography for this study. This select bibliography, with some annotations, is intended to help readers who want to read more widely on Zinfandel and its history.

Adams, Leon D. *The Wines of America.* Boston: Houghton Mifflin, 1973. A second edition of this work appeared in 1978, a third edition in 1985, and a fourth in 1990, all published in New York by McGraw-Hill. The first two editions are particularly good on Zinfandel and its possible origins.

Amerine, Maynard, and W. V. Cruess. *The Technology of Wine Making.* Westport, Conn.: Avi Publishing, 1960.

Amerine, M. A., and M. A. Joslyn. *Table Wines: The Technology of Their Production.* 2d ed. Berkeley: University of California Press, 1970. Originally published in 1951.

Amerine, Maynard A., and Vernon L. Singleton. *Wine: An Introduction for Americans.* 2d ed. Berkeley: University of California Press, 1977. Originally published in 1965.

Amerine, M. A., and A. J. Winkler. "Composition and Quality of Musts and Wines of California Grapes." *Hilgardia* 15, no. 6 (February 1944), pp. 493–673. This work, published through the California Agricultural Experiment Station, is based on extensive surveys done in the 1930s.

———. *California Wine Grapes: Composition and Quality of Their Musts and Wines.* California Agricultural Experiment Station Bulletin 794, Davis, Calif., 1963. An update of the preceding 1944 work.

Baldy, Marian. *The University Wine Course.* San Francisco: Wine Appreciation Guild, 1993.

Balzer, Robert L. *California's Best Wines.* Los Angeles: Ward Ritchie Press, 1948. Concentrates on a few premium producers.

Blue, Anthony Dias. *American Wine.* Garden City, N.Y.: Doubleday, 1985.

Blumberg, Robert S., and Hurst Hannum. *The Fine Wines of California.* 2d ed. Garden City, N.Y.: Doubleday, 1973.

Bynum, Lindley. *California Wines and How to Enjoy Them.* Los Angeles: Boelter, 1955.

Carosso, Vincent P. *The California Wine Industry, 1830–1895.* Berkeley: University of California Press, 1951.

Chorlton, William. *The American Grape Growers' Guide.* New York: A. O. Moore, 1859. Several later editions followed, containing excellent material on the East Coast hothouse grape culture, with good illustrations.

Church, Ruth Ellen. *The American Guide to Wines.* Chicago: Quadrangle, 1963.

Conaway, James. *Napa.* Boston: Houghton Mifflin, 1990.

Costa, Eric J. *Old Vines: A History of Winegrowing in Amador County.* Jackson, Calif.: Cenotto Publications, 1994.

Csavas, Zoltan. *The Louis M. Martini Winery.* St. Helena, Calif.: Louis Martini Corporation, 1983. Contains very useful information on this early producer of premium Zinfandel.

Darlington, David. *Zin: The History and Mystery of Zinfandel.* New York: Da Capo Press, 2001. This is a reprint of Darlington's *Angels' Visits* (New York: Henry Holt, 1991), with a new epilogue.

Draper, Paul. "Zinfandel." In *The University of California/Sotheby Book of California Wine,* edited by Doris Muscatine, Maynard A. Amerine, and Bob Thompson, pp. 223–234. Berkeley and London: University of California Press and Sotheby Publications, 1984. Draper is the CEO and winemaker at Ridge Vineyards, a leader in the production of premium Zinfandel since the 1960s.

Fisher, M. F. K. *The Story of Wine in California.* Berkeley: University of California Press, 1962.

Florence, Jack W. *A Noble Heritage: The Wines and Vineyards of Dry Creek Valley.* Healdsburg, Calif.: Wine Growers of Dry Creek Valley, 1993.

Francisco, Cathleen. *Zinfandel: A Reference Guide to California Zinfandel.* South San Francisco: Wine Appreciation Guild, 2001. Looks at current Zinfandel producers.

Haraszthy, Arpad. *Wine-Making in California.* San Francisco: Book Club of California, 1978. This volume is a reprint of Haraszthy's articles that were published in *Overland Monthly* in 1871–1872. Its importance here is the biographical essay on Haraszthy by Ruth Teiser and Catherine Harroun.

Hawkes, Ellen. *Blood and Wine: The Unauthorized Story of the Gallo Wine Empire.* New York: Simon & Schuster, 1993.

Hedrick, Ulysses Prentice. *The Grapes of New York.* Albany: New York Agricultural Experiment Station, 1908.

Husmann, George. *Grape Culture and Wine-Making in California.* San Francisco: Payot, Upham, 1888.

Hyatt, Thomas Hart. *Hyatt's Hand-Book of Grape Culture.* San Francisco: H. H. Bancroft, 1867. The first book on California viticulture.

Lapsley, James T. *Bottled Poetry: Napa Winemaking from Prohibition to the Modern Era.* Berkeley: University of California Press, 1996.

Laube, James. *Wine Spectator's California Wine.* New York: Wine Spectator Press, 1995.
Lukacs, Paul. *American Vintage: The Rise of American Wine.* New York: Houghton Mifflin, 2000.
Mabon, Mary Frost. *ABC of America's Wines.* New York: Alfred A. Knopf, 1942. The author liked Zinfandel and visited all major producers.
Massee, William E. *McCall's Guide to Wines of America.* New York: McCall, 1970.
McGinty, Brian. *Strong Wine: The Life and Legend of Agoston Haraszthy.* Stanford, Calif.: Stanford University Press, 1998.
Melville, John. *Guide to California Wines.* Garden City, N.Y.: Doubleday, 1955. Several later updated editions followed.
Mondavi, Robert. *Harvest of Joy.* New York: Harcourt Brace, 1998.
Olken, Charles E., Earl Singer, and Norman Roby. *The Connoisseurs' Handbook of California Wines.* New York: Alfred A. Knopf, 1980. A second edition appeared in 1982, and a third in 1984, both published by Knopf.
Peninou, Ernest P. *A History of the Orleans Hill Vineyard and Winery of Arpad Haraszthy and Company.* Winters, Calif.: Winters Express, 1983.
Pinney, Thomas. *A History of Wine in America: From the Beginnings to Prohibition.* Berkeley: University of California Press, 1989.
Prince, William Robert. *A Treatise on the Vine.* New York: T. & J. Swords, 1830.
Roby, Norman S., and Charles E. Olken. *The New Connoisseurs' Handbook of California Wines.* New York: Alfred A. Knopf, 1980. A second edition appeared in 1994, a third in 1996, and a fourth in 1998, all published by Knopf.
Schoonmaker, Frank. *Frank Schoonmaker's Encyclopedia of Wine.* New York: Hastings House, 1964. Six later editions have been published, through 1975.
Schoonmaker, Frank, and Tom Marvel. *American Wines.* New York: Duell, Sloan & Pearce, 1941.
———. *The Complete Wine Book.* New York: Simon & Schuster, 1934.
Stewart, Rhoda. *A Zinfandel Odyssey.* San Rafael, Calif.: Practical Winery and Vineyard, 2002.
Street, Julian. *Wines: Their Selection, Care, and Service.* New York: Alfred A. Knopf, 1948.
Stuller, Jay, and Glen Martin. *Through the Grapevine: The Business of Wine in America.* New York: Wynwood Press, 1989.
Sullivan, Charles L. *A Companion to California Wine: An Encyclopedia of Wine and Winemaking from the Mission Period to the Present.* Berkeley: University of California Press, 1998.
———. *Like Modern Edens: Winegrowing in Santa Clara Valley and Santa Cruz Mountains, 1798–1981.* Cupertino, Calif.: California History Center, De Anza College, 1982.
———. *Napa Wine: A History from Mission Days to the Present.* San Francisco: Wine Appreciation Guild, 1994.
———. *Wines and Winemakers of the Santa Cruz Mountains: An Oral History.* Cupertino, Calif.: The D. R. Bennion Trust, 1994. A collection of oral history interviews.
Teiser, Ruth, and Catherine Harroun. *Winemaking in California.* New York: McGraw-Hill, 1983. A general history of the California wine industry, with emphasis on oral histories from industry leaders of the twentieth century.

Thompson, Bob. *Notes on a California Cellarbook.* New York: William Morrow, 1988. This is a particularly informative survey.

———. *The Wine Atlas of California and the Pacific Northwest.* New York: Simon & Schuster, 1993.

University of California, Berkeley. Regional Oral History Office, Bancroft Library. The following oral histories have important sections on Zinfandel:

———. Draper, Paul. "History and Philosophy of Winemaking at Ridge Vineyards." 1994.

———. Foppiano, Louis J. "A Century of Agriculture and Winemaking in Sonoma County, 1896–1996." 1996.

———. Martini, Louis M., and Louis P. Martini. "Wine Making in the Napa Valley." 1973.

———. Martini, Louis P. "A Family Winery and the California Wine Industry." 1984.

———. Trinchero, Louis (Bob). "California Zinfandels, a Success Story." 1992.

Wagner, Philip M. *Grapes into Wine.* New York: Alfred A. Knopf, 1976.

Wait, Frona Eunice. *Wines and Vines of California.* San Francisco: Bancroft Co., 1889; facsimile ed., Berkeley: Howell North, 1973. The only book of its kind for nineteenth-century California wine.

Waugh, Harry. *Diary of a Winetaster.* New York: Quadrangle, 1972.

———. *Harry Waugh's Wine Diary, 1982–1986.* San Francisco: Wine Appreciation Guild, 1987.

———. *Harry Waugh's Wine Diary.* Vol. 6. London: Christie's Wine Publications, 1975. In 1978, Christie's also published volume 8, covering the years 1976 to 1978; volume 9, covering the years 1978 to 1981, appeared in 1981.

———. *Pick of the Bunch.* London: Wine & Spirits Publications, 1970.

———. *Winetaster's Choice: The Years of Hysteria.* New York: Quadrangle, 1973.

Winkler, A. J., et al. *General Viticulture.* Berkeley: University of California Press, 1974.

INDEX

Note: This index principally lists people, wine producers, grape varieties, organizations, printed materials, and geographical names. Authors and their works are indexed with the author's name indicated at the end of a work. Page numbers in italics refer to illustrations and tables.

TEXT: 12/14 Vendetta Medium
DISPLAY: Akzidenz Medium
DESIGNER: Jessica Grunwald
CARTOGRAPHER: Bill Nelson
COMPOSITOR: G&S Typesetting, Inc.
PRINTER AND BINDER: Thomson-Shore, Inc.